Feeding the Fame

Feeding the Fame

Celebrities Tell Their Real-Life Stories
of Eating Disorders and Recovery

Gary Stromberg

Jane Merrill

HAZELDEN®

Hazelden
Center City, Minnesota 55012-0176
1-800-328-0094
1-651-213-4590 (fax)
www.hazelden.org

ISBN-10: 1-59285-350-1
ISBN-13: 978-1-59285-350-2

Library of Congress Cataloging-in-Publication Data
Stromberg, Gary, 1942–
        Feeding the fame : celebrities tell their real-life stories of eating disorders
    and recovery / Gary Stromberg, Jane Merrill.
        p. cm.
        ISBN-13: 978-1-59285-350-2
        ISBN-10: 1-59285-350-1
        1. Eating disorders. 2. Celebrities—Mental health. I. Merrill, Jane. II. Title.

    RC552.E18S79 2006
    362.196'852600922—dc22

                                                                    2006043642

Credits and permissions appear on pages 243–244.

10 09 08 07 06   6 5 4 3 2 1

Cover and interior design by David Spohn
Typesetting by Stanton Publication Services, Inc.

To Leslie Pallas, my effervescent sister

—GARY

To Chris Filstrup with love and respect

—JANE

And to those who struggle to seek the light

The Bodily Beautiful

Ah, the bodily beautiful, how they are envied
for the perfect rhymes of their bodies' moons and stars,
how the world sets sail for the labial latitudes
of their lustrous skin, forgetting the bloody factories

within. But what of their burden, the daily swelter
in the spotlights of lust, the lovesick legions
and crush of attentive puppets, the ceaseless chatter
and charades of mating games, the splatter of night-

frightened moths who fling against their panes?
How hard it must be among fiestas
of permission and satin pillows to practice forbearance
and cleanse the spirit in the deserts of self-denial,

how hard to leave the shallows of sexuality
and immerse in the treacherous waters of love, to glimpse
the skull of time in the mirror's lie and the bones
of honesty inside those sublime impediments of flesh.

—Fred Dings

Contents

Foreword by Wendy Naugle

In 1984, *Glamour* magazine conducted a survey about women and body image and found that more than 40 percent of its readers were unhappy with their bodies. Chillingly, an expert told us, "Almost no woman, of whatever size, feels she's thin enough." When the magazine repeated the survey in 1998, the picture looked even worse: 53 percent of women were unhappy with their shape, 44 percent admitted to starving to lose weight, and 17 percent had tried vomiting. So when we embarked on a third survey in 2004—asking the very same questions to more than 13,000 young women—I was apprehensive, yet still optimistic. After all, a record number of women now own their own homes, run their own companies, and hold elected office: surely, I thought, we have made some progress when it comes to how we view the numbers on the scale.

Sadly, our body-image issues seem stuck in time. Twenty years after our initial queries, 42 percent of women reported being dissatisfied with their shape. How could things remain virtually unchanged? How much more must we accomplish before we stop wondering: do I look fat in these jeans?

As eating-disorder experts know, it's impossible to point to one factor that leads someone to starve herself, to binge eat, or to purge. It's likely a cocktail of genetic tendencies and environmental factors. The cultural factors, no doubt, loom large: for one, being thin isn't enough anymore—you must be sculpted and toned, too. (Think of some of the sexiest male icons of yore: Cary Grant, Marlon Brando, and James Dean never needed six-pack abs, yet could Brad Pitt have made his break in *Thelma and Louise* without them?) What's more, the very image of what we *should* look like is omnipresent—on TV, the Web, your cell phone or iPod. Celebrity weeklies document every ounce stars gain or lose, and compare women wearing the same outfit as if they were clothes hangers, not active, living people. If you're plugged in at all, then you're bombarded by images of beautiful, sexy bodies throughout the day. You can't even escape with "reality" TV, which suggests that "real" women—not just celebrities who can afford to keep a personal trainer, chef, makeup artist, and Botox expert on call—can achieve sample-size proportions and flawless looks. As if that's what it takes to marry a great husband and have a happy life.

Maybe we can blame those factors for the fact that the number of American women with an eating disorder has doubled in the last five decades, or that treatment centers are seeing more patients over age thirty than ever before. Women of color are also increasingly affected, as are men, who are trying to attain Ken-doll standards. And yet as damning as the environmental factors may be, many eating disorder sufferers I've spoken with point to much more personal triggers for their disease. Jenny remembered that when she was nine years old, her father told her she was the most beautiful creature on the planet. (She then felt obligated to fit that mold until she was well into her twenties.) Cheryl recalled her mother's silent pride when she admitted to eating a muffin and nothing else the day she started her first diet. Are events like these powerful enough to cause any woman to start starving or bingeing? Or did these women have an inborn perfectionist personality that led them to use food to express what they were really feeling? And in the end, how can we still be having a chicken-and-egg debate over the most deadly mental-health disorder?

Without more funding for research and treatment programs, we will struggle to find these answers. But it is our responsibility to take what we have learned and keep tomorrow's men and women from using food to control their lives or strive for perfection. The most persuasive way to do that is to share our stories, and that's why I applaud all the men and women here for speaking out and stripping away some of the stigma of eating disorders.

I am certain that after the publication of this book, the writers will hear from friends, acquaintances, and strangers who say, "You're the reason I got help," or "Your book helped me finally say something to my sister/co-worker/friend." Stories like these are one of the best antidotes to our body-image issues.

This book reminds us that we should not be without hope. After all, underneath the broad initial findings, *Glamour*'s body-image survey did find a few compelling signs of progress, most notably that women are beginning to value their health over their appearance. Only 10 percent of our most recent survey-takers had resorted to vomiting (a dramatic drop from just six years before), and 83 percent said they'd rather be slightly heavy and healthy than thin and unhealthy. Perhaps the solution is not to stop looking at our bodies, but to look at them differently: as a companion and partner through life, the very thing that holds us up, carries us through, and gets us to our destination after a long and fascinating journey. Who wouldn't want to cherish, protect, and celebrate a friend like that?

Wendy Naugle is the health editor of Glamour *magazine.*

Preface by Jane Merrill

While eating disorders have received ample attention lately, they have been with us through the ages. Among the royalty of ancient Mesopotamia, some queens could barely lift their immense bodies from their thrones. In religious traditions, monks have practiced extreme asceticism, and after eating and drinking rites in certain societies people worked off their misery in sweat lodges. Famously, citizens of the Roman Empire feasted, then vomited in *purgatoriums*—buildings or rooms devoted to that purpose.

Obscene eating was first given serious thought by the humanist philosopher and physician Rabelais in the sixteenth century. In Rabelais' encyclopedic folk epic, the heroes Gargantua and his son Pantagruel epitomized the unbridled appetite. Yet Rabelais postulated that obsessive eating was actually caused by a *rejection* of life's banquet. Such a denial of life perverts our natural inclination to virtue in pleasure. Thus Gargantua founds an imaginary monastery, the Abbey of Thélème, whose rules are nothing like the strict asceticism of the medieval monastery, but the epitome of laxness. This passage from *Gargantua and Pantagruel* describes Rabelais' idea of how to correct for frenzied disorder with harmonious social relations and thoughtful living.

> In their rules there was only one clause: DO WHAT YOU WILL! Because people who are free, well-born, well-bred, and easy in honest company have a natural spur and instinct which drives them to virtuous deeds and deflects them from vice; and this they call honor. When these same men are depressed and enslaved by vile constraint and subjection, they use this noble quality which once impelled them freely towards virtue, to throw off and break this yoke of slavery. For we always strive after things forbidden and covet what is denied us.

In our own time, the first person to document and publish her personal struggles with anorexia was the French philosopher Simone Weil. Her self-abnegation led to her tragic starvation, which she wrote about in a veiled manner, but at length. In fiction, perhaps the first work of art to focus specifically on an eating disorder was Franz Kafka's immortal and diabolical novella *The Hunger Artist*. Yet eating disorders have often moved under our radar, barely recognized as dysfunctional behaviors. Astonishingly, *The Hunger Artist* engaged literary critics for nearly a hundred years before a correlation was made between the fictive character's deadly game and the obsessive eating and dieting that debilitated Kafka and, under the guise of self-medication, may have contributed to his early demise.

Upon the release of our first coauthored book, *The Harder They Fall: Celebrities Tell Their Real-Life Stories of Addiction and Recovery*, Gary Stromberg and I began contemplating another. Writing *The Harder They Fall* had been especially rewarding because we saw the regenerative power of human beings who had hit bottom, then rose to the pinnacle. We interviewed stars who had waged mortal battles with drug and alcohol addiction, but survived the shame and despair of downfall and today lead lives of extraordinary accomplishment. We started to think about other social and health issues that would lend themselves to a subsequent volume.

With tabloids and television shows ridiculing eating disorders, and putting the stars onto scales virtually weekly, the topic practically begged for a more sensitive, questioning approach. Food compulsions and self-denials are so complex, and insinuate by such varied means, that a book of interviews seemed ideal for the subject.

Most of us are subject at least peripherally to the pressures of the beauty myth, but celebrities find their images under the constant scrutiny of media and fans. Remember how the no-nonsense Hillary Clinton changed her hairstyle with the weather when she first became First Lady? We decided the book would focus on people in the public eye.

And we set guidelines. We would include young people, but in all cases the individuals interviewed would have substantial awareness and recovery experience. We wanted to hear how they got past their problems and how the transformation of recovery was generated. How did they regain their health? How did they come to understand and express the emotions and fears that caused the self-destructive impulses in the first place? We found from the first interview that the celebrities who have suffered eating disorders and stood up and spoke out about their disease have a daring strength, self-knowledge, and warmth. Their personal accounts reveal unconventional, fascinating, and effective paths back to normal healthy body image and eating patterns.

Our empathy came easily because of our own past brushes with eating disorders, which, while not death-defying, were pretty awful. Gary's sensibilities derived from his early days in recovery from drug and alcohol addiction, when he found himself hyperaware of his relations with food. His addiction shifted in early sobriety to an obsession with eating. Not being able to drink or use drugs, he found he was able to "stuff his feelings" with food, and thereby avoid facing his personal issues. "It was a transference of my obsessions and compulsions to popcorn and ice cream."

In Gary's case, being aware of nutrition, he didn't "beat himself up with harmful foods." Rather, he indulged in choices he thought were benign, basic comfort foods like trail mix or oatmeal: "They weren't bad for me but nevertheless, in excess, they kept me from experiencing myself." He discovered he was as addicted to eating as to alcohol, and that his behavior was rooted in a chemical dependency. Finding himself often fixing something to eat late at night not out of hunger but out of a desire to numb out, Gary sought out a support group and eventually integrated his own recovery. He says that his first thought upon waking in the morning is still "What's for lunch?" But whereas before there was evidence of the disease of addiction, now he simply loves to cook and explore restaurants, and revels in working out and running. Gary's interest in pursuing this book was fueled by his strong identification with people battling addictive behavior and by his admiration of those in recovery.

As for my own history, my unhealthy fasting at twenty happened in the wake of losing my beloved older brother, Tom. Sometimes not eating is a metaphor for suicidal wishes. I was clear I didn't want to live or, if I lived, I wanted to remain in joyless mourning after my brother's fatal car accident. Within a year I had fled from home and was living in the Near East, wraith-thin, and somehow, as survivors do, functioning—teaching at an international school, traveling, and swimming for hours a day. I collapsed, was hospitalized, and the scare made me clean up my act. It wasn't overly hard, but at first I had not a clue about what a regular meal was. I had forgotten and had to relearn eating that spring. Soon I could give up the prescribed protein-fortified high-calorie milkshakes and eat normally again. In the hospital I had dreamed, half-delirious, of toasted cheese sandwiches and steaming cream soups—what my mother served me as a child sick in bed. That in a culture with one of the most delicious cuisines on earth!

For both Gary and me, experiencing derailed appetites, and then finding the happiness of balance and harmony, inspired us to find the interview subjects and ask them to speak on behalf of others. Thus began the journey of the book. It took a year to identify and interview all the individuals whom we wished to include. We tried to strike a balance of ages, disorder types, and also métiers: many of these celebrities are from the world of entertainment but there are also outstanding writers, a politician, and a sports star.

We hope this kind of participatory reporting makes all of us—authors, celebrities, and readers—insiders, as we springboard from our attitudes toward food, diet, and weight to understand others' struggles with serious addiction. We convey our heartfelt appreciation of the interviewed celebrities in progressive recovery who were willing to reach out to help others.

Acknowledgments

Our gratitude goes first to the individuals who welcomed us into their lives and gave us their stories.

We also thank those who led us to them: Gail Abbott, Stacy Abrams, Lesley Alexander, Bob Barney, Gerry Casanova, Jill Eisenstadt-Chayet, Suzanne Gluck, Erica Hoggard, Albert Imperato, Joshua Kosman, Sara Roberts, Alice Stewart, Sissy Terry, Beth Thompson, and Mark Williams.

There were others who gave the benefit of their fine minds to brainstorm and research the subject's many facets, and comment on the book's progress: Janie Chang, E. Christian Filstrup, Laurie Filstrup, Diane Glynn, Sherry Goodman Luttrell, Julie Merrill, and Rosalind Parry.

To work under the aegis of Hazelden meant the benefit of an extraordinary team, among whom we signal especially Becky Post, Mindy Keskinen, and Karen Chernyaev, as our personal editor a writer's dream.

While we both are attracted to moving to new places, we would miss one of the greatest assets of our town in Connecticut, the Westport Public Library, whose reference department cannot be beat.

Introduction by Judi Hollis, Ph.D.

"The very rich are different from you and me."

"Yeah, they have more money."

This wry quip, attributed to Ernest Hemingway, hints at the topics of separation and status, celebrity and power, and asks what distinctions really apply to us fragile human beings.

When sitting down or standing up to food, we all face the great leveler. Whether we count calories or pulse rates, binge at buffets, or work out incessantly at gyms, when it comes to our love-hate relationship with the source of all our energy and life, we humans are not all that different after all. No matter who, what, or how special we think we are, many of us show our humanity and frailty when dinner is served.

If we find ourselves obsessively looking forward to eating, if we find emotional solace when we eat to excess, we're misusing and abusing the function of food. We don't need to diagnose ourselves with an eating disorder. We are all on a food-use continuum that can quickly, and without our awareness, shade into food abuse. Food obsessions are not a matter of quantity or manner of ingestion. They have to do with an unnatural, obsessive relationship with food. The obsession emerges subtly and is often characterized by fear and self-loathing. Rarely can people pinpoint when the relationship becomes abusive. When does a cucumber soaked in brine become a pickle? The important thing to know is that once pickled, the cucumber is hard to find unless we do some deep and sensitive internal work.

Though I have long been credited with bringing the disease concept of overeating to public attention, I have modified my initial findings somewhat. Food Obsessives are not necessarily diseased persons, but rather supersensitive human beings. We are like the miners' canaries sent below the surface as a signal for noxious gases in the shaft. If the bird dies, humans dare not enter. Many of us sacrificing ourselves as obese, anorexic, or getting away with bingeing and vomiting, are signaling to our society the difficulty of living in this oppressive atmosphere, where bodies are scrutinized and souls are raped.

In *Feeding the Fame,* the authors deftly portray seventeen celebrities—some both rich and famous—who candidly and insightfully report on the degradation and humiliation they've suffered with their food obsessions. Entertainers and performers have long been associated with alcoholism or drug addiction. We all know the image of a tortured, brooding artiste hanging over a whiskey glass with a cigarette dangling and a line of cocaine waiting. But strung out on a bowl of Häagen-Dazs or stuffing dozens of candy wrappers into a purse? Where's the glamour or creativity in that? There's nothing cinematic in the pigging out—or in the contracting in.

These celebrities have pondered the issues long and hard, and the message is clear: insight is not enough to heal obsession. Ultimately, all had to realize that the body is not a costume to be altered but a conduit for channeling creativity and personal voice. I found most impressive a star who refused the doctor-prescribed drugs to courageously insist on living her own life with all its heartache as well as reward. Her pleas to stay conscious offer great hope amidst all the pressures to pursue "better living through chemistry." Similarly brave and honest was the admission from a recovering alcoholic who realized she had promptly transferred her obsessions from alcohol and drugs to food abuse. When nothing changes inside, the forms of self-destruction merely turn like a carousel on the outside.

Freud said we all have "an ambivalent commitment to both life and death." The drive to self-destruct is common to all obsessions, no matter what substance we abuse. With eating disorders, we deny or overfeed ourselves with the very essence of life, the fuel that stokes our engines. By restricting or overindulging that life force, we are committing slow suicide. Animals do not commit suicide. When we turn self-destructive behaviors around and stop abusing food, strangely, we move closer to our essential animal natures. Using food, the essence of life, for self-destruction is so unnatural that when we begin to heal, to view food as sustenance and fuel, we heal at a very deep level. Concurrently, when we own and accept our bodies, and find a healthy and disciplined way to fuel them, we rise to our higher spiritual natures. That drive to realize our higher selves helps us change as only humans can.

So if the drive to eat makes animals of us all, what distinctions, if any, should be noted for celebrities? Are their issues different from those of the average sufferer? Before creating the nation's first clinical unit for eating disorders, I worked as a counselor in several pioneering alcoholism centers, including the U.S. Navy's flagship program where we treated Betty Ford, who changed the face of women's treatment forever. Even then, we were clear about avoiding hierarchies of status. Officers had to attend groups with enlisted men, senators with first ladies; no one got special treatment. Still, we had two distinct patient groups, affectionately labeled "drunks" and "chunks." Alcoholics and overeaters, though facing the same personality problems and the same rigorously honest lifestyle requirements, were put in separate groups just because one abused a liquid substance and the other a solid one. We knew the similar personality dynamics of overeaters and alcoholics, knew that the same types of lifestyle and psychological changes were essential for lasting recovery, but still we illogically separated them.

There do exist specialized Alcoholics Anonymous groups for doctors, lawyers, writers, and artists, and even a "wings" group for airline personnel. Such specialized meetings are based on lifestyle and work issues—not on drinking patterns such as daily versus periodic drinker, or bar drinker versus back-bedroom housewife, or pure alcoholic versus multiply addicted. No matter what the manner of ingestion, it is a person's attitude toward the substance and what it does for him or her that qualifies each person for membership. Members use specialized groups to discuss topics related to their work, but must also attend other more general meetings to maintain lasting sobriety. Individuals who think they are too special, live too rarefied an existence, or focus on differences rather than similarities, are likely to drink again.

The celebrities speaking through this volume, whether actor, writer, supermodel, opera star, politician, chanteuse, or jockey, reveal to us basic human frailty in the face of food abuse. They also emphasize our similarities and speak authentically, seeking no special consideration for celebrity status. Their stories are carefully chosen for wide diversity, and all seem blessed with great personal insight—whether a result of good therapy, good Twelve Step programs, or sheer luck and pluck. Ultimately, their stories reveal topics that must be investigated by all recovering individuals.

For public figures and entertainers, the issues of boundaries and of energy consumption and release are paramount. Anyone with a food obsession must learn how to handle conflicts between self-care and others' needs on an hourly basis. How much can we let others penetrate us, and how much of ourselves can we give away? How do we handle the personae projected onto us by others? Public figures struggle with their audiences' projections, but nonpublic figures deal with all kinds of expectations from family, friends, coworkers, and society at large. How do we live when others see us as someone different from who we believe ourselves to be?

How do we conserve energy and then later release it at our best time? Celebrities struggle with these issues on a grander scale, but we all face them every day. If food is our fuel, then conservation and dissipation of energy are topics that must receive our utmost attention.

And if food is the problem, how is abstinence possible? When the offending substance or behavior is something unnatural or mind altering, then keeping it entirely out of our systems seems best. But to swear off food is a rejection of the life force, removing us from a natural state. How can we measure ourselves? Initially, Food Obsessives must make definite commitments and pay exquisite attention to what and how they eat. They must devise strategies and plan for going *toward* the substance. They must become super-conscious of and talk intimately about that favorite and fun topic: food. Failing to plan is planning to fail. However, ultimately, to be fully in recovery the sufferer must decrease the heightened vigilance. He or she must surrender to listening to the body, eating when hungry, stopping when full, and waiting with faith for a sane and "surrendered" relationship with that primary love object. We must eat regularly without bingeing or dieting. We have to eat from a position of neutrality, neither lusting after food nor fearfully running from it. We look at our eating behavior, focus on how we live, talk a lot about our problems, and eventually food becomes a quiet, background nonissue. It's like the great definition of humility: Humility is not thinking less of yourself. It's thinking of yourself less. Can artists afford to think of themselves less? What is the risk? Can we risk thinking less of food and thinking of food less?

Motivation to stardom and public life often comes from a deep longing to heal suffering. As I saw for years in our treatment centers and then recounted in the book *Fat and Furious,* many people binge or purge their family's disowned pain and anger. They have to separate from that pain, grow up emotionally, give up fixing Mom or men, and just do something about themselves. When taking on that seemingly smaller, simpler task, they find it a monumental feat to eat moderately, one day at a time, over and over and over again. Most who had fashioned themselves as superheroes and rugged individualists find that in order to curb their appetites, they have to surrender and acknowledge needing help. The lure of sugar and flour, cultural body-image standards, genetic propensities—many factors play into eating disorders. But each person depicted in this book did the personal work to surmise that "We have met the enemy and he is us." They also saw that they needed to quit "digging their graves with a knife and fork"—that food punished more than rewarded or soothed.

Reading *Feeding the Fame* I am reminded of Eugene O'Neill's poignant lines in *Long Day's Journey Into Night*. The consumptive son, Edmund, tells his father that he would have done better to have been born a fish. He describes his greatest moments of feeling truly himself while on the high seas, not bothered by any human contact. He said, "I am always a stranger, ever alone, always a little in love with death." No matter what path to recovery these celebrities took, all came back to loving life in their own way and on their own terms. Their stories illustrate that giving up food abuse, though painful, is worth doing. You will want to join in their journeys.

Judi Hollis, Ph.D., is the author of Fat Is a Family Affair, Fat and Furious, *and* Hot and Heavy. *She can be reached at www.JudiHollis.com or 1-800-8-ENOUGH.*

It suffices. What suffices?
All suffices reckoned rightly:
Spring shall bloom where now the ice is,
Roses make the bramble sightly,
And the quickening sun shine brightly
And the latter wind blow lightly,
And my garden teem with spices.

—Christina Rossetti, "Amen"

Molly Jong-Fast
(writer)

MOLLY IS FUNNY, hip, and wry. Her darkly comic novel *Normal Girl* features the nineteen-year-old daughter of famous people, circulating in a milieu of drugs and drink, who is accused of murder. Molly wrote it when she was nineteen, and a few years later published *The Sex Doctors in the Basement*, an entertaining and rapier-thrust-filled romp through her own bohemian childhood.

After earning an MFA from Bennington College, Molly became an accomplished writer without any practice flights—she's written for the *New York Times, Mademoiselle,* and other publications. She documented her own wedding for *Modern Bride.* Molly is soft-spoken, and before she replies she ponders—you can see the thoughts whipping through her mind. She has a serene air, as if she stepped out of an English castle or a Vermeer painting, where she'd be doing crewel work on a hoop, illuminated by a shaft of sunlight. One senses love as this new mother speaks of her young son and husband. She also seems to inspire affection in others; even the doorman of her apartment building smiles when he hears her name.

Where is the classic perfectionist, the high-strung woman who falls prey to anorexia? Molly is humble, sensual, and considerate. She is clear how it happened. Molly comes from a family of poets and writers on both sides: her father is Jonathan Fast, who is both author and social worker; her grandfather was Howard Fast, author of *Spartacus;* and her mother is poet and novelist Erica Jong, whose *Fear of Flying* proved the voice of a generation of women. Molly says her parents were exciting and wonderful; yet she wasn't taught boundaries and thus wandered in a wasteland of hip-dom before she made her own boundaries.

Molly lives in New York City with her husband and son, in a bountiful and more conventional life than she knew growing up.

—J.M.

My eating disorder is all about being a drug addict and an alcoholic. So the only times I've really been hot on my eating disorder have been when I'm sober.

I believe that I was born an alcoholic. Even very young I always wanted drugs. At about eleven I had a baby tooth that needed to be pulled and the dentist said to me, "I think you could just take Tylenol," and I said, "I don't get any Vicadin?" I was so upset. I really wanted Vicadin. And the dentist looked at my father, and my father looked at the dentist, and they were both like, "Hmm, there's something wrong here."

You know, I came from a family where one of my grandmothers was always either drinking or trying to get a drink. My father's mother was not like that but my father's father, Howard Fast, was just a real pain in the ass, and really horrible to my father. And it was just a really complicated upbringing and everybody was crazy and difficult. In the seventies when we were living in Weston, Connecticut, my mother used to have a Christmas party where everyone would do drugs, and people would drive off the side of the road.

What happened was that I was the kind of kid that, even really young, always wanted to be an addict. I thought that was a very glamorous and okay kind of ending. I didn't want for conventional things. For instance, I never thought that I would have an apartment, a co-op, or a child. Those were never the things that I wanted. I wanted, like, to live over someone's garage and shoot heroin. I was not very conventional in my goals, and I don't know that I knew that normal life could be available to me. I don't know that I understood that.

At about twelve years of age I began smoking pot a lot, and that was my manifest addiction. The second was drinking, but I had this innate tolerance for alcohol so when I would drink I had to drink so much to get drunk. I'd have fourteen vodka cranberries and feel fine and go drive somewhere. As I said, I think I was born to be an alcoholic. When I was about a junior in high school my drug addiction became totally unmanageable.

I got very into my eating disorder because I needed to get my schoolwork together so I could get into a decent college. And I stopped eating and started running. I would just run for hours. Every day I would run for an hour and then I would run up twenty-seven flights of stairs to my parents' place, in New York. It was really exercise bulimia. And then when I got to be incredibly skinny, I got really horrible. A lot of measuring and joyless deceiving. A lot of not-eating! I'd eat a loaf of bread and then I'd have to run for an hour to work it off. There's this eight-mile loop around the park I used to run. I was crazy!

There were these pivotal moments of recognition when I felt I couldn't do it anymore. Eating disorders are really explained by those constant resolves. This time is different; this time is different. You know you're screwing yourself and closing up on yourself. At the worst moment you look out and know there's an end, but you don't trust or can't find it. My feelings with my own eating disorder—when I was about thirteen I was heavy and very dejected. I had my shrink take me aside and say, "This time, Molly, you have to lose weight or you'll be abject and miserable. You have to get it together." And then I did, and then I went too far. It's almost as if I was too angry to ever be able to do things the way that would be good for me. It really was a long adolescent hostility towards people, and of course if someone tells you to slim down, if you are feeling rage you tacitly say, "You want to see thin? I'll show you thin!"

My family didn't remark on what was happening with me. They tend to be both very into dramatics and not that interested in dramatics.

When I went to college I got back into drugs. Then I was ostensibly fine because I couldn't kill myself with eating. Shortly after, I was swept away with the drugs—cocaine especially—and that took me along. The summer I was eighteen was the worst in my life. Right after I turned eighteen I just became a junkie. Not a heroin addict, but someone who did cocaine twenty-four hours a day. I had an apartment but I was a train wreck.

Supposedly I was going to college, but I was in the process of getting kicked out. That year was one long low in my life. Then it was very, very dark—a lot of chaos and senseless things happening. It makes me sad, so sad to think of any other person or myself that way.

Then, three months after my nineteenth birthday, I checked into treatment. And I got clean and sober and started a Twelve Step program. This was a choice I made myself. Oh my God! I was waiting and waiting for the intervention, and the intervention was never going to come. It's not so much that my family is nonchalant about drugs—by this time everybody had moved on from them—but that influencing anybody, even for the good, that's just not their speed. Everyone in my family tends to be so consumed by their own horrible childhoods, even well into their sixties, that I don't think that anyone can see the woods for the trees. I think they're so damaged. So then I got sober. That was November 2, 1997, and I've been clean and sober ever since—but I had to compulsively overeat to do it. I had a terrible trouble with that.

That's been a real struggle in my sobriety, trying to keep myself on an even keel. Now the therapist I work with has me journaling and telling about my feelings. I try to stay present and it's a totally different experience for me. You know, I have no reference. I come from a family where everyone was an emotional eater. It was a kind of disorder I was very familiar with all my life.

I believe that food was not only my first addiction but my most powerful. As a child it was always an issue for me. I was too heavy or, later, too thin. There was a lot of overeating and a lot of dieting and weirdness with food. Even before I understood what sobriety was, I always wanted to go to spas with my mother to dry out. The appeal was they didn't have alcohol there, and the portions of the meals were controlled. Part of my distress came from my addiction, but part of it was an inability to deal with the real world. And part of it has just been anxiety, and some of it is I really never knew how to nurture myself in any way but with food. This was a very pathological thing with me, that I didn't know how to be good to myself. And I knew that was really a profound, seemingly hopeless thing, that I couldn't care about myself.

There was a shade of an overdeveloped ambition to be unique and special, but it was more that I needed to isolate somehow and get release for the anger. I had so little confidence in who I was or wasn't: that factor alone disabled me from pulling out of the multiple addictions for a long time.

The causality is so complicated because I also felt the disorder was programmed in me. I was clinging to the problems because they were part of me, rather than exerting my freedom to get better. The disorder was the way I experienced the world and related back to it. Among my female friends, that was the way I related to them: through overeating or being the heavier one.

There are many explanations for my calamities. Certainly the eating disorder was a way of trying not to compete with my mother, sensing my creative talents would run parallel with hers, on some level. The eating disorder was also some protection from the incredibly overwrought atmosphere I belonged to. You know, I felt my childhood in the home and in the society I grew up in was overheated in a less than healthy way. It seemed in my childhood through my teens that I had no protection from the adult lives.

It was complicated, and as defense mechanisms go, it was a pretty good one: in the fact that it worked. I developed intellectually and even socially according to expectations but just had this problem with regulating my diet. However, the stigma and shame were a big thing, and it's only through my twenties that I have been able to get over that. I've had to be vigilant about writing about my feelings. This isn't a hobby, but has been crucial to integrating the elements of my self. And I try not to put myself in situations where I feel very vulnerable.

It feels as though every woman I know has eating issues. I'm happy that I'm aware, but I have to exert constant vigilance. I think also what's good is I'm really careful about the disorder in relation to being a mother, trying not to pass it on to my child. Obviously since he's a boy it's a lot easier, as the whole model thing—that false goal—is internalized by girls.

I see a lot of moms that I'm friends with going awry on this. Some of the things that come out of their mouths about food and their children are absolutely insane. For instance, I think one of the great things about having had all this therapy is thinking less about why I fell into the disorder and more about how I behave today, right now. Sherry Cosell, the psychotherapist I work with, does a Twelve Step eating disorder model that's not as hard-core as Overeaters Anonymous, as overcoming overeating, and is mostly about the feelings, less about the food.

I haven't binged in close to a decade. I do have issues. I may have had what I would consider a binge because I am hyperaware of departing from the middle of the road. But compared with what a normal person thinks constitutes a binge, it's not. I definitely feel I've been consistent about writing down my feelings: journaling, and being able to see, to be okay with, who I am, with my feelings, which was my core problem. I'm also so immediately alert to certain things, to acknowledging and handling emotions that were not okay before.

That cycle of self-punishment and rage—that I shouldn't feel that way, should hide or suppress my anger . . . in my view, so much about this eating disorder is women not feeling comfortable with rage. So then when I was so angry I would just eat it, which is such a brilliant double entendre. I think that was something I found myself doing a lot. I also think so much of it, for me, was about being nice and sweet no matter what the circumstances, just deflecting.

Now I can see mothers confusing their children about food. A person I know says, "I don't want to make my baby fat," when the baby's six months old. You're like, "Oh my God! This is a six-month old!" I tell her something like, "Could this be your problem? Watch what you do and deal with it."

I always thought it was so unfair that I wasn't a model. There are definitely a bulk of women in New York who are really anorexic but can make
it work for them, and I always felt so jealous that I wasn't one of those
women. Because if you have an eating disorder you're so sick—you have the
eyes of a junkie. You get into other people because your self feels hollow.

You want to suffer the most, too, on some level. I used to envy some
women who had this anorexic thing going for them, and now I don't, because I see how their pain is just like what my pain was. If not worse.
They're experiencing it constantly. The worst manifestation of it, that really
blows my mind, is these women of my generation or older who get pregnant and don't eat. It's profoundly disturbing to me and undeniably narcis-
sistic. If you can't remove yourself from the narcissism enough to raise a
child on healthy principles then you ought not have children.

But it's not all me in a critical mode. Having gone through the anorexia
and bulimia, I do have a sensitivity about these hidden, shame-filled disorders. I feel now that my job being sober, as long as I am abstinent, is to
be a good influence, or example of pulling through. There are so many
women in New York around my age with the problems I've had. In the status circles, and among young professional women, there is so much that's
considered okay that's not okay. Just the standard stuff, the food crazies.

The example of someone like Kate Moss, all fragile and weak-looking
and without the energy to even smile, is profoundly bad. All these people
want to look like her! I think that the undernourished, languid model is
the biggest example that these women get, and not much positive to
counter it. You should use cocaine and not eat, or even just not eat, as cocaine is frowned on by society, but not eating is equated with restraint.
Thinness is a social caste thing, about which I sincerely have come not to
care. My own appearance is interesting to me but not profoundly. Looks are
not what I am.

And this is new for me, a little revolt that signifies a step forward.
Everyone in my family was very involved in what they look like. My parents were raised pretty absorbed in appearance and passed that on. My father's mother was a fashion designer, married to Howard Fast. She was
more than a little attentive to how things looked. And my grandfather was

a philanderer, so he was interested in the way things looked. And my mother's parents—a painter and a businessman/drummer—commented on the visual aspect of things all the time. It followed that both my mother's sisters were painters. You wouldn't think that of a writer's background, but my immediate forebears are artists, and very myopic. For instance, my mother's mother always had people posing. She painted us grandchildren over and over. Then for a while she and my grandfather were making these dolls that looked like their grandchildren. It was really creepy!

So there was a lot of sense of what things look like and what they are. Especially as a writer, my mother fed for so long on the image of the rebel: looking like the troublemaker. Wanting to look edgy and writerly. I realized, from this, that phenomenon of looking different from what you are. I'd observe my mother wearing getups that were more edgy than her actual life, so there was that dichotomy—not looking what you are, looks that get attention. Not that this was a conscious choice, but an attitude that was formed in my early life.

I have a long way to go. Especially if I think of the larger sense in which life is a spiritual journey, I haven't even started. In fact, I'm starting, as I progress, to see how far distant is a completion or integration. I'm still really wrapped up in the rat race in such a way that it's counter to my own health. I mean, I'll be screwed if the whole goal of life is to grow spiritually! I work at it, but I'm nowhere near where I'd like to be. I feel all this the longer I'm sober and on an even keel. I'm not battling the symptoms so much anymore. But I'm still deeply damaged in some way that I sense I'll recover from, too, but I can't gauge.

I spent so long just battling the symptoms. And now I feel as though I've got them under control, but there's so much more that I can start to work at, on myself. When I say I'm far from where I'd like to be in the spiritual dimension, I mean the way it shows up practically, for instance in my daily tasks. Right now I'm just drowning under minutiae. All of a sudden I'm looking at the pile on my desk, and I'm lost and overwhelmed in it and asking, "How did this happen?" And my husband expects me to take care of paying the bills; my responsibility is to send the checks after he writes them. I only have to put the check in the envelope, lick the envelope, and put a stamp on it. I don't even have to put a return address on. And I swear to God that's problematic for me—like some sort of reminder that I may have control over the addictions but I'm still unsure at the margins.

Having a child and not a job outside the home probably affects me, changes my rhythms and I am glad for it; that's natural. I know that being a mother has helped me see everything afresh. "You're only as happy as your least happy child," my father said. Our emotional systems are webbed with our children's. Having a small child is really sweet. Meanwhile I think of what my parents endured through my teenage years. My dad's great, a social worker who teaches at Yeshiva and also works with the Red Cross during disasters. He added to that statement, "Unless you can ignore that child!"

So much of my eating disorder was characterized by rage. So much of a lot of these things is a sort of rage gone sideways, where I couldn't express it. Curiously, once you express it—and this came years later for me— it's not such a big deal. But for so long the abiding anger is like a ghost at your back. That's the big joke of addiction. Your feelings are so raw and fisted up that you can't deal with reality. You feel you got to do drugs, you got to kill yourself, and do this purging and starving, and then when you do let go of the rage you're like, "What the hell, that was it?"

The fear to be myself led to distorting my desires, appetites, emotions. That fear of oneself. Also, the last thing I ever wanted to do was to be "typical" to people. Because my parents had this horrendous divorce that went on for years and years, and they were so angry at each other for so long, I just interpreted a lot of normal human interaction as rage. I didn't understand that a day could be peaceful, or that a person's emotions could run smoothly, instead of being stirred and roiled up.

I also think this is typical of most addicts: I had no sense of gray. I was either the thinnest person in the room or the fattest. The drunkest or the most sober. With drinking that's pretty black and white, you're either drinking or not, but with food it was a matter of going way, way overboard—no minor diets or slight overeating for me, but hopeless excess. That's why it's so challenging for a lot of recovering addicts: you just have to experience and gain faith in gray. You have to get over the sense in which everything is either this or that.

You also have to cope with the judgments. When people see an anorexic on the street they'll gawk. Same with someone who is too fat. There are a lot more judgments than for alcohol or cocaine addictions, for instance, and a super-sense of shame. You even get approbation for being a good-looking cadaverous rock star, but other women scorn you if you're heavy. With my child I try to build a really good attitude towards food. The recovery goes on and on, and this is on a secondary level: another chance to exercise the being better myself.

So many lyres hang on this tree,
But it seems there's room for mine among these.
And this rain, sparse and sunny,
Is my good tidings and my ease.

—Anna Akhmatova

Andrea Marcovicci
(cabaret singer, actor)

WE FIRST REMEMBER seeing Andrea Marcovicci in the movie *The Front,* costarring as Woody Allen's activist girlfriend. Andrea is a spectacular performer whose patrician features, ethereal beauty, and entrancing voice are familiar from her many stage, television, and film performances, but she is unique and adored above all as the Queen of Cabaret.

Andrea grew up in cabaret, as her mother is Helen Marcovicci, a noted singer with a different, deeper voice, who sometimes dazzles audiences in mother-daughter numbers.

"Torch singer, spellbinder, heart-breaker" were *People* magazine's words for Andrea; *New York* magazine called her "the most throbbingly irresistible voice in cabaret"; and Stephen Holden wrote in the *New York Times* that "Andrea Marcovicci has an incandescent enthusiasm and a masterly balance between poignancy and wit." She has appeared regularly in the Oak Room of New York's Algonquin Hotel since 1987, she tours in her universally acclaimed shows coast to coast, and she has recorded thirteen CDs.

Andrea began her acting and singing career on the daytime television series *Love Is a Many-Splendored Thing.* She debuted on Broadway in *Ambassador,* a musical adaptation of the Henry James novel, starring Howard Keel. Her numerous off-Broadway appearances include *The Wedding of Iphigenia* and *The Seagull,* and she was hailed in the title role of an American Conservatory Theater production of *Saint Joan.* Her film credits include *The Hand* with Sir Michael Caine, *The Canterville Ghost* with Sir John Gielgud, and the star-studded documentary *Who Is Henry Jaglom?*

She was honored to usher in the millennium with the Chicago Symphony Orchestra. Lincoln Center commissioned both her Noel Coward show and her *Kurt Weill in America,* and she has performed at the White House.

Andrea's cabaret shows are her original creations: mesmerizing blends of song, storytelling, and self-revelation. Typically she comes onstage dripping in diamonds, shimmering in a glamorous gown, blowing kisses and extending greetings left and right. She is warm, witty, and by turns heartbreakingly tender and hilarious, interpreting a wide range of great popular music with unequalled depth and sensitivity. The audience is left tipsy with song, witness to an immortal tradition of performing that brilliant, gutsy, sexy women have dominated through the ages.

When you talk with Andrea personally, you feel drawn into the magic spotlight with her. She looks delicate and fine-boned but handles herself with such emphatic self-assurance that she seems to embody the power of the great song tradition where she reigns supreme.

—J.M.

I was leaning over this banister at a party last night, and a man said something so over the top. He left his wife sitting and came over to me. I was with an old girlfriend at the time, and we looked up, and he peered down on me and said to me something so extravagant that both my friend and I were sort of, "Oh, thank you!" I was with my friend, also a singer, Barbara Russell, and this man said, "You make my life worth living." Not quite, but along those lines, that over the top. I didn't know him and had never spoken to him. Or maybe it was, "When I come to hear you sing, you make my life beautiful." We both took it lightly, but it was such a remarkable thing to say.

As a singer I represent something. I don't do it consciously, but it's something that I have when I'm in performance style and in my element. It isn't constant, because you can see that I've had to fight hard to be in that place, but when I'm in that place I represent a kind of ebullience, a grace and femininity that just doesn't exist very much anymore. And it is a delicious, giddy femininity that is not sexy, so therefore every man and every woman can get involved in it. The appeal is not vampy in that respect so no man feels guilty getting caught up in it at dinner. Most women, when I'm singing, actually try to attract my attention so that I will direct that at the husband because they want that to happen. It evokes a sort of elegance from long ago. It makes people happy that that sort of elegance, a glamorous ebullience, a kind of life force that has to do with the essential feminine nature and charm, still exists—that someone can have that much fun wearing that much jewelry. And that it's fun. It's not about "Oh, aren't I rich, wearing this much jewelry?" It's about "Isn't it fun to wear this much jewelry?" This has a lot to do with the sheer love of life that is projected in performance.

So when I walk out on the stage wearing a four-thousand-dollar gown it isn't about, "Oh, I made so much money I can buy a four-thousand-dollar gown." I come across as someone who was either so entirely giddy on a man's arm that he bought her a four-thousand-dollar outfit, or that I worked so hard that I was able to purchase a four-thousand-dollar gown, and isn't that grand? There's nothing about conspicuous consumption.

Beyond the heady verve, the shimmer, is the darker stuff, especially a very vulnerable, edgy quality. There's a great deal of joy in it, but I think people know me quite well and they know also that at a moment's turn in the show a great deal of my trouble and sadness and breakability will show, and that I've been through a lot as well.

But right now there's not a lot of the great glamour of Hollywood of the past that I represent, to some extent, even though I'm a New York–based actress-singer. The music that I represent, that Fred Astaire elegance, that extreme grace, that cabaret grace, doesn't exist in this world very much. So when people come to a locale like the Algonquin, I project it out to them.

If this man I met last night has a very strong feeling for me, it's highly possible that at one of the shows I might have entered the audience and had my hand on his shoulder in a song. And it's highly possible that I was very direct or flirty with him during a song. This comes from the tradition of long ago—the cabaret singers who used to sing at tables. Mabel Mercer did that, and the next person that I'm doing a show about is Hildegarde, and Hildegarde did that and people just adored her. It was really hero worship for her.

Last night was a very interesting case in point. I opened the cabaret convention, and yes, I wore a gown whose original price was four thousand dollars. I got it for $2,800, and spent an extra God-knows-what on alterations, and the fact is I wore it with an unmitigated sense of joy. Somebody could tear me apart for twirling at my age in a gown like that. Sure, somebody who wanted to be cruel could say, "My God, what's she doing twirling at fifty-six?" On the other hand it's an honest twirl, and it comes from "Gosh, is this a pretty dress!" I think that the same joy is in my singing, my mothering, and in a good day. Unfortunately, being challenged in my life, that same joy is balanced by an equal amount of lows. And I think anyone who has been in severe trouble holding a life together knows exactly what I'm talking about—how you take those moments of joy and you run with them, because you know that they're fleeting. And you know that they're laced with the opposite. But I do project a very joyful and energetic creature. And I often am astonished at how those bursts of energy never fail me. They never fail me. They're always there when I need them, and thank goodness they are.

When I'm in residence here at the Algonquin—I just recently realized the extent to which I can allow myself that nightly joy. And it's time not to feel any guilt about it, as I've often felt very guilty at not being at home with Alice, but now I realize it's the time to inhabit that glittery dimension and say, "Well, I worked twenty years for that joy, I might as well experience it."

This work is—I am actually bipolar, but this work would make you so if you weren't, because it's bipolar work. I have a remarkable inner governor, like the governor on the steam heater, those little funny things you put on the sides of boilers. Well, I have an interior governor, which will sometimes keep me low during the day. And even depressed during the day. And I used to be so concerned about it because I'd feel very low and think, "How can I do the show tonight? I'm feeling so blue." I feel physically sick sometimes. I feel as though I can't do it, I won't do it. But it was just my natural barometer keeping me low, and then *va-room,* all the energy would come in at night. And it would always be there. I've come to recognize that feeling not as cycling to a depression—not a real low, but an unnatural, subconsciously imposed low—to save some energy for the night, to keep me a little low. And so now I recognize it and say, "Ah, that's the self-preservation low," so that I won't blow all my energy running around town shopping; I'll have some energy for the night.

I've had every issue you can possibly have and beaten them all. It's difficult for me to talk about one without talking about the others.

The first issue is unbridled manic energy. Naturally there is an enormous difference between an actress who waits for the phone to ring and a self-motivating, self-creating chanteuse cabaret performer. And with my central choice of career comes its own set of challenges and achievements. But if there was ever a time when you have to gather your own resources, your own belief systems and extraordinary courage, that's the time. Waiting for the phone to ring and auditioning is painful beyond belief, and yet once you get that job you are, at that point, interpreting someone else's words, you are—some people feel—hiding behind a character. I never did, because I was never a character actress, but you certainly have the protection of character. And you have directors, and it's a collaborative art, and what is produced is a collaborative work. But what I do is much freer and much more burdensome all at once, and leaves very little room for any kind of depression, because it's entirely private in the beginning. The idea comes from me. Okay, am I going to do a show about Ruth Etting or Fred Astaire or Hildegarde? It's entirely mine.

Sometimes I'm given some inspiration—for instance, the Hildegarde show my friend Lesley Alexander thought of—but once the inspiration is in there I have to run with it. No one is there. It's private. It's alone. I'm as solitary as any other writer would be. If I didn't have the discipline that it takes to plow ahead, there's nobody to ring my doorbell saying, "Oh, here's some music, Andrea, why don't you try that?" There's nobody there. But I also have the joy of knowing that every song that I have is a better script than I get going in auditioning for the latest episode of a sitcom or something. I have a song that has a beginning, middle, and end. I have a song that is written by Noel Coward. There's not going to be a better script that I'm going to audition for tomorrow when I get a phone call from my agent.

So there's extraordinary freedom in being the motivator. But again, if you're not on top of yourself, if you're not in control of your mood and emotions, nothing gets accomplished. So you really have to be a self-motivator to the max. Now once you're on stage, cabaret is the greatest kind of performance style there is, because it's all about you—you're it! To be responsible for the entertainment that night—and there is no fourth wall, there's nothing between you and the audience. It's completely improvisational; it's a conversation between you and the audience, not a play. Definitely a one-on-one between you and them: I think of it as a great date. That's how I've always thought of cabaret, as a great date between you and the audience. And it has to be structured in that way, with the first course and the second course and the third, just a magnificent evening out. All of this is a great deal of pressure and a great deal of fun. But it would be less than honest if I didn't say that it requires a lot of strength and ego. You have to stay balanced and you have to feel good in the mirror, and you're at the helm of everything, from the bottom of your shoes to your hair. It's a great responsibility. And when you think that I write all that dialogue—not write it down, but imagine and refine it all. I improvise it over and over and over until I like what I've said, and then and only then do I either tape it, or I'll write catch phrases down, so they don't get lost along the way. I've never written down a script. Never in the history of my cabarets have I written any of them down. And that's a big deal, too, because the act has to stay alive in my head.

I made a choice along the way to actively conduct my own career and not to be passive, not wait for the phone to ring but to have this very busy, active career. I mean, I can always memorize a song. No one is going to tell me that I can't be spending my day learning a song. I don't have to wait for permission. And that life of waiting for the phone, the audition, the approval, was very painful, worse for me than some people. For me it squandered my time. On the other hand, with those jobs came the camaraderie, the order—got to get up, be at the studio at 5:15 or 5:18, can't fall into very bad habits. And with the cabaret life you can fall into some pretty bad habits. You can say to yourself, "It's better for my voice if I sleep until noon." There are a lot of us who do. You can fall into depression, sleeping all day, living in the nighttime, and you can forgive yourself for that.

I've veered into terrible periods from which I have had to bring myself back. For instance, for most of a decade I never touched alcohol. I decided it would be healthier for me never to drink at all, because in our business the temptation to spend time after hours, to wind down with drinking or eating, is ever-present. Moreover, in my world to eat after a show is damaging to a throat. Who would know until you find that out? One of the only ways to come down after a show is to eat, and to eat is punishing, damaging, dangerous, the worst possible thing you can do. It's been proven it causes acid reflux to eat after a show and then lie down and go to sleep. You're breathing in acids, and eventually I did bring asthma and acid reflux on myself, eating and drinking after a show. Now it's absolutely no food after a show. And it's very difficult because if there's ever a thing you really need discipline on, it's the after-show, to wind yourself down in a healthy way. And I didn't used to. I used to be very hyper after a show, and spend a lot of time having champagne and getting into conversations, trying to sustain the high. And now I have finally disciplined myself in such a way that I can simply say, "Job well done," shake hands, and put the high— I find myself doing this now—I put the high back in the eyes of the people who have come to see me. I really deliver it back.

I had a therapist who told me that I was the channel for everyone's pain and happiness and worry and everything. There was a time a few years ago when I was experiencing such lows and only meager highs. It struck me that if I could be a channel in my shows—because I was receiving so much—it would be advisable to try to close the channel at night, before going upstairs and having all these dreams. Sometimes it feels as though I'm dreaming for everybody. I don't just dream for me. I've had vivid dreams my whole life. I have had nightmares that are absolutely out of proportion with what I live, and I have been plagued by them my whole life. My therapist says, "Well, maybe you are dreaming for the village!" And since I take in so much—I'm a lightning rod who feels the feelings of someone twenty people down, and sees that person and sees if they haven't felt connected, sees if they are having an argument with their husband: I see all this—so just recently I've noticed that afterwards I wind down better if I really take this time, when I'm shaking someone's hand, if I really connect in that moment. Now I close the channel a little bit, so by the time I go upstairs I feel there's been a real circle of energy that isn't open. That when they say thank you for a performance, I've really heard it, it's not just "Oh, yeah, yeah, yeah," that it's very important to them. I used to do that for them, rather than for me. Now, based on what I've been told about the channeling of their feelings, it's important for me to acknowledge their thank-yous and completely restore this unity of self, in a way that reinforces for me that most of this channel is closed. So that I can have peace of mind when I go upstairs. That we're all complete, that everyone's complete. Then I can go to my hotel room and do what I really love to do, which is to watch *Law and Order*.

I've talked to some other people who have had troubled pasts, either with food or smoking addictions or anything else like that, and *Law and Order* is the balm of Gilead. I had this conversation the other day with someone who had addictions—*Law and Order* is it for some reason! I think it's because there's a distinct right and wrong, a distinct beginning, middle, and end, and you just watch it like eating candy. I get a sense of peace of mind from an abstract exercise. Following the action of the show there's a puzzle involved. Similarly I sometimes do a jigsaw puzzle at one in the morning! Focusing the energies after hours. Giving the creating a rest.

I do have a history with anorexia. I had a history with almost every single kind of trouble that you can have in a woman's life. And I'm quite surprised that I'm still here, because of the difficulties that I've had to undergo and overcome. And I'm kind of surprised because I don't have anything to point to that would say "Oh, yes, of course, this happened to me in my childhood and naturally I would have all these disorders." I don't have any causality for most of these experiences. I think I was just born so sensitive. I was a very sensitive child. I always worried in a global way. Suffering for the village. This rang true to me with a jolt when I was told it by a therapist. A person like me, who was never able to live in the moment, was never truly able to enjoy what I should be enjoying, always worrying about the next thing, living a life of worry most of my life, doesn't make any sense. That I should have been so tortured by so much, when I was living such a great life and nothing was really wrong—doesn't add up.

My two or so years with anorexia was like going deaf and blind, arguably the worst time in my life, and it basically sprang out of nowhere. One of the things I want to counsel people about, speak up about, is that so many people think anorexia is a kind of choice. They think, "Well, she chose to be anorexic." There isn't a lot of sympathy for it. People think it's connected to vanity of some sort. She wanted to get thin and then thought it was very chic to get thinner and chose not to stop. And she doesn't like eating. Nobody understands anything about anorexia until she experiences it. It's so vastly different from the image.

From my understanding of it, anorexia is a nervous breakdown. Nobody understood that, and I resent to this day that the therapist I had at the time didn't immediately send me to her husband, who was a psycho-pharmacologist. He could have immediately saved me by putting me on some Valium or Xanax or something, and gotten me right up and out of the goddamn thing. Because truly it's a chemical imbalance. At the time, immediately because you've been dieting . . . that's the aspect of it that no one understands. Yes, it starts with dieting but what I truly believe is that the dieting itself sends you into some chemical imbalance.

I was going to a dentist before all this happened. And I was doing a lot of nitrous oxide for the dentistry. I wonder whether that also tipped some scales in my head because for me what happened with the anorexia was it went past anorexia to depersonalization anxiety. And what I didn't realize, after anorexia, was that there was anything worse than anorexia, and there was. Complete depersonalization anxiety where I left my body and I was not . . . You look in the mirror and you're not in the mirror, and you're here. And you spend the whole day trying to get back into your body. The whole day to get back in! Oh, it's the worst thing under the sun! It began with anorexia in my twenties. I'll never forget it. For many years I was scared even to discuss it because I feared that would reactivate it. I still have one or two episodes a year where I'll have the depersonalization thing—it's freaky! I'm not quite here! It's like an echo. You get a little chord in your head of music and you think, "I'm out! I'm not here, not here!"

I had been dieting. I had lost my voice. Somebody had told me to fast. And I fasted for three days—but still wasn't dieting in that way where you can think of nothing else but food. That's the other misnomer about anorexia: they think we don't want to eat. We think of nothing else but food. It's obsessive thinking. It's compulsive. It's OC disorder. You think of nothing else! It's the worst thing under the sun. I wouldn't wish it on Hitler, which was my line at the time. I would not wish it on the most evil person. It was that bad for me. Living hell.

I went on a fast. I ended up in the hospital because my intestine had shut down. When I got out of the hospital I was 109 pounds. I thought this was beautiful, and that was the beginning of the end. I'm five foot five and a half, and I was ecstatic. I know now that this was the beginning of my brain chemistry going askew. But they had done a spinal tap and given me a headache that was so fierce that they gave me some steroids. And within two weeks I went from 109 to 120. Well, that freaked me out, because I had seen myself suddenly at 109 and thought I was beautiful, and from that went to 120. I went mad! What if that kept on going? I felt insane. So for the next year, to get from 120 to 115 where I thought I should be—which already is crazy, I should be 130 or 135 with a frame like mine—I descended into madness. It was a madness of such proportions that I cry for her; I cry for that girl.

There was support hose at the time that supposedly would take weight off you if you wore it every day. I wore not one but two pairs. I would try on my jeans five, six, ten times a day, putting on the same pair over and over, as though they were a scale. I'd eat one something and try on the jeans to see whether they still fit.

Eventually I got so sick in my brain I could not go upstairs in my own apartment. I had a beautiful two-floor Manhattan apartment and I couldn't finish it. I couldn't do anything, just saw it as overwhelming. My world was narrowing down until I could not even pull my tired, heavy legs up the stairs in the apartment where I lived. I couldn't get off the couch.

I was living with a boyfriend who loved me but couldn't understand a word I was saying. I would sometimes go out to Greenwich Village and stand in front of a pastry store and cry. I would want the pastries because they would represent my father to me. I denied myself, of course. I tried throwing up but couldn't because that would break blood vessels in my eyes and I was too vain for that.

It was disgusting and strange. I would sometimes chew a box of cookies but spit them out.

The psychiatrist I went to see didn't understand. Had she given me Xanax it would have helped. I was in a state of severe anxiety. She kept saying, "As bad as you feel, you function, you'll work through this." But although I functioned I was nuts. I was on a soap opera and would think crazy things—like I really lived on the set, not the home that I have. It was awful!

Then I went out to do something in Los Angeles—and in those days I didn't drink—and I had a glass of wine and suddenly I felt fine. And then looking back on it, it was chemistry; I was missing sugars. But of course I thought it was the wine. And it was also getting away from the boyfriend, because I was really fundamentally not doing something I wanted to do. And, reviewing my life, when I fundamentally cross the line of choosing something that some part of me doesn't want to do, deep down in my bones, I go into unbelievable anxiety. Even if it's some small thing. I mean if I agree to some lunch date and I on a deep level have not wanted to do it, for reasons of my own, it can come out in all sorts of ways. Had I not moved in with that particular man at that particular time, would the onset of the anxiety have led to anorexia which led to depersonalization anxiety? Would it have happened? I don't know. My father had died, and I also had this chemical imbalance from having low potassium when I initially got sick. The whole episode started with low potassium from over-dieting.

My feeling is that to treat anorexia correctly would mean to see it as an episode of anxiety that needs to be dealt with by anxiety-suppressing drugs like Prozac or antidepressants immediately. Get these kids on the right drugs. Stabilize their serotonin levels. Don't even attempt to treat the food issues until you can treat the rest of it, because they are chemically so askew and we have no way of understanding how their minds are working. It's a mental illness of such proportions. When you see Dr. Phil, whom I enjoy, trying to deal with a girl of sixty-seven pounds who's eating one celery stalk for dinner, you can't deal with the behavior until you have the chemistry of the brain working normally again.

I look back on it as sheer hell and yet as something more. Beating everything that I've beaten in my life is positive. Beating this low-level depression that I have to beat is lifelong. I'm bipolar and take the right medicines for it now and that's just great because finally the treatment is in sync with the disorder, but inexplicably for me, with all of my great joy, and gifts and talents, to be given the steady dose of depression . . . You know I get so fed up! But I beat it and will for the rest of my life. But it is a foul depression. It is a foe at this point that I have to fight. My mother doesn't have this—she's Miss Fine. It isn't showing up in my daughter, either. All I can point to is that my father was elderly and there was a sense of fragility, but that's not enough. There are none of the familiar explanations you look for.

Meanwhile people didn't see it in me. I asked my brother and he said, "You were such a happy kid!" Now I'm really getting to the bottom of everything, because I have my daughter to consider and cannot be anything but great for her, because my husband and I have separated and I want to make sure that I'm the best mom in the world. He says, "What *are* you talking about?"

I know I was worried a lot, and that only now do I feel as though I live in the moment a great deal. I know that I'm troubled by dreams but that nothing is going to get me down anymore. I know that I can give a great deal of joy and that the people who come to hear me sing—I have heard them say dozens of times—that it's life-changing for them. I know that there is a natural warmth that I can project. I know that no matter how down I get that I always beat it. I conquered anorexia, generalized depression, and smoking (which I got caught up in). I don't drink, which is not an easy thing to say. I keep my weight stable and that's not easy to do. And right now I stay thin even though I eat all kinds of foods and I am not particularly paranoid about foods. And the love of my life called it quits, and I'm functioning. And I've had to learn—through many sorts of wisdom, without counting on one wisdom—to let go and to love with an open hand and an open heart. All the stuff that I used to make jokes about. "Love the bird as it flies." I used to say, "Better kill the bird, it should be dead if it's not with me!"

Now I love with an open hand and heart. When I first separated from my husband—we live in two homes and see each other a lot—I thought, "You're trapped; you're going to regress; that's it." Before that I thought I'd beaten it all, my mind would never be caught again. You know what it's like to experience your mind as separate from you, your mind as your nemesis. My mind is at me, tricking me, doing this to me, as opposed to everybody else just going along, never at odds with their minds . . . But I'm not sick. I'm living, experiencing all the feelings, yet staying well.

Anorexia was what came before the crack-up, the manifestation. The food has almost nothing to do with the anorexia. Sometimes there is an echo but no more than that. The moment I realized that the anorexia was founded on some severe fracture, and it would take more than resolving the eating problem to fix it, I really cracked up!

Above all, it isn't a personality defect for me, but Weltschmerz. I'm accepting at long last that I am the conduit for Weltschmerz, otherwise I wouldn't be such a good singer. I was hearing that from my first psychiatrist but thought it was such bullshit! Now I believe it. How could I do what I do with no particular training or effort? How could I know that it's appropriate to look right into the eyes of someone with that lyric that they need to hear? And they come up to me afterwards and say, "Oh, you must have known my husband died." And I do know, or do feel it. I know the person who needs the shoulder rubbed, or the special hug or treatment. I feel it or know it.

Why do I have no fear whatsoever? Is it just practice? No, it's not just practice. Why can I be out in the middle of that audience singing the way I do? And now my protégée, Mar, she can do it at thirty. No, there's a little magic going on, something extraordinarily special that has been legated to me. And maybe someone like me has a breakdown when there's a gap in the universal connection, when the connection has dropped away for a bit and we're falling through the crack. That's what it felt like. I felt like the earth had great big holes in it and I was about to step into one. I was convinced that the next step was going to take me into a drop in the earth of some sort.

As time goes by I have a particular attachment to, as schmaltzy as it is and sort of "that old thing," but for me it's always been the song of songs, "The world will always welcome lovers as time goes by." It's getting richer and richer for me, that song . . . "It's still the same old story, a fight for love and glory, a case of do or die."

Because it's really that for me. There are times that I think, "Oh, I'm going to San Francisco; there's always the Golden Gate Bridge." I shrug. "Well it's there." But it's that fleeting thought of "Oh, yeah, sure, you can jump from the Golden Gate." But for me it's a daily battle to wake up as I do, low, and go to sleep as I do, blessed and proud of my day. And, you know, I do it every single day. If you want the artistic great gifts that you have, maybe it's a small price to pay, to just roll with the ups and downs, and acknowledge and manage them as the day goes on. Because I'm now seeing staying in one piece and not dropping off into quicksand as daily battles. Harness the sources of agony because they are also sources of energy that have to be harnessed as the day happens, and they eventually become this spirit that comes out through my throat, heart, lungs, and eyes. And my clothes! There are times when it's all about the clothes! And out that inner darkness comes at night. Or, by the same token, out it comes in a direction when I'm doing my shows and I'm directing other people—the exuberance of grappling with your suffering. The same thing that made me cry in the morning—doubt, loss, fear—can be given as a direction to another actor and be "used," as we say, when I'm directing someone. That same morsel of pain that I was experiencing in the cycle of my day I can give to somebody else, and it connects me with others in a dynamic way. We all have to think of our individuality as a gift, and mold that gift as the day goes on. Okay, I'm going to use you and make you into something beautiful by the end of the day. That coal-into-diamond analogy comes often to me.

There are still going to be some days when the anxiety or sadness or worry is unmanageable. But if you don't seek a quick, destructive fix, if you don't starve or poison yourself either by eating things you shouldn't be eating or drinking things you shouldn't be drinking, or smoking or drugs, if you don't poison yourself with somebody who's going to treat you badly, if you can stay relatively pure and listen to your heart during these waves that are going to come in a day or month or year, whatever they are, you should be able to channel those energies creatively for your aspirations or your art. Fundamentally it's about leaving something behind, even if it is that man who said, "You make my life more beautiful." You make my life more beautiful? Life? What are you saying, life is more beautiful because I sang you some songs?! That's pretty cool!

Frustrated in their ability to find a solution to their problem in reality because reliance on food for safety (bread crumbs to mark the path) fails them, Hansel and Gretel now give full rein to their oral regression. The gingerbread house represents an existence based on the most primitive satisfactions. Carried away by their uncontrolled craving, the children think nothing of destroying what should give shelter and safety, even though the birds' having eaten the crumbs should have warned them about eating up things.

—Bruno Bettelheim, *The Uses of Enchantment*

Mike Huckabee
(governor of Arkansas)

IT'S ALWAYS PREFERABLE to do interviews for a book like this in person rather than over the telephone. Eye contact and body language make the job of shaping a personal story much easier.

So on a chilly winter morning I headed out of the lobby of the historic Peabody Hotel in downtown Little Rock, Arkansas, on my way to the state capitol building to interview Governor Mike Huckabee, a man who has had major issues with overeating and has been in recovery for some time now.

I decided to walk the mile or so to the capitol, to let the fresh air clear my head in preparation for our talk. Within a couple of blocks of what looked like a miniature version of our nation's capital, I came upon a little restaurant that took the starch out of the seriousness of what I was about to do: CJ's All You Can Eat Country Buffet. I felt as if I'd encountered a candy store in the diabetes ward of the local hospital. What on earth did Governor Huckabee think of this joint, its doors literally at the steps to his office?

Upon entering the capitol building, I prepared myself to be

carefully scrutinized by the now-customary airport-style security apparatus. A drowsy-eyed, overweight guard asked me if I had anything to show him. Upon answering, "No, I don't," I was waved in without even a further glance. I've submitted to tougher security checks at my local movie theater than I did on my way to see the governor of the great state of Arkansas.

The rotunda of this impressive building is replete with oversized portraits of ex-governors of the state. Men with colorful names like Jefferson Davis, Daniel Webster Jones, George Washington Donaghey, and Tom Jefferson Terral led the Razorback State, but where's the portrait of Bill, I wondered? Must be an oversight, I concluded.

I was directed to the governor's office by a friendly guard, and upon entering the reception area, I was asked the purpose of my visit and told to take a seat. I immediately noticed a guest book resting on a pedestal. I signed it, wondering if I would now be on the governor's Christmas card mailing list.

The reception room is home for all manner of gubernatorial memorabilia. Bypassing the photographs of obligatory poses with high-ranking government officials, including several with a smiling George W. Bush, I was particularly struck by a Plexiglas display case some four feet high housing a full-sized stuffed wild turkey gobbler. The plaque beneath it noted that the governor "harvested" it in 2001. Also prominently displayed is a head of a whitetail buck deer that he shot in 2002. Better be careful what I say, or I could end up on display as well, I thought.

After a short wait I was escorted into the governor's office, where Huckabee greeted me with a warm handshake and direct eye contact that put me right at ease. Without much in the way of formality, the governor proceeded to tell me the story of a long-lived eating disorder that he has not only come to terms with, but has turned into an advantage. A politician willing to talk candidly about a personal problem such as an eating disorder—one who found a solution that works—is someone who would probably get my vote. Listening to his compelling story did nothing to change my mind.

—G.S.

My issue with food is childhood based. Growing up in a family where we didn't have a whole lot, food was sort of the one constant. We didn't get to go on vacations, have new cars, own a nice home, but the one thing my parents tried to make sure of was that there was food on the table. I think that like a lot of kids growing up in the South whose parents had gone through the Depression, it was like the one thing that they had to make sure that we had. The result of that was we were always admonished to eat everything on our plate. Throw nothing away. There was no such thing as a leftover. You do not throw food out because that's throwing money away. Kids are starving in China . . . I ate for more kids in China than probably live there now! I ate for half of Asia!

As a child I didn't really have a significant weight problem. I would have interludes, maybe in the third grade, or later, maybe in the eighth grade, where I would gain some weight and get a little chubby. Then I'd cut back on my eating and try not to get overweight, but I came from a family that had a history of obesity, and it was futile.

When I reached my adult years, after college and after marriage, I found that as my activity diminished and my metabolism also began to slow, I could eat the same amount of food and I would gain a little bit of weight. You know, I don't drink and I don't smoke. I never engaged in those vices, but eating is something I could do without any social penalty. In the Deep South, an all-you-can-drink bar would be dishonorable but an all-you-can-eat buffet is an absolute, divine right. As a result I found that my stress could often be relieved by just eating. Snacking, eating late at night, junk food. Obviously I must have had a lot of stress in my life over the years, by the amount of weight I gained.

I would go through periods where I would get really big and I'd say, "I've got to do something about this," and I can remember several different times. In 1982 I lost thirty pounds, in 1988 I lost forty pounds. I sort of got my weight under control but never changed my lifestyle. All I did was focus on weight loss without changing my activities. I didn't engage in an exercise program, I simply said, "I'm going to lose weight," and I would target a specific amount of weight to lose, and go do it.

In my forties my weight problem returned. I had one bout in 1996 where I lost probably fifty pounds. I'd gain weight, I'd lose weight and get back closer to where I needed to be, but again, it was just weight loss. The focus was on weight, not health. I never made the transition of changing my personal habits. Within a year and a half the weight was creeping back, and then I got to my all-time high in 2002. That year my doctor sat me down for a serious talk and said, "Without a real lifestyle change, you're in the last decade of your life, and here's what's going to happen." And then he elaborated what this would be like, and it was not a very pleasant picture. He explained how diabetes begins to take over a person's body. How it affects everything from eyesight to the feeling in the extremities, problems with the feet, and heart problems. And I thought, "Good grief, this is not exactly how I want the last chapter to be written."

And so, former governor Fran White—he had been elected in 1980 and served two years and was defeated by Bill Clinton—was a good friend of mine. I had appointed him state bank commissioner. Frank had come to the point of retirement. He was sixty-nine years old and was here in my office telling me he was retiring. He and his wife were going to do a lot of traveling. Frank had gained an enormous amount of weight and was in very bad shape. I told my wife that night, "I was with Frank today, and gosh, he's struggling just to get across the room." He was short of breath, and then one week later, to the day, I got a phone call telling me that Frank's wife Fay had come in and found him dead on the floor. Massive heart attack, dropped dead. It really shook me up. I had just been with him the week before, and even though I knew he was in bad health, still his death came as a shock.

That, along with my own issues—I just said, "Hey, I got to make some changes. I'm not going to last to sixty-nine. I won't even get that far." And I wouldn't have.

A friend of mine had spoken to me about a weight loss program at UAMS, the University of Arkansas Medical Science campus: our medical school, associated with our university. He said, "It's really a good, solid program." I said, "I've got to do something," so I contacted them and asked for a description of the program, and decided to give it a try.

Really, the difference for me was that this was the first time the focus was not on just losing the weight. That's the wrong issue. Skinny people can be unhealthy, and people who are somewhat overweight can be healthy. But health is a lifestyle, and it's about what we eat and how we maintain the activity level of our body. So I decided what I really needed to do was to alter my lifestyle.

The first part of the program at UAMS is learning how to eat right, and detoxing your body from a lot of the things that you're used to. That was really helpful—kind of cleansing the system. The early days were a lot of meal replacements with shakes or salads. I ate a lot of vegetables, but what I've basically done is eliminate fried foods, processed foods. If it's highly processed I stay away from it. I don't eat refined sugar. I avoid it completely. I avoid partially hydrogenated vegetable oil in all its forms. Essentially I just try to eat food that is as healthy and natural as I can find. The manner of preparation is either grilled, baked, broiled, and not fried—which for a Southerner, you have to understand, is truly a challenge.

The reason Southerners fry so much is not just a cultural taste; it was actually an economic necessity. You take a very thin slice of very cheap meat, beat the heck out of it to tenderize it, bread it, then fry it, and then make gravy and pour it on top of it. Add potatoes, and pour gravy on top of that, and you have a very inexpensive meal. You're getting meat, but what you are really getting is breading and gravy . . . and grease. A lot of it. And a lot of calories. The name of the game for many of us growing up was just to get enough calories to sustain life. It was not about becoming overweight. We ended up doing that. In the early days in the South when people were having to work, and gather their firewood, and even walk down the trail to go to the bathroom, because they didn't have indoor plumbing—I always had it, I want to make that clear—but in my parents' day it was gathering the firewood, it was walking to school, walking to work. Not having indoor plumbing until they were grown, so everything involved activity. So two things happened: we got to where we didn't have to be as active, but we continued to eat the things that were culturally normal to us, and in greater portions.

The key lessons I've learned are, number one, to focus on health not weight. Weight loss as a goal fails, because a weight goal has a beginning and an ending. Gee, I weigh 290 pounds, I need to weigh 180 pounds, so I have a start point, but when I finish I say, "Okay, now let's celebrate. I'll have a double fudge sundae." A lot of people can lose the weight but they don't know how to adjust their lifestyle to make it permanent. And the second thing is while weight is one of the indicators of health, it is not the only one. What you also need to know is blood pressure, blood sugar, hemoglobin rates, cholesterol counts, pulse and resting pulse rates. Those are things that really give a person a much better picture of his or her health. Weight is just a snapshot of one aspect of health, but certainly not the whole thing.

One thing that I've dealt with was learning why I gravitated toward these comfort foods. There's a chapter in my book, *Quit Digging Your Grave with a Knife and Fork,* called "Stop Allowing Food to Be a Reward." I remember the day that this occurred to me. I was out on a walk, and I was smelling honeysuckle, and I was thinking about being a five- or six-year-old kid on a summer day, with the smell of honeysuckle in the air. How innocent and pleasant life was. I started to realize that there were certain foods whose taste or aroma took me back to times of carefree living as a child: some of my most pleasant memories, whether it was of a birthday cake or the special treat I would get if we won our Little League game. I realized that I'd grown up in a culture where we were rewarded with food. If I went to the doctor and didn't cry when I got a shot, I'd get a candy bar. If I went with my mother to the grocery store and I didn't make a fool of myself in the aisles and throw stuff in the cart or knock down large displays of canned goods, maybe I'd get a pack of gum at the checkout stand.

In other words, rewards were often food. Birthdays, special occasions, that's when we got treats like cake. If you were good you got ice cream. You got to indulge in foods that essentially had no nutritional value. If you were bad, on the other hand, those things were withheld from you. "Okay, no dessert for you today. You made a C. You should have made a B or an A. No dessert, just eat your vegetables." So we grow up with this programming that's been encoded into us that says, "When you're a good person you get to eat all the candy, ice cream, or all the junk you want, but if you're bad, we withhold those things and we force you to eat carrots and broccoli and celery." Without ever knowing it, this gets imprinted into our brain, and so we get to the place where as adults, we get to make our own choices. There's no mother over us saying you can or you can't.

So what do we do? We tell ourselves, "We can." And we do. So if I've had a tough day, people chewing on me all day, I can go home and say, "I'm not as bad as they think I am. Have a bag of chips. I'm not really that bad. Have a bowl of ice cream." That affirms that I'm good. That affirms that I'm all right. I deserve to be rewarded, not punished. So I came to realize that some of my indulgences were ways of dealing with my stress and ways of giving myself affirmation that I had failed to get in the world in which I lived.

Without trying to be overly analytical about it or make this some moment of couch time, I really do think that those subtle influences can have enormous hold over us. The key thing is to realize that that's why it's so easy to succumb to it, and to change the mind. What I learned differently this time, and why it's become my new lifestyle, is that I identified for the first time what caused me to be drawn back to my bad habits. And I realized that you couldn't build good habits into your life until you identify and confront the bad ones that are already there. Because whatever you do regularly and consistently, in other words, whatever becomes a habit, is not engrained. It's like a groove dug into your psyche, and you tend to get back to it when there is tension, strife, or conflict. It's always easier to fall back into the groove than it is to go against it. That's why so many people say, "I tried and I tried; I failed and I failed." My response is, "Keep trying." It requires changing the habit, identifying why you have it, confronting it, and building new ones. But get rid of the old one before you build a new one.

I thought I would just die without fried foods and things like that. You know, once in a great while I may think, "Boy, wouldn't it be great to have a plate of fried chicken?" But interestingly enough, I don't miss it that much, and amazingly I don't really miss sugary things either. I eat sugar substitute things so I'm satisfied with whatever sweet needs I have. Now when I encounter something that's made with sugar, I find it distasteful. It tastes syrupy.

Right before Christmas a friend of mine from Fort Worth, Texas, sent me a box of these coconut macaroons that he said were "to die for." Probably literally! These huge, big macaroon cookies that he found at some bakery, and he sent me a box. He said, "I know you don't want them, but just pinch a little bite off one of 'em and then let your staff eat them." So out of curiosity I took a pinch, but because it was so sweet, it didn't really appeal to me. It's like, "Okay, I tried it, and I can tell him I had a bite," but as far as wanting to eat the whole thing, like I used to—no way!

That's been my biggest surprise. I found that once I detoxed my body and the stuff got out of my system, it wasn't that difficult to say no to the junk. A lot of that was learning about the physiological effect of hypoglycemic foods. You know that old potato chip commercial, "Bet you can't eat just one"? It's physically true. When you ingest things that instantly turn into sugar—be it potatoes or foods that have been highly processed, and therefore your body doesn't think it's eating because it's not having to work to digest—it's simply passing empty calories. Then you try to eat more because even though your hands have said you've had food in them, your brain has been tricked. It's thinking you haven't had the process of your body digesting anything, so your brain is saying, "Feed me," so here you go. As you're doing that your blood sugar is beginning to kick up because of this processed food. That causes your insulin levels to spike, and then that demands that you "put some more food in me." I found that once I broke that pattern, I didn't find myself wanting to keep eating. I was eating things that were satisfying, and that need to just keep on eating and gorge, where I couldn't stop, just disappeared. It was an amazing, exhilarating experience for me!

Exercise has also helped me tremendously. I may be as addicted to running as I once was to food, and I wouldn't have it any other way. I ran my first marathon a year ago. I found myself getting up this morning and going out to run in the rain. I thought, "I would not have gone out to get the paper in the rain three or four years ago, and here I am out running in it." I feel very disciplined and focused in my life today. If I have a goal, like running a marathon, I create a training schedule and I'm pretty rigorous in keeping with that schedule. That helps me to have a pattern. The energy I get from running is better than the feeling I get from eating something and then having that crashing feeling a half an hour later. That's something I don't miss! I used to overindulge. The moment I was gorging on something I would think, "Wow, this is so delicious." And then about a half an hour later, your head is spinning and your blood sugar has taken a dive, so I don't miss that at all.

Given how overboard I'd go, I'm lucky I was spared and only had the one addiction. God was good to me. I had no natural inclination towards drugs or alcohol. As a teenager, obviously everyone's offered it, beer and everything else, and I smelled it. But I never tasted beer. I'm probably the only adult human being in this state who hasn't. Not that I was so moral or made such a great decision. When it was offered to me and I smelled it I didn't like it. I thought, "Hey, that smells like something that's ruined and spoiled, not something I want to drink." I will never forget when my friend said, "You have to develop a taste for beer." And my answer was, "If I have to develop a taste, that means I don't have a taste. Why would I try to make myself like something that right now my nose says, 'This is hideous'?" And that was it.

What I went through was a transformation in my lifestyle. There's an old me and a new me and sometimes there is something that will make me extra aware of it. Not having to test a chair before sitting down, for instance. There was a big moment in November 2003. President Bush visited Little Rock for a luncheon speech and, as is the case with most presidential visits, his appearance made front-page news the next day. The article showed a photograph of the president pointing me out in a crowd and calling me "skinny." Having that written in the state's largest newspaper was pretty good.

When you feel most alive find out why.
That is one guest you won't greet twice.

—Rumi

Dixie Whatley
(TV and radio journalist, sculptor)

IN A WORLD THAT tends to specialists, Dixie Whatley has followed two muses. One of the most successful woman in television journalism, she has also explored her artistic nature as a cartoonist, illustrator, and sculptor in stone.

After earning a bachelor's degree (graduating Phi Beta Kappa) and a master's from the University of Southern California, Dixie launched her career as a journalist in Los Angeles. At KCOP-TV she worked as a news writer and fill-in anchor for the late-weeknight newscast. Then she moved to KTLA-TV as a weekend anchor and reporter. It was here that fortune smiled upon her.

Dixie was noticed by the producers of *Entertainment Tonight* and signed on as anchor, reporter, and New York City correspondent in the very early days of this hugely successful and innovative show, from 1981 to 1986. Later she cohosted *At the Movies* with Rex Reed while she continued her fourteen-year stint as a popular film critic and arts and entertainment reporter for WCVB, the ABC television station in Boston. She also hosted the internationally syndicated TV show *The Star's Table.*

Dixie has been a reporter/anchor on four Emmy Award–winning news programs and received the Los Angeles Press Club Award in 1979 for best television news writing for coverage of the Iranian student riots in Los Angeles.

Among the manifestations of her artistic side are the illustrations she created for the *Los Angeles Times* over a six-year period while she was also working on TV. She designed the graphics for the Oscar-winning documentary *Scared Straight* and is a published photographer.

Now Dixie and her husband Brooke Cobb, a retired investment manager, divide their time between Boston and Naples, Florida. Her work in Boston includes hosting for Public Broadcasting Service programs and reviewing films for WMJX radio. In Florida's warm climate she applies her creative energies to her large stone sculptures. Again, both of Dixie's muses are at work.

Ever the observer of our national trends and fads, Dixie says that the camera has always made people look heavier and that celebrities are getting thinner. In her words, "The media is very guilty of putting forth ridiculously thin images of women."

A scintillating conversationalist, interested in everyone, Dixie Whatley is remarkably un-jaded. One notices both her caring nature and her skill with a barbed comment. Today she lives a happy life, flying with all of her creative energies engaged.

More offbeat facts illustrate Dixie's well-known effervescence: She flew in an F–16 with the Thunderbirds and got a 9-G pin for reaching 9,000 miles per hour. For the year 2000 she was asked to contribute a new Necco candy slogan, putting "2000 kisses" on those little hearts. She has performed with the Boston Pops, as well as other orchestras, reading such works as "Yes, Virginia, There Is a Santa Claus" and *Peter and the Wolf.* Last but not least, Dixie has been queen of the Crew of Tucks Mardi Gras parade, with Eugene Levy as her king.

—J.M.

I am a stone sculptor. I'm strong and muscular, and I can re-form unwieldy, ugly hunks of rock into creations of grace, whimsy, and beauty.

Sounds like the entertainment industry, doesn't it?

For many years, I was a television journalist. I was thin, really thin, once upon a time. Not a pretty picture. Well, actually, a really pretty picture, in the weird world of television. TV is peopled with strange, lanky creatures with thin bodies and big heads. Somehow, when captured by a camera of any kind, these creatures morph into stunningly gorgeous beings. These beings are worshipped near and far as the epitome of perfection and desire.

How warped is that?

It's tough to work face to face with the aforementioned, some of the most beautiful people in the world, and hold your own. I did it for years . . . and for the most part, I held my own. But if you ever want to be aware of how you look, the TV arena is the way to shove yourself into your own face and do a hard-core comparison test.

Long ago I realized that all the myriad issues about weight and eating disorders and addiction boil down to one simple thing: feeling good. Feeling good mentally, physically, emotionally. And if you don't feel good, you try to do something about it: exercise, yoga, bungee jump, sleep, chant, drink, drugs, smoke, or eat. And all too often, my feel-good solution was food. It simply made me feel better. And it was more convenient than bungee jumping. Ice cream and a good book, hunker down in a little cocoon of my own making and under my own control, and block out the bizarre world of television politics in which I had to live but didn't understand. At all. Still don't. And along with the stress of politics in that world comes the single priority that can make on-camera people even crazier: the fact that "look good" is vastly more important than "feel good." And if food is your "feel good," you've got yourself a problem.

A few years ago I moderated a forum at Harvard University, hosted by the Harvard Eating Disorders Center. I was chosen because I'd moderated many events, not because of a weight issue. I'd never discussed weight publicly. As a member of the media, I said in my opening comments—as anyone with half a brain and a TV or newspaper or magazine will agree— "The media is very guilty of putting forth ridiculously thin images of women." I also joked a bit about thin actresses (hey, I was the moderator; had to keep things upbeat), and was roundly taken to task by a Harvard student and actress who knew whereof she spoke: Natalie Portman. She chastised me for sniping about Calista Flockhart and other rail-thin actresses. Okay. I had said I was jealous and gave voice to what too many of us think when watching such slender women: "I hate her." (That part was, of course, a joke.) Portman said we shouldn't speculate about their health issues. We should discuss why this image is being encouraged. She's correct, and she has earned the right to comment. She said she was first questioned by a director about gaining weight when she was eleven years old. Now *that's* sick.

So she was caught up by those weird, warped values. As is Flockhart. (Just a guess, I admit. She may just have the metabolism we all wish we had.) As was I, in the lunatic world of on-camera media personalities. And for those of us who have faced weight and food issues for much of our lives, it's even harder to get thin and stay that way. For me, that was the case.

Food softened stress. In college, everyone went underground to study for finals accompanied by bags of candy and chips and other horrible crap food, which gave us the energy boost to study and ace tests. Me too. It was easy to rationalize. "I'm studying. I can eat junk." Now, there's questionable logic.

I suppose I could blame bad eating habits on childhood. Serious deep-fried southern cooking. What? Fried is fat? Eat more, weigh more? Who knew! I never really made the conscious connection. Sure, I was a kid, but even a kid can figure out that if you eat more, you weigh more. I look back at the dreaded school pictures and see a little butterball from third through fifth grade. Mom always said I never had an "awkward age," all knees and elbows. Of course not: I was a chub! I remember at age eleven wearing a sweater on the playground on a hot day because I was self-conscious. Now by high school, I was on the homecoming court and in the Rose Parade as a rose princess. But that chubby self-image never really goes away, no matter the outside positive reinforcement.

Being chubby as a child made me that much more physically self-conscious later, even though the chubbiness was gone. It's that classic thing: you see what you fear when you look at yourself. Now that never drove me to anorexia, but it was like a low-grade chronic condition. That chubbiness predisposed me to have to fight weight and to have a not-so-great body image. Combined with a television career, it made for a lot of conflicting emotions and self-consciousness. I never intended to be a broadcaster, to work in a field where how I looked was so important. As a child I was an artist, and art was what I intended to do, although by the age of thirteen I was a paid "journalist," writing a column for the local newspaper. The interest in journalism was encouraged, for both my sister, Susanne, and me, by our mother, who had been a writer of drama and comedy for CBS Radio Network in Hollywood in the 1940s. My sister is currently a radio news anchor in Los Angeles, and has been for many years.

As an undergraduate at the University of Southern California, I did political cartooning for the paper as well as writing, taking art classes along with courses for my journalism major. I finished a semester early and went to work doing advertising, public relations, print writing, illustration, radio, and TV, while earning a master's in broadcast journalism and getting involved in live television and radio.

I was blessed with being a pretty young woman, and that certainly helped me get jobs. At that time you didn't have to be itty-bitty teeny-weeny. I was average size; I wasn't fat but I wasn't thin, and that was fine—they called it healthy. I got my first TV job in my hometown, Los Angeles, and then the next there as well, as a weekend anchor and weekday reporter, when I got a call from Paramount . . . "Dixie, we have this brand-new show called *Entertainment Tonight*."

It had been on the air for a couple of weeks with a three-host setup, and they wanted to give it more of a news format. So: hire a newscaster. We met. At the time I was saying, "Is there really enough news in the entertainment industry to sustain the show?"

So much for that.

I did both jobs. I anchored the newscast on the weekends, as the "serious" anchor, and cohosted the mostly fluffy *Entertainment Tonight* during the week. But I was not ready for the politics of *ET.* I felt like I was being turned into a bimbo. I had no input into what I read on camera, and I did nothing but read the stories, no reporting. Of course, that was the job I was hired to do. Nothing personal, that was just the way the show was set up, but I had a difficult time with the role. And, working seven days a week, with the stress. And I began to suffer from depression. But I couldn't turn to food as I had in the past, because I'd gain weight. In fact, I figured I should lose weight to be more what this strange hybrid of news and Hollywood needed for a host.

We had a wonderful wardrobe guy. It was he who suggested I consider dropping some weight. So I did. I went on a doctor-supervised diet; I went to the gym and dropped a bunch of weight. I looked great, by TV standards, but sure didn't feel so good.

I became a gym rat for the adrenalin boost and to keep slim. But that wasn't enough. We all have our attributes. I've always felt that my legs were not my best asset, and the people who ran the show kept wanting me to hike my skirt up to there—and to there. I understood why, but I didn't think it was flattering for me, and no one was there to give me pointers on how to sit to best show my legs, so I was uncomfortable. Not only because I wasn't completely thrilled with my legs, but because I was bright and funny and had no idea how to bring my own strengths to the table.

Years after *ET* I did a radio news conference with Howard Stern. When I introduced myself, he and his cohost Robin Quivers sang "Na-na-na-na-na-na"—the *Entertainment Tonight* theme song—and the next thing out of Howard's mouth was "They canned you." And I said, "Yeah, they did." What are you going to do, lie to him? And he said, "I remember you were the one with the great legs." I replied, "No, Mary Hart was the one with great legs. I was the one with the great breasts."

It actually stopped him for a heartbeat, then he laughed. So you've got to go with what you've got. It's silly to fixate on wishing for something that will never be, until leg transplants become the norm. Did it really matter that much? Probably not. But remember that one of the big hooplas about my replacement, Mary Hart, was her great legs.

When you're in broadcasting you realize quickly that everything is personal. They always say, "No, it's not, it's business," but it is personal. If somebody says, "You're too tall, too short, too fat, too thin, wrong color hair, wrong eyes, wrong race," it's personal, whether they want to admit it or not.

So either you're able to divorce yourself from it, or you get nuts, and I really had a difficult time with that. I wanted to do the work, I believed in and was energized by it, but I was sensitive about image and vulnerable to the doubts about my living up to the image. I took all the remarks about my weight or my appearance extremely personally. I'm naturally spontaneous, but I was becoming more and more self-conscious.

In television there's no two ways about it. You become hyperaware of staying thin. And I did. As a result, I really cut back on eating a lot. It was particularly stressful because all my life I had considered my intelligence my best asset, not my looks. I think if you enter beauty contests from the time you are a child, or you aspire to be an actress, where your appearance is essential, then you are more aware of looks as part of a package you are marketing. I'd never focused on being seen, so getting hit full force with image was something I wasn't prepared to handle. "How do you look? Is your hair right? Do you need to do this or change that?" Those questions, day in and day out, reinforced my insecurities.

A major influence on my life, too, was that my touchstone was gone. My mother died a couple years before *ET.* I didn't have that voice of logic and reassurance in my life. And I was still mourning, although I don't think I realized it.

I ended up getting depressed. I assumed it was just the stress but eventually realized it was full-fledged depression. Not knowing what to do about it, I kept up all the work. And before going on the air I'd drink three cups of coffee to rev myself up, just to be able to cope with what was going on.

Now there's a happy coupling: depression and hyperawareness of how I looked. Because I was a news anchor and reporter, not an entertainer, I never dressed like one. I'd put on a suit, fix myself up nicely, and do a news show. All of a sudden I was wearing tight sweaters. It really bothered me, but I didn't know what to do about it. And—reality check once again—that was the job.

Even so, I fought for equality with the cohost. Mind you, this was a time when women were finally starting to emerge as equals in news. But this was not news. My male cohost always opened and closed the show and reported any story that could qualify as "news." As a newscaster and journalist, that really bothered me. I felt diminished and relegated to a distinctly secondary role. Again, we're talking about image—the role and the ensemble: sweaters, big hair, and heavy makeup. I'd made a strong foray into the news business earlier, and I knew I was undoing some of the respect for which I'd worked so hard.

A few years later I ran into Mary Hart, the longtime host of *ET* who replaced me, at a national convention. (No, she never undermined me, to my knowledge. I did that just fine all by myself, thank you.) We were sitting with a couple of other on-camera people, and she said, "Dixie fought the battles, and I won the war." That was a very generous and kind thing for her to say, and it was true. Everything I fought for she eventually did in the show: opened it, closed it, and became not only equal but the top person by far. And it's worked perfectly for the show. So I was actually right, but at the time I was labeled a pushy, complaining bitch. When women fought for equality at that time, the woman was labeled a bitch, while a man was considered strong and assertive. And much as we like to think that's changed, I really don't think it has. But of course, changing the direction of the show was *not* my job. All I did was annoy the bosses. And it goes back to that vicious circle: if I didn't look as I did I wouldn't have gotten the job, but then I was labeled the bimbette. Not that people said it to my face, but it was pretty obvious.

A few years later, I experienced a prime example of the stereotypes about attractive women. I was cohosting *At the Movies,* a national film review show. My cohost, the absolutely delightful Rex Reed, and I were on *Hollywood Squares,* sharing a square. Joan Rivers was center square at the time. A contestant was asked the question, "Which of our celebrities, along with Joan Rivers, is a member of Phi Beta Kappa, the national honor society?" The contestant, correctly, chose me. Talk about a backhanded compliment. Who'd think the pretty girl could possibly be the one with the brains to get into Phi Beta Kappa? And the contestant deduced the logic correctly. Ah, image.

At *ET,* I took it all too seriously. You have to have iron confidence to step into that kind of position. The pressure made me worse. The more people pressured me, the more they rolled their eyes if I couldn't read a story in one take, the more nervous I got. And coming from live newscasting, I probably goofed much more, since there was a second chance at a take. (*Entertainment Tonight* was live on tape—done as if it were live, then sent by satellite across the country an hour or so later.) It got to be a joke: the more pressure they put on me the more tense I became on the set. At one point the director—who's often called the voice of God because you hear his voice descending from the heavens—started placing bets with the other people in the director's booth, wagering on whether or not I'd make it through a read. Everyone heard it. He was trying to lighten the tension, but of course it only served to make me even more nervous.

The chipping away at your self-image accumulates if you allow it to. It's one big package, the way you look, feel, and speak, and it's rooted inside you. It's not the weight, the clothes, and the hair. Your image is you, and you cannot divorce yourself from it. That's what makes it so difficult to be an on-camera person, an actress or actor. You are labeled by the way you look. And if you don't look as they think you ought to, if they force you into a mold, you feel very pressured to *become* that image. It becomes much more important than who you are, or what you may be able to bring to the table creatively.

Also, on television there's a territoriality. It's a complete luck of the draw if personalities work well together. If one is much more assertive or selfish about wanting to have the last word, the tougher person is going to triumph. But the fact is that the most successful on-camera couples are the ones who show respect for each other, share the duties, and make each other look good.

When under this pressure, your attitude towards your diet becomes a factor because you are trying to maintain artificial standards. When I got really depressed I turned to food. After gaining weight I went through a few fad diets until at one point, through the doctor-supervised diet, I was able to get to my target weight sensibly.

Prior to the healthy weight loss I turned to food when I was down. Subsequently, in later years, I relapsed and went back to turning to food. That was undesirable, but so was the hyperawareness of staying thin and avoiding food. I know. I did the whole "Go pick up the pint of ice cream, eat the whole thing" routine that a lot of other people do, too. Self-medication. Turning to food for solace. I was trying to get rid of depression, and there is no doubt that having to focus on how I looked made me worry I'd be thought chubby again. It put weight in the forefront of my mind. Being out of the spotlight, out of the grind, I have a much more healthy body image. It's a different planet!

After *Entertainment Tonight* I did other shows, including a long stint on local news in Boston. There's nowhere near the nastiness and "backstabbing-just-because-you-can" kind of craziness that goes on at a network level, but it's still there. I did arts and entertainment on a politically oriented news show, so my work just wasn't deemed that important. I understood; I'd been a news anchor, and that was fine in many respects, because I had a great deal of freedom to choose what stories I covered. While in Boston, I was also hired to do *At the Movies,* so again I had two jobs. But when that show was canceled, and I lost, once again, the national exposure, I started to gain weight.

A few years later, I lost my first husband after a long illness. And at that point, something changed in me. I separated myself from some of the negative aspects of my job. I watched someone I loved die—someone who so very much wanted to live. And, along with so many other things, it made me realize how absurd the backstabbing, rumor-filled aspects of TV are. So much works against people being encouraged and *allowed* to do a good job. I still did the best stories the best way I could, but I became stoic about the slights, and removed myself from all but the work itself.

Since I left the business, I'm in a place I want to be. I don't miss the pressure and stress. Some people thrive on stress, but I didn't. Now I'm doing what I want. I have plenty of time to exercise, and I'm much better adjusted. In the world of television you succeed if you rally when you have to fight and scratch. Or when someone is screaming or undermining you, you can go around them—or you see it coming, see the people with the knives drawn and dodge them. I couldn't see it. I couldn't understand why someone would undermine me, so I never would defend myself. Usually, I wasn't even aware I needed defending. It was beyond me why anyone would badmouth or backstab me for little or no reason. I never took any enjoyment in the game or understood how it was played. The simple dynamics of this type of work are that it's a high-tension environment even when there's nobody out to get you, and it's a scramble just to stay where you want to stay. I was battling the stress, and my discomfort was expressed in weight. When the answer to "Why are you doing this?" is "To make a living," for a creative person, that's not enough.

Now that I do what I love and have always loved, which is art, I have found my muse. Stone carving gives me great pleasure. To be able to create from a chunk of rock, to make it look light and airy, organic, transform it into something totally different from what it was—that's a wonderful outlet. I love the physical aspects as well: heavy stones, diamond saws, pneumatic tools, chisels, dust and noise, and working with the earth's most basic material. And when I show my work to a gallery or juried competition, they don't want to know about me. It's about the work. And I'm doing very well with it. Now this is satisfaction! And, perhaps most important, I have a wonderful and loving husband who loves me for me.

I survived and am living proof of the old adage, "What doesn't kill you makes you stronger." But I know many, many people who did not come out unscathed. A woman I know, a former anorexic, still can't have a bowel movement without a laxative. When she tried flaxseed and other more homeopathic answers to the problem, she ended up in the emergency room. Another friend, a former model, is wearing dentures at forty-five years old. She was bulimic; the stomach acid she regurgitated over and over rotted her teeth. Another guy I knew in the music industry put a hole through the membrane between his nostrils after a ten-year coke habit. A *big* hole. His doctor told him he was lucky that was his only lasting problem. And we all know the endless stories of death and destruction from these pitiful and often lethal methods of self-medication.

I still do weekly radio movie reviews, go on TV shows as a commentator or film critic, and guest host on PBS in Boston. Most enjoyable is filling in for Emily Rooney, Andy Rooney's daughter and a veteran of TV news. She has a show in Boston, which has a wonderful format: two topics in a half hour, and it is a delight. (On TV you wait until someone offers you a format and try it and see if you're good at it. Only rarely is the format truly formed around the talents of the individual. For me, Emily's format is fabulous.) Now that the pressure is off, I have a comfort level for my image and body weight. I like being muscular and not especially thin. I still maintain a little excess weight but that's something I can deal with. There's not someone standing over me with a whip to lose it, or even worse, not saying anything but silently judging me.

My wonderful, insightful father used to occasionally quote Abraham Lincoln to me when I was down. "Folks are just about as happy as they set their minds to be."

Yup.

these hips have never been enslaved,
they go where they want to go.
these hips are mighty hips.
these hips are magic hips.
i have known them to put a spell on a man and
spin him like a top.

—Lucille Clifton, "homage to my hips"

The Barbi Twins
(former celebrity models, animal rescuers)

SIA AND SHANE BARBI became an international sensation modeling as the Barbi Twins. There were the covers of two top-selling issues of *Playboy* magazine, the comic book featuring them as heroines, their nomination as official pinups of the U.S. military, and four worldwide best-selling calendars. Indicative of their iconic fame was the fact that men from Prince Andrew to Saddam Hussein owned Barbi calendars. They are the perfect pinups, so you have to wonder—as of the star of the movie *Simone*—"Are they real?"

Then one day at the peak of their career the twins took a sabbatical. They stepped right through the image and began to talk about their battle with bulimia and to express their views, which proved that they were very real indeed. They wrote a book that shared their experience and hope, *Dying to Be Healthy*, and toured the country giving lectures at universities.

Something about the shots of the Barbis is not typically girly. In many photos the Barbis appear almost equine: their silky manes, big eyes, heads held high, their lithe muscularity from head to toe.

And finding the Barbis was like locating two wild horses, or maybe unicorns in a primordial forest. We felt them looking at us, judging, deciding over several months whether to trust and approve, peeking out at us, then disappearing again, like four eyes in a painting by Henri Rousseau.

Then I overheard Gary discussing, with great interest, the twins' latest project—and Gary never feigns interest. Sia and Shane wanted to expose a perversion among animal lovers, a phenomenon they call the "rescue syndrome": a neurotic impulse to rescue animals, far beyond normal concern for animals' well-being.

I admired the energy and verve of our exchanges with the Barbis, and respected their decision to "out" their eating disorder to the media at the height of their fame. Yet I had some skepticism about them as, shall we say, thinkers. Hadn't my grandmother told me that extreme beauty and big brains are almost never contained in the same person? And hadn't I met some models when I worked at an erotic men's magazine in the 1980s? None of us on the editorial staff—men or women—visited with the models on their breaks during shoots, the word being that these girls suffered from arrested development, having co-opted the sex-object stereotype.

So I prejudged. I figured two women who had built their fame on their Barbie-doll looks wouldn't be the brightest bulbs. Then Gary did the interview, we all began to converse, and I found myself adding Sia and Shane to my mental list of people I would love to spend time with. What an about-face! I learned that they are smart and cool, that despite modeling since childhood they are far from superficial, that they are intellectually serious, strong-minded, and vivid communicators. Then there's the twin thing. Their conversation is like an exteriorization of one person's thinking. Ideas arc between them. I asked my daughter, a savvy attorney who is a twin, what she thought was going on. Nothing mystical about their being in sync, Emma said. "They share an understanding and have a very similar way of expressing things because they shared the womb and their lives from day one." Yet there is still something uncanny about how the Barbi twins' thinking processes flow into one stream, and there is something feral and untamed about these lucid, purposeful, quick-thinking sisters— something that evokes Pegasus.

—J.M.

Gary: Okay, we're recording. Do me a favor and please identify which one of you is speaking.

Shane: We don't care if this interview is mixed up as to who is speaking. Not at all. We've switched personalities anyway. A lot of times my sister has the audacity to take over my life.

Sia: Yeah, and I've seen her sign my signature, so don't worry about it.

Shane: We literally have the same life story, but I'll tell you what is so weird about twins. Sometimes we get mixed up about what happened to each other.

Sia: Yeah, a little codependency there. We're not sure if a certain experience happened to her or to me.

Shane: It's true.

Gary: Well, I don't know if we can sort that out today.

Shane: Exactly. We'd need another therapy session for that.

Gary: Okay, Shane, you want to start?

Shane: No, Sia, you start.

Sia: All right. This is Sia, but it's Shane if I goof up. My sister and I are compulsive overeaters, in recovery. We're compulsive overeaters, bulimics, and I'd say we're alcoholics who don't drink. And we are codependent. We started attending a Twelve Step recovery program when we were really young. We truly take everything one day at a time. They say that our disease is genetic, which in our case is true. Everyone in our family did drink, so it was both environmental and genetic. We were predisposed to addiction. We were also influenced by our environment. It started out for us with obsessive compulsive disorder [OCD]. My sister and I were extremely neat and clean. We organized too many things, like our mother's closet. We were always washing our hands and our feet. That should have been clue number one that something was wrong. When people ask us, "When did this start?" I can't really put a date on it, but there were those clues. The OCD moved into other addictive personality traits.

Gary: In your early childhood, I assume.

Shane: Very early.

Sia: It probably started when we were around eight. Growing up with a gay mother was an influence on my sister and me to live with a secret. We learned that we had to lie in order to be accepted, and that is very alcoholic behavior. It's a shame, but society made it too hard on our mother and us to be honest about the fact that she was gay.

Not that I want to out her about being a homosexual, I want to out the fact that we had to live with a very heavy secret that we felt was shameful. We thought we were doing something wrong because we had to lie about it. This was our family, and that's all we knew. And when people say, "How does it feel to have a gay mother?" Well, we don't know how it feels to have a heterosexual mother, let alone not be a twin. We are oblivious.

We grew up very codependent, my sister and I, which automatically happens with twins. From day one we became each other's identity. People would ask our mother, "How are the twins?" Not "How's Shane?" or "How's Sia?" but "How are the twins?" So the OCD and codependency started right away. Plus having the secret that our mother was gay and, I should add, alcoholic—we learned to lie at a very young age. Our whole world was about keeping a normal image, and as real a one as possible. I remember as a young child my biggest dream was to be normal because I knew that my sister and I were abnormal. We wanted to fit in.

Our love for animals also started when we were very young. The way we did it, wanting to rescue animals and losing our identity in the process, was codependent. We wanted to find anything that needed help and help them. I would say that was very sweet. When I look at other people who do that, I think it's a sick need to want to go and rescue, and we had that need intensely at a very early age.

Shane: We actually wrote a book when we were little, called *Civil Rights for Animals,* which my mom published as a children's book.

Sia: We were distraught by the fact that animals did not have rights. It was kind of funny, because as young children we became super-fanatical. We just couldn't handle suffering. Anywhere we went. When we went horseback riding, or we went to the beach, our mind was, "How can we save an animal today?" We'd spend a whole day at the beach feeding the seagulls. If there was anything that washed up on the shore that needed to be thrown back, we took care of it and felt fulfilled.

Shane: Holidays were the toughest. We'd actually try to go feed animals on the holidays.

Sia: People feed the homeless on holidays; we would feed the animals.

Shane: When we'd go horseback riding we felt bad for the horse, so most of the time we wanted to do what the horses wanted to do.

Sia: I wanted to get on the horse, a control issue, to control that horse, but at the same time I wanted to rescue it.

Shane: When we went to the stables, we'd take the horses out and let them eat grass and rest, and make sure that they had fun. We'd pet and massage the horses. Not that we did any good, but we thought that we did.

Sia: Our mother said, "You two girls have unusual empathy." But I think it was just our sadness, that we looked at everything as the glass half empty. There was a void inside of us that we tried to fill with food, or by helping others that we perceived as suffering.

Shane: Excuse me, but it is so much my nature to embellish her thing rather than add my own. Can I do that?

Gary: Please do.

Shane: I'm so into this . . . Holidays were painful for us. I don't think it's like that for most kids. There was a lot of crying during the holidays. There was lots of sadness. We would try to alleviate the pain by helping. I still feed the homeless on Thanksgiving, because I want to take my mind off of me.

Sia: It's getting out of our disease and working the Twelfth Step to connect and contribute.

Shane: We try to make an effort to do that.

Gary: But what was all this sadness about?

Sia: I can't quite put my finger on it, but a lot of it was pretending we were the Waltons, when we're really the Addams Family. It wasn't a real family like what we saw on TV. There was always a big secret in our family.

Shane: It wasn't only that. I just believe that we didn't have a childhood. When people look back on their childhoods, typically they have happy memories.

Sia: We were basically caretakers. I felt this need to take care of my mother. When we were very young she left our father. That made us sad. Now I understand. She wanted to get well and find recovery, which was the healthiest thing she could have done.

Shane: Our mother did her best in her given situation.

Sia: Yeah, she had a sad life. I felt bad for my own mother.

Shane: I heard this about adult children of alcoholics, that they had feelings that most kids don't. Maybe we should have been living as kids, and developing our own ego boundaries or whatever that's called, but we were busy caretakers.

Sia: She was a good mother in that she didn't make it obvious how hard life was for her.

Shane: Do you know that we did not invite kids to our house because we felt shame and also we were protecting our mother? We felt her pain.

Sia: I remember the times she would break down and cry, and she really didn't want to do that in front of us. It was so hard on her.

Shane: At least that was our interpretation.

Sia: Can I go back a bit and say that our grandfather grew up in a recovery program, but my father did not continue that, and my mother did leave him because of his alcoholism. She wanted to get well herself and not be so codependent.

Shane: You know what's so funny? My sister and I have had more blackouts than most down-and-out alcoholics.

Gary: Explain that, please.

Sia: I always tell my story as a collage because the timeline is so imperfect because of all the blackouts.

Shane: Yeah, but what's really scary is my sister's memory is much better than mine. If you ask me my life story it would be blah, blah, blah.

Sia: I had more blackouts than my sister, so maybe I learned to deal with things that were painful by just not remembering, and just moving on, where my sister would remember all the details.

Shane: Okay. As a therapist by profession, our mother was also in the rescue business, plus she was a sponsor. She would befriend people in trouble and have us around them. So we had to relive the alcoholic life over and over and over. She would work with people who were at rock bottom.

Sia: Not to out our mother here, but we felt she gave a lot of attention to her patients. It's amazing we didn't turn into drug addicts or alcoholics ourselves.

Shane: We were jealous of the relationships she had with her patients and her sponsees. She would tell us, like a good mother, why we were prone to alcoholism. She explained it so well that it really did turn me off.

Sia: I want to attribute our success at never drinking to her making us go to meetings as young girls.

Shane: I was on the point of saying that.

Sia: I don't think it was our nature to want to go, but we got life tools very, very young. When we started working the Twelve Steps we already knew what we were in for. Mind you, our father was drinking during this time. We were with him on weekends.

Shane: Actually, we went from home to home to home. We stayed with our mother, sometimes with friends, and we were also separated.

Sia: And switched. One with our mother and one with our father.

Gary: Tell me about this.

Shane: Okay, but this is a part of my blackout.

Sia: I can't believe how open we are about this!

Shane: Our mother would always try to set us up in a good, healthy environment. That was important to her. Her life of sobriety was also important to her.

Sia: She would bring home too many unhealthy people, so when she had a chance she'd place us in what she thought was a healthy environment— usually the home of a celebrity friend—where we wouldn't be exposed to unhealthy and alcoholic people. These homes were mansions with pools and such.

Gary: And you would be there for short periods of time?

Shane: Yes, not only were we split up, but we learned to adapt to wherever we went.

Sia: We became big people pleasers. All I recall of these experiences was that nothing was secure and stable, except for food.

Shane: And I judged each home by the food we had.

Sia: I remember going to other people's family events on holidays. I would purposely starve myself beforehand so that I could enjoy the high of all the food.

Shane: Yes, I did that too.

Sia: I remember getting to eat an ice-cream sundae at some big movie star's home and thinking, "Wow, this is nice."

Shane: We loved to watch scary movies while eating ice cream with chocolate syrup on it.

Sia: I can't recall whose house it was or what the house looked like, but I can describe the bowl that held the ice cream, and the sundae had Hershey's syrup.

Shane: You're right, that was it.

Sia: And it was a white bowl, very thick, like a porcelain bowl.

Gary: Okay, can you move the story forward for me?

Shane: No, we're stuck on this sundae, Gary!

Sia: Our mother was friends with some very famous people, and therapist to some, too. I believe that in itself is dysfunctional. High-profile people live in their secrets. Famous people call it privacy but it's secrecy. They don't want anyone to know anything about them. With all due respect, it causes an unhealthy connection with other people.

Gary: How did that impact you?

Shane: We thought that everyone went through what we were doing.

Sia: It didn't impact us, except for the fact that we weren't allowed to talk about this stuff.

Shane: Some of these people were leading a double life, not wanting people to know they were gay. Even though they were friends of my mother it was not to be talked about, that they were living a gay life. So it was more secrets.

Sia: Another thing: our mother did not say that she was gay until we were around eighteen.

Shane: We just knew instinctively. When she told us, it was like, "No shit. Is that the big secret?"

Sia: You know, it's funny. We never chose to become actresses, even though we had those connections, because they look like the loneliest people I've ever seen.

Shane: And the saddest people.

Sia: They're so isolated. Which is just the opposite of what I got out of the Twelve Step meetings. In that respect I thought, "My God, if you're ever a celebrity you're going to be the most isolated, paranoid person. The dishonesty of having to live a double life!

When we were seven we got our first Social Security card and SAG card—Screen Actors Guild. We wanted to work to earn money for freedom, for us to get a new life. I wanted everything to be different. We also became Girl Scouts. My mom, being gay—she was very femme. We went the opposite way. We were very tomboyish, wanting to get into horses. My dream was to move to Texas and be around cowboys: everything opposite of my mom.

Shane: My mom would always hug us and try to make us feel loved. She tried to set us up in good situations: going to a good school, things like that. But we also spent time with our father. That was part of their agreement. My father was still drinking.

Sia: You know, it's funny, when we were around all those celebrities and all their money; I pictured myself with a backpack on a horse, purposely living very poor. We saw our parents go from rags to riches over and over, and

I preferred the rags because you didn't live in fear. The people that had all the money and all the fame were miserable. They constantly lived in fear of losing it. So I wanted very much to live in simplicity. Then I never had to fear losing anything, even desire anything. I think that's why to this day my sister and I dress like bums.

Shane: Probably, but would you not "out" me!

Gary: Okay, you guys: now tell me a little about the food.

Shane: It started at an early age. I remember relating everything to food. We would go to someone's house, and I would check out their refrigerator. If it was full of food, it reminded me of family: comfort, safety, happiness, and security. We would judge our friends by what they fed us.

Sia: One of my most delightful memories is of an actress, whose name I won't mention, who had a birthday cake on some TV talk show. We got to eat that cake while watching it on TV.

Shane: It's funny, but nothing else impressed us except food. Food and animals.

Sia: If one of these celebrities had a horse, they were famous in our minds.

Gary: Or a full refrigerator.

Shane: We became Girl Scouts at an early age, which was a little too frilly and girly-girly for us. Maybe it was the Brownies. Sia, were we Brownies?

Sia: We loved brownies, but we were Girl Scouts.

Shane: We really wanted to be Boy Scouts. We liked everything boys did.

Sia: So what we did was order boxes—no, cases of Girl Scout cookies. We kept them in a neat stack, because we are OCD, in our closet. Then we ate them all! We were supposed to sell them, but we ate them instead. So that's how our dishonesty started. We thought we'd deal with this later.

Shane: We would lie, cheat, or steal to have those cookies.

Sia: We were looking at jail time.

Shane: We didn't know what to do once we ate them all. We were out of control. We were thin too, so people laughed at our problem. We would eat everything in sight.

Sia: I remember thinking, "I'll eat that now and worry about the consequences later."

Gary: Did you get into trouble over the cookie theft?

Sia: We have a mutual blackout on that question.

Gary: So you both might still be wanted?

Sia: Hey, we were drunk on cookies. There may still be a warrant for our arrest, but I'll never know.

Gary: So you never really got in trouble.

Shane: I think we did, but we were so high on the cookies, who knew?

Gary: I have an image of the two of you in your Girl Scout uniforms, hiding in the closet, stuffing your faces with cookies.

Shane: Exactly. The buttons unbuttoned—especially where the stomach is.

Sia: As you can imagine, we got no awards or badges. Unless maybe there was one for eating.

Shane (to Sia): Do you remember the best Christmas of our lives? Eating the Oreo cookies?

Sia: It wasn't Oreo cookies, it was Hershey's Kisses.

Shane: Okay, so we have different views on our best Christmas. I remember our father got in big trouble with our mother. All he got us was candy. And Mom's lover brought us a case of Oreo cookies. Maybe I worked on the Oreos and you worked on the Kisses. It was utopia.

Sia: It was a little bit overwhelming because I'd think, "What's next?" Because that high—just like an alcoholic's—would get less and less, and the craving would get more and more. We had to have sugar in our systems to even connect with other people.

Shane: Also, at an early age we each had paper route jobs, and afterwards we would eat together to reward ourselves for the work. We binged, but we grew tall, so we stayed thin.

Sia: Now, mind you, we would once in a while do modeling jobs, because it was big money, but we hated doing the girly-girly body-obsessed things.

Shane: Yes, we certainly did.

Sia: What's really funny is we fought our mother's image. She was actually very sexy. It really bothered us. Our guy friends would make remarks. Our teachers. Everybody wanted to go out with her. We were kind of protective of our mother.

Shane: I think that's why we became a little butch, a little masculine. It was almost as if we were taking on the masculine figure, protecting our mother, and wanting that attention ourselves.

Sia: Not wanting her to go out with men. I actually didn't mind her hanging out with women.

Shane: Actually, that was very comfortable.

Gary: Tell me how old you were when you started modeling.

Sia: Oh, seven. We did Sears & Roebuck catalog modeling and commercials.

Gary: Your mom put you into this?

Sia: Actually, we wanted to do it.

Shane: All of our friends did it, and we were always asked to do it because we were twins. And they liked twins because of the child labor laws. We could trade off. One would be tutored while the other one worked.

Sia: Quite honestly, our mother didn't want us to do it. She had been in the business; she was a model and a beauty contestant. It was our choice.

Shane: Because it looked normal, we thought that modeling would give us a way out. Freedom.

Sia: We were always looking for a way out of our lives. That's for darn sure.

Shane: Escaping was our big thing.

Sia: It was our ticket out. Even though we were around very wealthy people—we even stayed at wealthy people's homes—we felt this poverty, a kind of suffering.

Shane: We saw how our parents went from rags to riches, rags to riches.

Sia: I'm sure things were amplified, in that as children of alcoholics we were feeling things other kids didn't. I couldn't believe how other kids would bash their families! We were very protective of our family. Even to this day. Our parents did the best they could, given what they went through. Both of them had a hard life. Our father lived to see us. The best thing our mother did was she never, ever badmouthed our father, which I thought was brilliant. She let us come to our own conclusions.

Shane: It's funny, while growing up we wanted our mother and father to be together. We would ask our father, "Why don't you marry our mother?"

Sia: As we got older we saw that he was very dysfunctional. He had a life that didn't look healthy. I definitely saw my mom's life working and being a lot healthier than my father's life, but I didn't see that as a kid.

Gary: Was your father drinking during this time?

Sia: Oh yeah, throughout his life. Which was sad because he had a father who had got sober.

Shane: Toward the end he became a dry drunk. He never got into a program. He had that negativity, a victim blaming the world.

Sia: He turned to Christianity, big-time. Thinking that was the answer. We were all going to hell.

Shane: Seeing my father's life—it was so sad. He remarried, which was very difficult for us. It's funny, I didn't mind my mom with other women, but couldn't accept what my father was doing. I look back on it and I'm glad he got into another family. He wanted it so bad, but the jealousy was horrible with me and my sister when we were young.

Shane: He married several times, but when he married a woman with kids we were very jealous.

Gary: Okay, ladies; let's go back to the food.

Sia: Can I put my cigarette out? I feel like I'm in therapy! (Only kidding! We don't smoke.) So, going back to when we were kids, we were also into

sports. We wanted our bodies to represent a horse. Not just an athlete, but a horse. We liked being muscular.

Shane: Yeah, that was weird. We always had long hair. Why? Because it let us wear a ponytail, like a horse. We loved horses so much that we wanted to become them.

Sia: That's why we got into sports: because we wanted to be fit, muscular, and run like a horse.

Shane: Oh my God, what weirdos!

Sia: Going back to food, my memories of my father are that he tried to make us part of his new family by getting us all together and going out for ice cream. I remember getting so high and happy. Or we'd go to a coffee-house and have french toast or pancakes. The whole family united. Sunday breakfast.

Shane: We lived for that. The only time I could get along with my new family was with food.

Sia: The other family—they were good people, but we were still very jealous of them. We had to give up our father, and now he's got the family that he's always wanted.

Shane: Yes, that jealousy really kicked in. People ask me, "Are you ever jealous of your sister?" How can I be? We are so codependent and enmeshed. I never liked to see my sister suffer, because it was like my going through it.

Sia: I don't know if this relates to food, but because of the jealousy with our father and feelings of abandonment—I think that's why in high school we started going a little bit on the "cheap" side.

Shane: We were cheap with money, cheap with our looks. We felt we were abandoned by all mankind because we didn't have an available father.

Sia: We saw that our mother, being so beautiful and sexy, could get whatever she wanted. And mind you, our mother would say, "Looks don't count."

Shane: What a liar!

Sia: So we started looking like tramps. Twin tramps. It's funny, we stayed virgins pretty long . . . not too long.

Shane: But we would not cut our hair. Long hair represented women who could attract men. We noticed with our mother, all the women had short hair, and they were gay.

Sia: Now you might ask, "How does this relate to food?" Well, we didn't get into therapy until later. We fought it because everything that my mother was, we didn't want. We got away from our Twelve Step program, but we still didn't drink. We know that weakness in us. Food was our drug. We'd say to each other, "Let's get high."

Shane: Yes, we would say that, but we meant "on sugar." People don't understand the sugar highs you can get, but it affected us just like a drug. Our eyes would dilate, our mouths would dry up.

Sia: And we couldn't stop talking. We were just speeded up.

Shane: We would attack our favorite food group. Junk food. Pastries, candy, ice cream, and fat. Mostly sugar. We were not interested in real foods.

Sia: All the fattening "good stuff." We felt normal and happy, and high chemically in our brain, when we ate this junk. It was like we could now enjoy life.

Shane: My memories of childhood are of deprivation.

Sia: Our mom taught us how to medicate ourselves.

Shane: Can I tell you something? Our mom would actually lock the refrigerator and hide her treats, so we learned to be thieves.

Sia: Now mind you, we were never fat—until lately!

Shane: We're both three hundred pounds!

Sia: No, but we were alarmingly thin, even anorectic, while in our heads our body image was so poor we thought we were Orca or Free Willy.

Shane: We also didn't want to develop, although I liked being a girl, with the long hair and everything.

Sia: Developing also meant being fat. The curves represented extra weight.

Shane: We always wore baggy clothes except when we went through that cheap stage. It was weird. We would fluctuate from being sexy, tan, and showing off our body, to feeling like we were just being molested and putting on all the clothes.

What I learned in therapy later, if I can jump to the future, is that I was told over and over by therapists that eating is a sexual issue. Like molestation. And I couldn't figure out where that came from, except for feeling icky. Maybe that's what we did, we would fluctuate from being sexy to feeling awful by overeating.

Sia: And dressing with a ton of clothes and sunglasses. That was a big deal. Hiding our eyes.

Shane: Yet our eyes were nice.

Sia: They were the only feature that we didn't ridicule.

Shane: People would always tell us how pretty and blue our eyes were.

Sia: Because we were always living a secret, we felt that if we wore sunglasses, people wouldn't be able to tell that we were about to turn into pumpkins.

Shane: There were also times where we would wear long sleeves because we didn't want to show our arms. Our childhood desire was to be a nun, because we loved how they covered up.

Sia: I'm going to need a therapist when we finish this interview.

Gary: *I'm* going to need a therapist.

Shane: I forgot how wacko we were!

Sia: Can you believe the dichotomy of wanting to be a Catholic nun and then going on to do *Playboy*?

Gary: And also wanting to be a horse. You guys wanted to do everything and then some.

Sia: Yes! Amazing, isn't it?

Gary: It's remarkable that you seem to have the same attitudes about everything.

Sia: Everything. Twin dysfunction. I've heard that many twins are anorectic. I can see why. It's all about control, and being enmeshed, and trying to find your boundaries.

Shane: In addition, we were also trying to find our boundaries with our mother. I didn't want to be a gay-fully dressed sheep, so I went Texan, to the ultimate masculine men, so I could define myself as different from my mother.

Sia: So back to food. I judged people by what they put in their refrigerator. You knew how boring a person was if all they had was alcohol in the fridge? We're not going to mention names, but we stayed at very famous people's homes, which we thought were utopia because of the refrigerators.

Shane: We became big people pleasers. All I recall of these experiences was that nothing was secure and stable, except for food.

Sia: Our father would go into bars when he was taking care of us, when we were very young. He would give us a lot of money to go into the doughnut shop next door, while he became drunk. In order to hide his disease. Or he would let us stay in the car, and tell us he'd just be a minute. But he'd lose track of time. He'd come out and give us some kind of reward for being good.

Shane: We also saw—oh, this is sad!—that he would be with a woman who was stealing money from him. We would see this. We saw all these people that used my father. He was a wealthy, very successful architect. So when much later my sister and I got screwed by managers or businesspeople, we would always say, "We are our father." We could see that people were using us.

Sia: Back to holidays . . . Besides wanting the food, it was a big day for us to give everybody a gift. It didn't matter if it was the postman, it was a big deal. My mother says—even though I think she's wrong—how wonderful and giving we were. I don't think it's normal for a child to be that giving. I think it was shame and guilt, and people-pleasing. Kids should not have to feel a need to give to everybody. At the stables we gave presents to the immigrant workers. No one gave them presents, but we did. Also the horses: we gave the horses presents, and the animals in the shelter.

Shane: You know what's funny? I'll bet my sister didn't say this, but we didn't have the money to give these presents, so we used to steal it.

Sia: Or we recycled gifts.

Shane: We were generally on a roller coaster with money. My mother was climbing back up, but my father had a lot of money, then no money, and back and forth.

Sia: We had a big belief in God. A big desire to pray all the time.

Shane: That's what got us out of stealing. I condoned it at first. I thought I was Robin Hood.

Sia: That's true. We shoplifted to get people what they needed. We justified this because it was never for ourselves.

Shane: As an example, we would give the Mexican workers extravagant gifts. These were workers at the stables, and everyone treated them very poorly. Horrible, and we experienced this pain for them, so we would make their Christmas really nice. It was a big deal for us.

Sia: We wanted everything to be like a Shirley Temple movie. She was always so poor, sometimes adopted, and whenever someone would adopt her, they'd feed her what she wanted.

Shane: In grammar school, *Charlie and the Chocolate Factory* was my favorite. I would just think about those cubes of chocolate. I must have been drooling. I looked forward to lunch more than anything else in school. Eating out of a lunch bag would drive me nuts.

Sia: Being OCD, we had these perfect little lunch bags with our names on them, spelled perfectly, and the crinkly sound and smell of them . . . Our OCD mixed in with our food compulsion was unbearable.

Shane: You're right. Oh my God, I'm being drawn back into my past again.

Sia: Back in high school I thought if I were fat I wouldn't get the attention of men, and that's what I wanted. That was my ticket away from my pain. So we started dressing sexy. I knew that depriving myself of food would be okay if I was popular with guys. So we battled wanting to be a nun and wanting to be more of a whore. It's amazing we didn't become prostitutes. I wanted attention from men.

Shane: We became the ultimate teases. We wanted to keep our virtue with God.

Sia: Okay, but let's go back to food. We started dieting when we didn't need to, just to be beautiful.

Shane: It was so weird, because we were thin to begin with.

Sia: It was something to do to bring control back into our life.

Shane: To set a goal. To make ourselves beautiful, because we thought this was our means to attract men.

Sia: We would starve ourselves, which led to our binges. By high school we had the up-and-down, roller-coaster kind of eating.

Shane: We tried every crash diet you can imagine. Once we ate only watermelon for a week. We ate up to six watermelons a day. Another single-fruit diet was oranges.

Sia: In our book *Dying to Be Healthy,* we tell how we had a friend of ours lock us in an apartment with nothing but distilled water for forty days. Only we got so hungry after ten days that we tied a couple of bedsheets together and climbed out of a third-story window. We were barely able to walk, but we somehow ran to a convenience store and gorged on candy and pastries.

Shane: There was no such thing as normal eating with us. It was either feast or famine. And it's funny: our mom, who was a top alcohol and drug therapist, didn't recognize this. She didn't think that anything was wrong with our being so thin, but I did. It was a type of insanity. A discipline—and boy did we love discipline!

Sia: Right, we even wanted to join the military—besides being a nun. As far as our food went, we loved to starve ourselves and then reward ourselves by eating to celebrate.

Shane: We started to gain weight at around eighteen.

Sia: Who knows? Our body image was so off.

Shane: When I look back at pictures we don't look fat.

Sia: Also, our eating patterns were really extreme by now. We had done every conceivable diet. Dieting started our weight issues. If you want to get fat, diet!

Shane: We did the egg and water diet in high school. I mean, how extreme is that?

Sia: I'll tell you what made us so crazy. Our stepmother gave us a book—a fanatic's book on health. It was about becoming vegetarian. Drinking wheatgrass juice. Oh my God, this was the ultimate high. Fasting on wheatgrass juice. My father was also into health. He would make these health food shakes and take vitamins.

Shane: He was ahead of his time. Same with my mother. Both of them were into health and they actually made us vegetarians. It's funny, because then we would go off into protein diets.

Sia: Only to lose weight—but we felt guilty eating meat. Somehow we knew, growing up as vegetarians, that protein and meat diets were unhealthy. So when our stepmother gave us that book it was almost like finding a religion.

Shane: My mom was a hippie so we liked this kind of living because it coincided with the type of eating we did. We thought if we had a spiritual life we wouldn't get fat.

Sia: I remember reading about this one saint that didn't eat. He lived on a Catholic wafer.

Shane: We loved the idea of being the very best at anything: the very best at school, the very best at sports—we were such perfectionists. And then we found that there was a saint that fasted for thirty days or a year, I forget how long. But I would get high off of the idea. Of course I'd have one last day of bingeing, then I would do this insane thing of never eating again. I actually got high off the thought of it. Wow, we'd be thin—but we also would not have the dependence on food either. How many times did we do a forty-day fast?

Sia: We also went to Texas and did these twenty- or thirty-day water fasts. Then we wanted to move out there and make this our life. It wasn't a fat farm, it was the opposite. This was Texas, and we loved the idea of cowboys—the down-to-earth mentality. And yet we loved to eat like hippies. It was this crazy dichotomy. I wanted to dress and act like a cowgirl, be a rodeo queen. The eating brought us into this compassion for animals: not eating them, or even going to rodeos.

Shane: So you can see, everything was related to our eating. Our whole lifestyle.

Sia: The big reason we went into modeling was that we saw it as a motivational tool for us to diet.

Shane: My mentality was, before we become three hundred pounds—because I always had this fear I was going to weigh three hundred pounds, which we of course never achieved—we would do this last modeling job.

Sia: The modeling would also serve as a document that we were actually thin at one time.

Shane: Yeah, before we became three hundred pounds.

Sia: My thing is, now, that if you really do believe you are dieting for health, you can succeed and be abstinent or you can eat, without the confusion or extremes . . . For us the goal of being healthy was also an excuse to eat as much as we wanted. Our salads by this time were the size of your dining room table!

Shane: We were grazing, by this time, day and night.

Sia: Grazing? Eating. Grazing was a euphemism for bingeing. We abused health foods as another diet.

Shane: Our calendars were marked with the days we fasted. Not the calendars we kept as models, but our private calendars. Those were, by the way, always animal calendars.

Sia: I truly felt that I molested a child when I overate.

Shane: Speaking of molesting, let's go back to my sister. She was a cutter.

Sia: Oh, don't say that! You're outing me!

Shane: Just a little bit. I thought my sister was bizarre.

Sia: This is how sick I was. I thought I was like a saint. I wanted to be like a saint; I didn't think I was a saint. Let me really make that clear. I had just finished reading about Fatima and I thought that if I suffered for others, and for animals, I could take on their suffering, take away their pain. Wash away their pain and mine. I couldn't stand to see innocents suffer. Babies, animals, et cetera. I was also thinking about being a veterinarian at the time, and I thought that I wouldn't be able to do this if I was averse to seeing blood, so I started practicing on myself. Cutting. And I would take a needle and thread and see if I could sew a small stitch into my skin. It was mind over matter.

Shane: She was sick. We both were.

Sia: I feel that most of my life has been about dieting and setting goals.

Shane: We really didn't have high goals, nor did we expect to be in this business as long as we did, because we are very private—which is contradictory to who we project. It's so weird that we would do the opposite of who we are.

Sia: We are very private and modest. We were asked once by *Entertainment Weekly* what our goals were, and my sister said, "To own a doughnut shop," and I said, "I want to own an island, so I can get away from everyone and be three hundred pounds." They thought that was hilarious because most people say, "I want to be an actress" and all this, but I was dead serious. I just lived to get out of the business and be private and let people see me eat and be out of control.

Shane: It was scary getting famous because we did not know what we were in for. We thought we could just do our work and go hide, but the whole world was looking at us. So if you go into a supermarket and you're buying crap, you better say that there are a bunch of Girl Scouts in the car.

Sia: That's why early on, we decided to talk about our problem. I believe we were the first ones to do it on national television.

Shane: I kept thinking our secrets are our sickness. I wanted everyone to fathom this.

Sia: I knew our disease was extremely harsh. Our principal thing was bulimia, and an addiction to exercise.

Shane: We didn't recognize that we were bulimic, we just thought we were super-disciplined. We never got into throwing up until we got these multi-million-dollar jobs with modeling and all that. We would exercise, my sister up to fifteen hours straight, me up to eight hours. I never saw that as being obsessive. I saw that as being super-disciplined.

Sia: It wasn't fifteen. I think it was around ten.

Shane: I would at least break up my exercise. Listen to how I justify this: four hours in the morning, four hours at night. My whole life: losing weight to be thin, and then eating.

Gary: You guys purged as well?

Shane: Yes, we got into that later. Now I was really good at it, unlike my sister.

Sia: Nothing to brag about.

Shane: Yes, but I do recall your being a little jealous.

Sia: I've said before that I'm never jealous of my sister, but I was jealous about that. I wanted to purge, but I couldn't. I saw it as a defect.

Shane: She was sticking everything down her throat and nothing would happen.

Sia: Yeah, I'd look at a toilet brush and think, "That's going to go down my throat." I might blow up but I don't care, I'll do whatever it takes. For the life of me, my stomach would not regurgitate.

Shane: We loved each other as binge buddies. We started living together for the first time when we were modeling. It's very dangerous, living with your binge buddy. It was uncomfortable for me to throw up my food when my sister couldn't. I felt guilty. So then we got into laxatives, which made us both throw up. That was dangerous. That's when my sister overdosed.

Sia: We took so many, up to a hundred at a time, that we became like pharmacists, learning which ones worked.

Shane: We learned about these in Europe. We were doing fashion shows. We were bingeing and purging. The Louvre was not an art museum to us: we went there just to say we'd been there. And then our whole mind was, "Okay, let's find some French pastries."

That's all I remember. We stayed at the most outrageous hotel, and we ordered everything on the menu. They probably thought we were having a party in our room because we kept ordering food.

Sia: We were in the Caribbean once and all I could think about was certain binge foods I wanted flown in. At the end of our shoot, of course, so we could stay thin until we finished our work. And we were taking laxatives all during this time.

Shane: I had to go to the hospital in France. I had starved so much that when I binged I thought I split my insides open. All they diagnosed was acute constipation. They gave me magnesium citrate. And I lost more weight. I thought, "This is the best discovery."

Sia: You know that we were abstinent from alcohol and drugs, but this was our drug: the laxatives. And I never ever thought about doing any drugs, but this was legal. I just thought this was the greatest thing in the world.

Gary: How did this come to an end?

Shane: It came to an end when we started walking the line of not dieting and not bingeing. We called it abstinence. But it was very hard. If we abstained too much from eating it became a diet. If we abstained too much from purging it felt like we were going back to compulsive overeating. So our abstinence became tighter as the years went on.

Sia: It was pretty loose in the beginning. I'd say, "I'll allow myself three binges a day." We were always wanting to quit Hollywood.

Shane: Every time, after a job, I'd say, "I quit." There was freedom in that.

Gary: You made a conscious choice to stop using the laxatives?

Sia: Well, truthfully, the laxatives stopped working.

Shane: We had multi-million-dollar jobs that people say they would "die for," and we were not expecting the success that was thrown at us.

Sia: That's why I don't like to see them put anorectics on TV. It's still body obsession, and we know weight should never be a goal. It should only be a by-product of healthy living. When I went to church once, a minister came up to me. A bunch of people were there eating lunch, and he said, "Here, have a cookie." And I said, "Oh no, I don't eat cookies." I thought one would be the whole box. And he said, "Come on, it's from God," and I thought, "Oh my God, how can I turn this away?" The minister said, "Health takes the mind off of the body, not on the body."

So I said, "Okay, give me that cookie."

Shane: When I was really out of control. I was going to all of the Twelve Step meetings, and my mother said to me, "Twelve Step meetings are supposed to embellish your life, not be your life."

Gary: So you got into Twelve Step recovery and it started to work for you. What is your life like now in relation to food?

Shane: I'm married. I can actually apply my Twelve Step program to my marriage. I really truly know what it means to live a day at a time. Marriage is a dangerous world, and I'll relate its perils to the ones with food. "Okay, I'm going to binge today, and starting tomorrow I'm never going to eat sugar." It's such a bad expectation and such a setup to fail. That's what marriage does. It says, "You have to be with this person forever." Never cheat. Never do this. And I really take my marriage a day at a time. It gives me that freedom: "Today I'm going to do just this or that."

Sia: Neither of us has a need to fix someone. And we're no longer attracted to raving alcoholics. I really do like to connect with people who are recovered.

Shane: Yes, I like people who have hit rock bottom and come back.

Sia: These days I don't feel the need to rescue or fix someone else. I turn it around and think, "What can I learn from this?"

Shane: It's all about working our Twelve Step program. We tell people that doing a Twelve Step program is not like becoming born again, it's about putting in the effort and surrendering to your eating disorder.

Sia: Unlike alcohol or drugs which, when you stop, you know if you are doing well or not. With food, it's very difficult to gauge when you slip into compulsive eating.

Shane: We know that weight is just a symptom.

Sia: Yes, today I try to practice three things. Being grateful, humble, and honest. And I struggle with all three every day. But so long as today was better than yesterday, I feel I'm making progress, and that's good enough for me. I've also changed my rescue mentality to doing charity, and I now see how it benefits me, instead of focusing on what I'm doing for others.

An East African Fable
Tongue Meat

A RARE REFLECTION on the relationship between our emotions and our body weight comes in the form of this fable from Kenya. A traditional folk tale, its depth and truth reverberate past its Swahili origin. It is provocative because it reveals how our state of mind influences the shape of our bodies. It is affirmative because it offers us a means to transcend sadness and reorder our lives. The story is easy to remember and has been retold in many folk tale collections. As a keepsake it speaks eloquently to our personal understanding of eating disorders.

———

Long ago a sultan lived with his wife in a beautiful palace, but the sultana was very unhappy. Each day she grew more listless and irritable, and she began to waste away.

In the capital near the palace lived a poor man whose wife was happy and healthy. The sultan summoned the poor man and demanded to know the secret of his wife's happiness. "I think it's because I feed her meat of the tongue," he said. So the sultan ordered from the butcher all the tongues money could buy— of cow and lamb, fish and lark—which the cook then prepared by roasting and salting, baking, boiling and frying, in all kinds of exquisite dishes. The sultana was made to eat these foods three or four times a day, but still she withered away.

The sultan was desperate. He called for a litter and made his wife trade places with the wife of the poor man.

An odd thing happened. While the sultana immediately began to thrive over at the poor man's house, the poor man's wife, now dining on palace fare, languished. Soon she grew as frail and miserable as the sultana had been.

More baffled than ever, the sultan dressed in a disguise and went to secretly spy on the poor man. There was the sultana, healthy and strong, with luminous skin and a smile on her face. What could the secret be?

And the sultan saw the poor man coming home at night to his new royal wife, telling her about things he had seen in the day, laughing and talking with her. Next he would take his banjo and play music and sing her songs, and then they would talk some more. And they would tell each other stories, and the poor man would amuse her until late at night.

At once the sultan understood: "So that is what is meant by 'meat of the tongue'!"

Every soul is a celestial Venus to every other soul.

—Ralph Waldo Emerson

Maria Conchita Alonso
(actress, singer)

BORN IN CUBA, raised in Venezuela, and schooled in Spain and Switzerland, Maria Conchita Alonso started her performing career as a beauty queen. In 1971, at just fourteen, she won the Miss Teenager of the World beauty pageant. Crowned Miss Venezuela and a runner-up for Miss World in 1975, she subsequently ventured from modeling to singing and acting. Soon Maria garnered fame as one of South America's best-selling recording artists, also playing in Spanish-language feature films, before moving to the United States to become one of the most popular Latina actresses in Hollywood.

Maria has costarred in movies with some of the leading actors of our time. She won raves for her role as Robin Williams's Italian immigrant sweetheart in *Moscow on the Hudson*. She played alongside Michael Keaton in the romantic comedy *Touch and Go*, Arnold Schwarzenegger in the futuristic *Running Man*, Edward James Olmos in *Roosters*, and Nick Nolte in *Extreme Prejudice*. Maria was Sean Penn's doomed lover in *Colors*, acted opposite Tom Skerritt in a TNT remake of *High Noon,* and also starred in *Predator 2.* Her performance in *The House of the Spirits* was praised by John Simon, perhaps America's toughest movie critic, as "hot in both senses." She is now a regular on the hugely popular television series *Desperate Housewives.*

She was the first South American woman to star in a Broadway show, playing Aurora in *Kiss of the Spider Woman.* Maria has received many honors as a Latina performer and does active fund-raising to benefit Latino organizations. She lives in Beverly Hills.

We adore Maria's spirit. After our interview with her she traveled to Mexico to judge an *American Idol*-like reality show. From there she wrote to us:

> I love life, but it's an everyday struggle, happy struggles, angry struggles, mad ones, easy ones, and it will never end, I believe, but as long as we take it with a smile on our faces, we will be able to go through it happily. It is always so important for me to read my fan mail through my website. They lift me and make me strong, they give me energy to keep going, as I give it to them. It's like a partnership. If we can make each other happy, we would live in a better world.

Maria is still grappling with her challenges, but through the words she speaks, her own power and truth come through like sunshine through a lattice.

—J.M.

I have always been both very outgoing and had a life to myself only. I've been known in Venezuela since I was a kid for a little nervous tic that

I've had, where I move my nose. A big emcee from over there said that I'm bewitched. I named my dog and my music company Tabatha, who is the witch's daughter [on the TV sitcom *Bewitched*]. All my life I felt I could do anything I set my mind to, but I had anxiety. Sometimes the anxiety was too much to bear and I would suffer, without stopping from acting, singing, or the dancing I did for exercise. Just suffer and crave to be alone.

If you come from a background that is well-to-do or educated as I did, your world is the same here, there, everywhere. For me my movie career led me to America, where I found it to be very similar to Venezuela. I never had a culture shock. It may be different from Cuba—I have no idea, since my parents left their homeland when I was a baby—but we are all from the Caribbean side of the world. I went to Washington State University, as well as schools in Switzerland and Paris, so I'm used to this lifestyle here, or Europe, or Latin America, and experience no shock at all.

That problem of disordered eating came from men, from a boyfriend and how he treated me. It really didn't come from my family. From when I was very young we had family all over, because we all had left Cuba. I was put on a plane by myself when I was seven years old to go visit my cousins in Puerto Rico. I would spend a month there, or Christmas or the summer. Being separated from my family was never an issue, because I was with my cousins, aunts, and uncles, and then my parents would come. I am used to being on my own.

So, in my late twenties, when I was first anorexic and bulimic, it was undeniably because I had a boyfriend who made me feel that I was fat, when in reality I wasn't, because that was a time in my life when I was doing three, four classes of jazz and ballet a day, every single day, and one of aerobics. All together I was doing six classes a day of exercise. So I was in one of my best body forms.

People thought he and I were an exceptional couple. He is very sweet and nice, and amazingly talented and handsome. He projected his unhappiness onto me. He himself wouldn't eat because he wanted to be a rock star and was striving to be skinny. He was not a bad human being at all, a very nice, good man. It's just that he was miserable in his career being a very good artist and not seeing results, while I was exploding in my career here in the States. I guess that was a way for him, without even knowing it himself, to feel better by controlling me in that way.

I talked to him a few years later—by then he had kids—and he felt very bad about it. He was very sorry and didn't mean it. And I knew it was so, because he was not an evil guy acting with premeditation to injure me. I guess he was going through his hell, and the way to run away from that was to unconsciously make me feel bad so he could control me.

Before that it never occurred to me to worry about body image. I had no idea there was something called anorexia or bulimia out there. My parents owned a spa. It was the first spa in Venezuela, a private spa for women only, and a very successful one. My mother grew up with sports all her life, in Cuba and continuing in Venezuela. When nobody thought of that—it was still years before Jane Fonda came out with her exercises—my parents had the consciousness that exercise was the only thing that kept you young and healthy. Yet there I was, not caring.

I wasn't fat, but maybe I was a little chubby for being a teenager. Even like that I was Miss Teenager of the World—not being the prettiest one of all the girls, or not being the skinniest of all of them—but I won it because of my personality. My mother always said that was the most important thing. She said, "Your personality is the only thing that will make you win among other people." Just because of my personality and my smile I should have confidence in me and how I presented myself. I can hear her say, "You can't compete with outside beauty."

So I was always enthusiastic and unafraid in modeling and acting, where people can lose that natural confidence. But I did not want my mother to criticize me, the way a ballet dancer might feel. So I would hide condensed milk underneath my bed. Condensed milk is something very typical of Latin people. We love condensed milk. It's very sweet and we put it in our coffees and Pepsi. I would put it in everything. So I was addicted to condensed milk, although you could say it was an addictive tendency that might have disappeared later if I had not been teased and criticized badly by a boyfriend.

When I announced that I didn't want to study anymore, my mother said, "Then you have to work." I went to work in my parents' spa. I taught aerobics to the ladies and jazz to little girls. I was in my late teens when all this happened. My mom would say, "Lose weight. Look at you. We have to be an example. We own the gym, a spa." It was like being a dermatologist and your face being all messed up. It was something that I wasn't concerned about, however. I still didn't care. For instance, I wore my micro-mini bikinis without hesitating. I went to the beach no matter what. A perfect body was something that wasn't important.

Then I was Miss Venezuela for the Miss World contest in London, and I was the second favorite since I got there. And because I was very nervous I gained weight. I became friends with the bodyguards and everybody, so we had lots of cocktail parties and all that. I would eat and eat and eat, out of anxiety and nervousness. In the last few days I saw I had gained weight. I had to buy a new swimsuit, and a new night dress—the gown. I became one of the seven runners-up at the end. Before only my mother spoke about my weight; now my father did. Chiming in he said, "You lost the contest because you gained weight! You lost because you're fat!"

Of course I was in the spotlight, so even there it came through the ear and went through the other. I had a wonderful time in London and I didn't change my attitude of living spontaneously. I didn't stop eating. I continued living my life.

Next I lived in Spain and worked there as a model, but then I gained more weight because I was having too much fun, and eating whatever I wanted, so I returned home. My first modeling assignment, despite being nineteen years old, was to play a mom, because I was chubby. Still, it was never really an issue. I was comfortable with myself and people gave me compliments, and the big factor continued to be my mother's philosophy: She always said that most important in a person is their spirit and character, what's inside. I wasn't concerned as much with surface as many other girls, though I grew up also being taught that you must take care of your skin. Since I'm sixteen years old I put creams on my face and body, and I thank God I have great skin now because of that.

There was no other girl in the family to hear about beauty, just me, since I have two older brothers, but the eating disorder had nothing to do with my modeling or performing—it was the boyfriend, I'm a hundred percent sure.

I'm a Latina and the majority of us are not toothpicks. We have hips and butts and well-formed legs. Someone like Beyonce or J-Lo, that's how we are. For me they're normal; it's not, "Oh my God, look at their butt!"

No! But my boyfriend would say, "Look at you. Look at how fat you are. Look at your legs, they're so big." Once he started he kept it up more. "How can you eat that? Look, it's going all to your legs, and then there'll be cellulite." So I stopped eating. But I was not the only one. He was a musician who wanted to be very skinny like a rock star, and he would not eat either.

That went on. For four months I was anorexic. Then I was bulimic for a year. It became an ongoing fight until I went to get help. We all know that like alcoholism, it's something that you have. Although you stop or you do it ninety-nine percent less, you have to work on it for the rest of your life.

Conquering an eating problem is very gradual. Little by little you realize you are not a slave anymore to something you were before. A doctor helped me. A medication helped me. I was supposed to take a half pill in the morning, a half in the afternoon, and a whole at night. That would calm my anxieties, and I continued to need it for quite a while.

The worst was when my anxiety mounted. I would eat like hell. Certain foods could trigger it, like creamy stuff or fried stuff. Things like that open something in me where I want more and more and more. For the anxiety, the medication really helped ease my reflex to go off into an eating jag. It calmed me down so I could handle the sick impulses. I used to go to the doctor three times a week, and then twice, and finally only once a week, and then I stopped.

In retrospect I see the anxiety was general rather than *about* anything. There were absolutely no career anxieties, for instance. I was doing all my huge movies and had a number one huge album out that I was touring to promote. It quickly got so that certain foods triggered the anxiety and the disorder, but the source of the anxiety had everything to do with love and men. I've always been very intense regarding men in my life. I give myself a hundred percent and more. So that's what it was.

Part of being healthier is changing the type of men I look for. I think that took a long time, and I'm only starting to see it in better judgment and better rapports. I like strong men because I never needed a man to give me anything. I was also raised that you should only have a man to love you, not maintain you in your life.

I also like a man to give me presents. Why not? Sometimes it's been hard for me to accept an expensive present because that means, in my mind, that I'm going to owe the giver something. I've rejected a few big huge presents from men because of that, and each time I'm like, "Am I stupid or what?" But that's the way I am. If a strong man proves to be too strong and domineering, then I say goodbye. On the other hand, I also like it when I can be the strong one, I can be protective and be the mom. But then after a while I also get tired of that. So because I like both types I guess I like them all. So it's complicated.

Typical men thinking to get involved with an actress or a woman in the beauty field are overinvolved in her looks. I've had a few of those. It does happen still, up to now, because of the men that I might look at in my surroundings. However with my last two relationships I did learn something, and as I just broke up with a boyfriend right now, I do not want a boyfriend. I want lovers. I have to be in that state that is different from all other relationships, where you admire and seek each other above all others. That's the way that I think I'm going to find the man that finally at the end is going to be the one. I think he's the most wonderful, he thinks I am, you're on each other's side and not critical, and you hope the bubble doesn't burst.

Also I have learned to hold back, and with a lover—not a life partner— you still can. I lost myself and jumped into a relationship very fast, the way I did with the boyfriend who damaged me. Then I get to know the person and then it's like, "Oh God, we really aren't good together." So now I don't want to jump into any kind of relationship but to grow in a lover relationship. I carry through what I say, so I am sure before it happens that this is what I'll be doing next.

Men pay abnormal attention to a woman's looks if she's on the screen or a model. They are aware beyond the natural pleasure in someone's attractiveness. I've had two other men who have made me feel insecure about my looks—making three including the first one who turned me to anorexia and bulimia. In each case, looking back, I see it was the man's way of controlling, that was rooted in his insecurities, a well-hidden side.

When I had these problems and suffered dire consequences I went on with my career, and went out, but it was very tough. I was having to be public, because at the peak of my eating disorder I was promoting my music every-where. I was on a promotional tour and had to meet people constantly and give many interviews. I had lunches and dinners with famous people and with fans. In my mind, I was crying that I wanted to be hidden, really to be alone. After doing an appearance or contest or role I was obligated to do, I would eat and eat and eat. I couldn't find myself at all and it was out of des-peration. And then, good-bye, out with all the food! Yet I still kept up meticulously with everything I was doing. Only if I didn't have to I wouldn't go out, because I didn't want to go out and see the food and not be able to control it. Where I used to love parties, I was tormented by them.

The people managing my career and working with me had no idea be-cause I never looked sick. They thought I loved life and was spirited and happy-go-lucky. If they'd seen me naked they could have figured it out, though, because I remember sometimes my neck on my shoulders looked like the neck of a chicken. Besides that, because you don't have enough en-ergy to exercise when you are in the state of anorexia and bulimia, I had to stop exercising and dancing. All my muscle deteriorated into fat. The firm-ness of my body became soft, and then because I was eating bad things a lot of cellulite came out. So dressed I looked fine, I didn't look unhealthy as many do. I never reached that state of looking what I call "dead alive." I think my parents would have known just looking at my eyes. But they didn't find out because they were over there in Venezuela, and I was over here.

The bulimia destroyed a lot of my gum tissue. I had lots of surgery. A few dental jobs worked their success, but the damage to my gums and other tooth problems were because of the acids that come out into the mouth. I was lucky that I didn't lose my front teeth and was able to have the gum surgery.

The disease was very lonely, but I didn't get better all alone. Basically it was the doctor who helped regulate my emotions with medication and taught me how to eat again. I was able to enjoy eating finally as before, understanding that it wasn't going to be bad for me. I had a little carbohy-drate book with me all the time. If a tomato had two carbs I wouldn't eat a tomato!

Finally what happened was I couldn't sleep anymore because I had an open hole in my esophagus. So every time I lay down to sleep the air would come out of that hole, and that would make it very painful to be lying down. It felt as if a knife was cutting my esophagus and through my chest. And then one night I saw myself in a big magnifying mirror. It was the kind where if you take a good look you see everything. And I saw all the little vessels in my neck and face that had broken, from the throat up. I also had little blood dots everywhere on my skin. That's when I got scared and called my girlfriend. I was sobbing: "I'm going to die, I'm going to die, I'm going to die." At that time I was in New York City on a promotional tour, so she came over to the hotel. I told her everything and she recommended the doctor in Los Angeles who helped me get well.

For no one is this a problem that comes and, just like that, goes. It altered my life. It was admitting I can't handle everything alone. Coming from my background and winning the big movie roles and prizes, this was a little disturbing, but also I am glad for it. I feel more connected, not a personality that is hiding out. Once I spoke out, that was when I felt my power all come back. And peace. I've never been one to keep things to myself. My scene is to be outspoken. Once I let all that out, it made me feel so much better. Instead of "Oh my God, what am I doing?" it was, "Oh, I'm so strong I can even talk about this and I feel great." And I make it like, "Yeah, man, look, it's great." Not a joke, because it's not, but incredibly I can talk about it even lightly. I can laugh at myself, at certain things, instead of crying because I did those insane things. As long as you find the solution to it you should be happy and talk about it. I can look stronger and higher up to me for having been able to speak about it than if I had kept it inside. So for that reason I'm a better, stronger, more confident human being, less scared about anything. I don't care what people say or think: I never cared in my whole life. And it made me more content with who I am.

> *Just what was this problem that has no name?*
> *What were the words women used when they tried to express it?*
> *Sometimes a woman would say, "I feel empty somehow . . . incomplete."*
> *Or she would say, "I feel as if I don't exist."*

—Betty Friedan, *The Feminine Mystique*

Barbara Niven
(actor)

LATE BLOOMERS ARE OFTEN wonderful people; in acting they are highly improbable as well. Yet, at thirty, Barbara Niven—a wife and mother from the sticks with a high school education—chased her lifelong dream and became an actress. As soon as it seemed remotely possible she could make a go of it, Barbara, along with her little girl, moved to Hollywood and soon became a star. She succeeded because she is outstandingly capable and also because she's a natural, projecting her sheer, sexy vivaciousness in sparkling on-screen performances.

Barbara is one of the busiest actresses in Hollywood. She has starred in numerous television series, including *Pensacola, Fraser,* and *Las Vegas,* and in many made-for-TV movies. At New York's Shakespeare in the Park she played Kate in *Taming of the Shrew* to great reviews, and she has had leading roles in feature films, especially thrillers and mysteries, notably *Alone with a Stranger* and *Rumble.*

After we interviewed her she went on to shoot a western for

Hallmark's *Mystery Woman* series, playing Annie Oakley, the star of a Wild West show, opposite Bruce Boxleitner. A "true John Wayne/Maureen O'Hara scenario . . . romantic comedy as well as murder mystery," was Barbara's description. This note came from the actress: "I'm shooting guns and riding horses! I even got to rear up on a beautiful white horse four times. What a rush! . . . Gee, did I say I love my job?"

—J.M.

I was always a chubby kid, and an overachiever. Most people with eating disorders—cutters also, now—are overachievers, if you look across the group. At least for me the sickness was always about trying to be perfect. Back when I was in third grade I did so much extra-credit work that I was getting migraine headaches. Every line in my report card was A with four pluses on it. I did all that extra credit, so they had an intervention with this little third grader—me, my teacher, the principal, and my parents. And they banned me from doing homework the rest of the year. I was totally an overachiever, which is good for my business now because it revs you up: you've got to work very hard to have a career in acting. And driven is how I've always been.

I was an avid reader, not getting out and playing as I should have done. When the whole teenage period hit, there I was, this chubby kid with glasses. When I was about fifteen I heard my mom talking with our neighbor, her best friend. They were talking about how, yeah, my mom when she was young was hospitalized because she couldn't keep food down; she'd been throwing up. And everybody else was disgusted by that, whereas I thought, "Oh my God, that's like a secret weapon!"

So I started doing that, and I did drop weight. I did everything. I used to binge eat. I used to horrendously exercise, wrap myself up in Saran wrap. Nobody knew that I was bulimic and all, and I'd never heard of it.

Neither of my sisters had an eating disorder. My younger sister was always skinny, which was horrible for me, being the overweight one. I was chubby with a silver front tooth and glasses, but always the sunshine of the family. We also had a high stress level in the family, coming down from my parents, which nobody could discuss. I was the sunny overachiever trying to keep everybody happy, because if I made everybody happy, nobody would explode and life would be good for everybody.

Yet, looking in the mirror didn't prevent me from wanting to be seen, to perform. Ever since I was a kid I remember looking in the mirror and practicing my movie star poses at ages four and five. My mother would apologize to people. She didn't want a Shirley Temple and thought I was being a baby, but I knew I wanted to act. When we used to go to the beach, all of us, they would lose me and find me in the front row of somebody else's home movie. Inveterately in front of a camera! I loved a camera then and it's the same now. I love a camera better than a live audience. I don't know how weird I am, but acting has always been my shtick and my ideal element.

Adolescent anxiety and self-consciousness were like my unique problem for which I had a unique solution. In those days it wasn't outed. Nobody ever talked about it or knew what an eating disorder was. So I just kept it a secret forever.

Then when I had my daughter, Jessica, I ended up gaining seventy pounds. I didn't worry about this, didn't do anything to restrict my diet. I thought with the experience of giving birth that bulimia had just vanished. Instead it lay in wait. I ended up being quickly bulimic all over again and wondering if I could ever get over that and be the healthy mother I wanted to be.

But at the same time I discovered exercise as being healthy. That has helped keep me on the straight and narrow, because I eat really healthy, and I work out, and I always do best when I feel that I'm an athlete.

In my business a lot of times you are stranded at people's houses, and there are dinner parties and all that. I just always had my ace in the hole. If I was required to go eat somewhere, I would go to the bathroom as soon as I could sneak it in, and go and throw it up. And I was married to somebody pretty prominent in Hollywood, and we were required to attend parties and events all the time, and also to eat late. All of this just causes such a panic in someone who has an eating disorder.

What I did was go into the bathroom, all dressed up, in one of these exclusive Hollywood restaurants. Often somebody in the next stall would be doing the same thing I was. And then, you know, you'd come out and nobody would ever talk about it. So I just did this from the time I was fifteen until about forty-five.

The watershed came when my mother passed away. It all kind of happened quickly in one year: I was kind of confronted with my sickness and decided "I have to stop." All my sisters converged in Portland, Oregon, and we helped Mom pass with hospice. My mom, she was stubborn like me: she set the record of going the longest without food and water before she passed, for any hospice in Oregon. So each day we tried to do whatever we could to help her.

The stress was unbearable. I was performing the tasks I could, but then was going in and throwing up three or four times a day. Then came the reckoning, when my oldest sister, Shelley—I think she saved my life—was outside the bathroom and confronted me. She said, "I know what you're doing. You've got to get help. If you don't make a call now I'm going to do it."

I was so mad at her! I was so angry at the exposure. I was ashamed and fearful—the whole bit. Shelley wouldn't let me do my dinner out thing either, the remainder of the visit. So I ended up calling the eating disorder clinic at UCLA and talking to the head of it.

The other reason I had to do it right then was that my daughter was also going through a lot of stress. She was sixteen, and having her mom gone—me up in Oregon, helping my mom pass—aggravated it. All the cheerleaders at her school had eating disorders. They all binged and purged. One day I got the call that Jessica had fainted during cheerleading because she'd been bulimic and also was not eating. So I decided at that point to face myself, crawl out from the pit. I brought Jessica into therapy and me into therapy. I realized, "I've just got to stop her from suffering from my disease."

So that pivotal moment, when my sister confronted me, is what soon after got us both into therapy.

It took a long time because it's not about food. You have to discover what it's about, and for me it's just my way of handling stress. It's about trying to maintain perfection all the time, which is ridiculous. And now what I do is operate on a whole new program. And luckily my daughter doesn't have any residual problem; we stopped it soon enough. Jessica is just great now, and it's not an issue for her. I had it for much longer. It's always when I'm under stress or when I am conscious suddenly of feeling really full. I clench! It must be like being an alcoholic: something triggers it and that panic starts setting in again.

The way I resuscitate is I talk to somebody about my state. I take action by that means. So for me, getting rid of the secret made me not sick anymore. I don't know if that's true for others. I don't want to assume what they're doing is the same. It's a manifestation of how you deal with things. I just let up on myself some and realized, too, that other people aren't perfect, and they're happy. It's crazy how we push ourselves in this society. Once I let out the nature of my disorder, I've related to people better, because I don't keep a part of me secret: I don't hit up against a barrier of concrete, and neither does the other person.

I do wonder about the origin of my overachieving. It might be genetic. It's interesting that my mother, me, and my daughter all suffered from it. Is it in the genes or behavioral? Who knows? I have no inclination whether this response to stress is in my wiring, or is a learned response that has been passed down. I know that my daughter demonstrates the same intense drive to achieve that I do. She did a two-year master's program in one year and got straight As. Even her adviser remarked, "Well, we're a bit of an overachiever, aren't we?" But we just need—and this is the reason I speak out about my history of this disease—we just all need to let up on ourselves and everybody else. And take a big sigh of relief and say, "Hey, we're all cool. We're in this together."

Bulimia should have killed me, or damaged my esophagus or bones or teeth—all those unhealthy years. You especially worry, if you've had this, about the invisible effects, because you can have bone loss if you're bulimic or anorexic. I'm most fortunate because I had a bone density test, which says that at fifty-three my skeleton is 110 percent of a thirty-three-year-old's.

That sounds perfect to me. By working out, I think I must have erased the damage I did. It seems reversible.

The part of my disorder that is really incredible is that nobody knew. I was married and he never knew. As an actress, I was fastidious about everything. Even looking back now, I think it's almost impossible that people didn't realize I had this problem. I'm that good an actress!

What I like to do now is use a little bit of humor and even push it in people's faces. I spoke at the first annual eating disorder seminar in Ohio this year. I said I would love to do this, only instead of a podium I want a white porcelain toilet out there on the stage. And that's what I used. And you know that damn thing still affects me. I walked on stage, walked around it before I said anything. Then I just started describing how I felt. And other people in the audience felt the same way. It germinated this huge emotional thing. It was a magnificent experience, because people just don't talk about their eating disorders. If they did, they would discover that in a certain way it's idiotic and funny. You've got to have a little humor and put it in their faces, so they get over the shock of it. And there were women who helped put the seminar together who have bulimia or who've had eating disorders, and at first they couldn't even look me in the eye. By the end of my presentation, some of them at last cracked a smile and were, I hope, able to have more of a dialogue with it.

I was grateful I got the chance to take part in that event, and again, speaking out about the troubles with eating keeps me not sick. The more I dispel the secrecy and the more I'm "out" the better it is for me. On the other hand I have found I cannot talk with other people who are under siege from it. I have an eating disorder message board on my Web site, but I can't get into the details of people's conditions. I cannot share with them other than to say, "You've got to get help!" because it triggers all my old stimuli again, and I get weird again about it. What I can do is maintain that an afflicted person has to get help. I'm adamant about it. I'm tough on them about it.

"And you have to talk to somebody who has training in this issue," I say, "Because nobody else can do it. And it's not about food. You have to figure out your own personal reasons why you've taken on this pattern, and what it's doing to you." But if I talk to them—I've heard that before, too, from others—I am pulled in. There are so many message boards. For cutters it's the same: they often just help each other stay sick! The more you talk about it with a fellow sufferer, the more the bad impulses can stir up. I can't participate and be with that person who is still in the throes—not unless they take the help and run with it. If they just want to stay sick, I'll be damned if I'm going to get sick with them.

Friends of mine are in touch with this. I feel I don't have to hide it from them. I was recently doing a really stressful movie in San Francisco, and just needed to let someone know. So I talked to a friend there that I'd made on the set. And once I do, it's like all this pressure and panic that have started building up are let out—literally, the pressure goes from my mouth as I talk about the feelings. Then a sense comes, "I don't have to do this. I can wait and this urge will pass. I can do this."

But the residual anxiety is always there, and I'm sure it always is going to be there. Will I be this frail little ninety-year-old woman who has eating problems? I have to endure and weather it, because it's a special experience of my life.

I accept my drive, too. I mean I crave working out, I don't just like it. I feel like kind of a warrior athlete! I love keeping my body feeling like that now. That's why I work so much as well. The rigor makes me vital. As a result I get in tune—with my body, spirit, everything. Then there's the most important change that overrides everything else: not feeling I have to be perfect anymore.

Jessica, when she graduated high school, was in a dance program and her fellow dancers highlighted her and let her choreograph. She used the text of a poem I'd written about my disorder. It was her celebration and victory dance for having a brush with an eating disorder and getting over it too. She danced in and out of a big mirror. It was so moving, amazing. I was very proud of her. For each of us it's the case that what doesn't kill you makes you stronger.

You know what? Trying to be perfect means failing every moment, being racked with it. I'm a real giver for everybody else but I don't let a lot of people know me. The root of that is a fear, from when I was young, that

I'd think I wasn't perfect enough to keep up the level of contact. Many others who have eating disorders seem to be the same way. If we let our hair down and let people into our lives, it's a lot better. In my case that's also better for creativity, for acting. The more I've embraced my neuroses and idiosyncrasies the more accomplished my acting's been. Because I don't have to put anything over on people any longer. All the little weird stuff I am, and the little misshapen things, like my crooked mouth, I accept. I love me now. I just love where my body is. Despite the aging process I'm doing great and feel in the best place I've ever been. That's akin to where my daughter was when she choreographed and performed the dance.

I'm the opposite of a diva. I don't exhibit extremes. My whole thing was not being able to do confrontations, just trying to be the perfect little girl, basically. Not letting anybody know that I wasn't that image, believing those kinds of feelings could bring me down if I gave in to them. Which was why I tried to hide fears, flaws, and whatever was unresolved—and get them out by throwing them up. That's what I would do, get to zero. If I was really stressed it was so calming to throw it all up and kind of get into this zero, get back to zero, kind of zone out. That's what the purging would do to me. Actually I was completely aware it wasn't food I was voiding from my body so much as it was emotions and situations I couldn't "digest."

It helps me be healthy that I'm totally living my dream. It all feels natural even though I'm an unlikely woman to be starring in movies and acting for a career. I didn't even start to act until I was thirty, in Portland, Oregon, as a single mother. What motivated me was a little newsletter for my ten-year high school reunion. It said, "Our class is going to have a ten-year reunion, what have you been up to?" This hit me like a ton of bricks. At thirty I hadn't even started my life. I was just living for everybody else, and that's where I talked my way into an internship at a news station and lied my way because I didn't even graduate college—I just got married and had a baby. My first story sold to network, then I discovered acting and saw that the news wasn't for me because I like making people feel more than that. When I began acting I thought, "Oh, Lord, this is what I was meant to do!"

I've made a living acting for twenty years, and that's not supposed to happen. And now, in my fifties, I am having the best career time ever. I've starred or had lead roles in seven movies back to back. I'm just shooting as a guest star in *NCIS* this week. The day after that, I take off for Canada where I shoot a starring role in another Lifetime movie. Somebody just called and wants me to veer off to Vancouver to see if they can put me into a project for a week there. I feel I've connected with my purpose.

Jessica is living her own dream too—that's a lining to my life, like my good secret. Her dream is not in this business. What I taught her to do is to connect with her destiny, to make sure she didn't settle. To find your dream. And it's not important how much money you make; if you live what you love to do, you'll wake up every day happy. All you have to do is cover your bills, earn enough to be solvent, and you're going to love your life. To me that's the best secret. Jessica is like a little hippie girl—I'm so proud; she's my hero. She has a bachelor's in anthropology and environmental studies and a minor in African studies. She speaks Swahili and has been to Kenya. She has her master's now in environmental education, so she spent the last two years in Costa Rica. Jess really wants to make a difference in this world. She stands up for the underdog. Without people like her, we might as well roll over now.

It buoys me up to know that despite the fact I had these terrible problems when she was small, I was an adequate mother. She wrote in her college application—her headmaster at Buckley here in L.A. read me part of it—that the day that changed her life was the day that she and I climbed into that twenty-six-foot U-Haul, pulling a ten-foot trailer down from Oregon. When everybody said "You can't do that." Not only were they berating me for being a single mother trying to take my daughter from Oregon to L.A., but to aspire to be an actress? We knew it was scary, but I knew I had to try. And Jess was beside me all the way, and she said that showed her to go after her dreams no matter what. It gave her the courage to realize her idealistic goals. When we made the break with the past she was ten. We went off into the wild unknown and Jess supported me in my dreams, and she always has. I'll do the same for her.

Everything is possible. Look what we have done for one another. I would have died had it not been for my sister and my doctor. When you're in the middle of this illness you feel like, "Oh my God, I'm trapped and there is no exit." And it's like binge drinking where you can do it every day, for me two or three times a day, forever. And all your electrolytes go bad and you don't remember being anything else than in this ruined self. I remember thinking: "Please just let me die now, because I can't do this anymore." It was like if you go falling backwards into a black hole and there is nothing to hold onto.

I couldn't have recovered by myself—you need to turn to people who care about you. My sisters and others gave me support, and the doctor totally helped as well. It was a whole journey for me. I had to take in all my old photos from when I was a chubby kid. The therapy was an intense three and a half years. The disorder was twisted up inside my self. It was the me I had known for thirty years, so I had to learn, and am laying down all the time new tracks. I remember having a few hellish times trying to get out of the black hole—pulling myself out. Once I got off the freeway and called the doctor in a panic. "I don't even know which way I'm going," I said. "What am I doing?" Every fiber in your being wants to maintain what you were, in the power of your addiction devil. The change for normalcy and serenity is really scary. Gradually you do what other recovering addicts do. You learn the reasons why you were messed up, and after you uncover that, you substitute other good behavior. Disclosing all the sorrowful secrets means a special lot to me, as I grew up so repressed. If I feel panic, something I do is cast my mind to all the new growth in my life. For instance my daughter's performance of my poem "Perfect." That was pretty powerful. It was such a victory for each of us.

Now I actually feel beautiful and whole. That self-acceptance is partly a secret of getting older: you get wisdom with the wrinkles. Some of us just get calmer. I don't like the signs of aging—who does? But I am aware of having grown strong. I am so happy, on top of my game in my career of acting. And man, I'm doing my best work ever, and life is great. Every day I wake up excited.

I awaken and oh God
it's still here
THE PANIC
I cringe and lie still
and do a quick once-over
of my enemy
my body
my flesh
Am I fatter than yesterday?
I can't be
I didn't eat
but God I feel
gross
ugly
out of control

I jump up
stare into the mirror
and hate what I see
eyes that stare back
in a face too round
a body too fleshy
too disgusting
too much
too much
not perfect
yet NEVER
PERFECT

—from "Perfect" by Barbara Niven

*And for thirty years he so mortified his body that never did he eat wheaten
bread nor vegetables, nor drank wine, nor used salt to season his food . . .
He fasted always, never eating until the evening; and when he took his repast,
he first put ashes into his mouth, and then ate a barley loaf.*

—Jacobus de Voragine, "Saint Germain,"
in *The Golden Legend*

*You can't eat the orange and throw the peel away—
a man is not a piece of fruit!*

—Arthur Miller,
Death of a Salesman

Shane Sellers
(jockey)

SHANE SELLERS WAS A world-class athlete: a jockey who survived
decades of starving himself and risking his life to stay at the top of
his profession. As he describes it, "I don't have a lot of happy memories now." Indeed, he has seen his share of tragedy as well as
triumph.

Sellers fell in love with horses and racing when he was around
eleven. His passion blossomed into a twenty-six-year career during
which he won more than four thousand races and earned more
than $130 million in purses.

While he loved the sport of thoroughbred horse racing, Sellers
learned about its "dark side" as well. Every track has weight assignments for jockeys, depending on the horse's age, sex, and skill level,
and the distance of the race. Even though he was a small five foot
three, Sellers's natural weight was close to 150 pounds, far in excess
of the 110- to 112-pound range required of him.

The only way he could "make weight" was to take extreme
measures. Starving himself, sessions in the "hot box" or sauna,

running for hours in heavy sweat suits, diuretics, and, worst of all, self-induced purging, which jockeys call "flipping" or "heaving." Doctors call it bulimia.

Retired, and now at a healthy weight, Sellers still spends time around horses and racetracks, now as an owner and trainer. He's also heavily involved in trying to reform the sport he loves, pressuring the industry to create reasonable standards for jockey weight so that current and future riders won't have to place their lives in the kind of danger he and others did for so many years. Sellers says, "I don't want to be remembered for what I did on the racetrack. I want to be remembered as somebody who made a change in our industry, for the good of the sport and the riders."

—G.S.

What I experienced during my riding career was quite a bit different from a bulimic or anorectic. I might have heaved five, six, seven, eight, or even ten times a day when I was at my worst, but it wasn't because I wanted to do it. It was because I had to in order to keep my weight at an external limit. This didn't start up as an emotional reflex; it was a way of life for me. When I quit riding—I weigh upwards of 150 pounds right now—it wasn't nothin' for me to quit eating, and throw up, and all of that other bullshit. It was a rider's way of life. This differed from someone who looks in the mirror and says, "I'm fat and I don't want to eat," or "I'm going to throw up my food." It's quite a drastic difference. Mentally these people are in a condition where they progressively lose control, where I had an iron control. I would throw my food up—and I would do it seven, eight times a day—because I couldn't keep nothin' in, because I had to stay at 112 pounds.

I started riding races when I was eleven years old, and naturally, I weighed 65 pounds: I was very, very small. When I was riding on the match tracks in Louisiana, which is non-pari-mutuel [no wagering]—there's no rules, no weight limit, no age limit. And when I turned sixteen—at sixteen you can become an apprentice—I became an apprentice. At that point I think I weighed 113 pounds. I didn't fight my weight; I didn't know how small you had to be. I had to be 107 pounds with my saddle and everything else, so the first thing they did was, the older riders taught me how to heave: which means, to us, to throw up your food. So they put me in the back room in the toilet, and taught me how to put my finger down my throat and heave. That's where it began.

I started heaving, and everything I ate I heaved. I would keep a little bit of something, maybe a slice of ham, something in me. You just learn how to survive. You learn how to keep your strength. How I did it, now that I'm looking back, comes down to pure will; it was my only way to make weight.

My family was very poor. I was supporting them, including my parents, when I was eleven years old. I had nobody, nowhere to turn, no other way out. I made a decision when I was eleven that this sport was my only way out, and nothing was going to stop me, boy! Except God, and any bad luck falling and hurting myself. So the actions to control my weight were something where I didn't have a choice.

I didn't heave that much then. I would heave big meals when I was sixteen. I really wanted to eat. It became a problem because I knew I could get rid of the food. So then I would eat all I wanted. And I wouldn't eat a little portion; I would eat until my stomach was filled. I followed every other rider, the older riders; that's what they would do. You wouldn't eat just half of a sandwich in between races. If I had two or three races off, I would go in there and say, "Give me two hamburgers, a large order of french fries, and three Cokes," 'cause I was eating until I could hold no more food down, because I knew I could get rid of it. Knowing that I could get rid of it, I was starving to death! I mean, I'd nothing in my stomach.

But I wasn't heaving once or twice a day. Then the older I got—eighteen, nineteen, twenty—the bigger my body started growing. I continued to mature, and as I was maturing it became harder and harder for me to keep my weight down. And that's when I got to heavin' seven or eight times a day.

What I needed to do, the objective, was to keep my weight at 112. I don't know what my natural body weight was, but it was very much higher, since now I'm steady at 145. I retired in 2000 because of an injury, and that's the first time I was ever off of work for more than three or four weeks. When I would be off I would jump up to about 120, but I would never let it get higher than that, because it's too hard to get off. I could take off seven, eight, nine pounds, and it was doing my body some good to go up in weight. I would put it on, jump the nine or ten pounds in a matter of three days. But when I retired I jumped up to 145 right quick. It feels like heaven!

Because I rode year round, riding was all I knew. I rode over a thousand races a year. And I was at the top of my game. I got up to third leading rider in the nation. So I was making an unbelievable amount of money, and there was nothing that was going to stop me. And I didn't rankle about it. I felt normal because everyone around me was doing the same thing, everywhere I went in the country. That's just the life of the jockey. Ninety percent of the jockeys were either heaving, or if the riders didn't heave, they ate very little, they watched their weight, and they got in the sweat box and pulled three or four pounds a day of water. So neither one was healthy. Worst-case scenario, riders are doing both, heaving and sweating—and that's all over the country.

I did an HBO special a few years ago, which was nominated for three Emmys and won an Emmy, about the lifestyle of jockeys: what we go through and how jockeys become bulimics. How they learn the routine of throwing up, heaving, daily. The last year I've been fighting the industry to change the weight system. And I got 'em up to a minimum of 116. We've made some strides but we had a kid die three months ago. He pulled seven pounds in the hot box, and he died. You never hear about it in sports news. When you have a guy die on the football field of a heart attack, it's major news, where hardly a soul ever heard about this. Three weeks ago we had another kid die. I rode with him and his name was Chris Harrel, and when he was riding I'd ask him, "Why are you doing this?" I mean, he was tall, and he'd sit in that box and pull six or seven pounds a day, and throw up every ounce he ate. And he broke his collarbone about six months ago, and he ballooned. He put on thirty-five pounds in two, three weeks, and then when his shoulder was healed he started getting it off, and he pulled twenty-something pounds in three weeks, and it killed him. He died: his organs just shut down. But who ever heard of that?

Most riders ride at two to four percent body fat. Any doctor will tell you: under five percent body fat you're cannibalizing your organs. So there's a major problem in this industry, given the nutrition of kids today. You look at a thirteen-year-old kid: how many do you see who weigh under a hundred pounds? It's absurd. It's not going to happen. In Australia they banned the hot boxes and jocks' rooms. But Churchill Downs and Arlington Park, and a bunch of other racetracks, it's not accidental that they have hot boxes that riders abuse. They put the facility in there for you to kill yourself! A hot box is not like a sauna that you go in just to sweat, like in a gym. These guys get in there and are abusing their bodies and pulling five, six, seven pounds a day.

Then you go in the bathroom where they got six stalls. Five of them are regular toilets and one of them's a heaving bowl for you to throw your food up in. These racetracks are promoting bulimia, and they know the riders are doing it. They know you're throwing up your food.

When is the government going to step in here and say, "Whoa"? In my eyes, when this kid died in the hot box the racetrack should have been held criminally responsible.

The clerk of the scales, those riders, all the people at that track knew Chris had pulled seven pounds. How much more time will pass before people who participate in the sport and the officials that regulate it will take responsibility for the riders' well-being? But business goes on as usual and this kid just died, nobody heard about it.

About ten years ago there were three college wrestlers that died pulling weight, and the intercollegiate wrestling industry stepped in. They said, "We have to come up with a solution for these kids. Otherwise the sport will be banned." Now you can't wrestle at 175 and then say, "Aw, I can win at 155."

Most sports have governing bodies that test athletes. For instance, gymnasts and triathletes are tested, and if they are under five percent body fat they can't participate. We're the only athletes whose well-being is held in disregard. It's a multi-billion dollar business and the industry doesn't protect you.

A body fat measurement is the only means I know to effect a change. The weights need to be changed, first of all. But you can't just change the weights, because if you raise the weights ten pounds then there's going to be somebody heavier that's going to try to get down. So you're going to be in the same trap. You need to raise the weights, then you need to put a stipulation that the rider needs to do that weight naturally. There has to be somebody that oversees it, though. Because as with those three wrestlers that died, they knew what they were doing to their bodies. We know what we're doing to our bodies, but when you have a dream you just do it.

Riders don't have education. We give up our education at sixteen. That's another wrong I'm fighting, and it's related to the weights. A sixteen-year-old is not mature in mind or body. Sixteen is too early to say "This is it" for your education. A jockey is not mentally capable of doing his best when he's a boy. As a sport, horse racing's fast and dangerous. But that's the bottom line of it. The top line of it is his body isn't even finished growing. The minimum age to ride has to be eighteen. This gives a kid time enough to be mature, and gives his body two more years to see if he can naturally do the weight.

So far the industry doesn't care. For three years I have fought for changes you can't dispute. Don't they know these kids are dying? Meanwhile the people who run the sport are telling us, "No, shut up! We don't want you to interfere. You're making waves here." I'm the bad guy . . . In Australia they had three kids die from pulling weight in the hot boxes. They banned the use of hot boxes in the jockeys' room, and they raised the weights. That's what I call caring.

When I started as a young man I was desperate to succeed, because I came from nothing and had nothing. So now you start to get successful and your life works, and you're getting money, yet you're still going through this. At what point do you open your eyes and act for your real self-interest? What occurred over the passage of time is that I decided, "Enough! I'm not going to do this anymore!"

I blew my knee out in an accident, and I couldn't come back—that was the end of my career. I stayed off almost two years, and then I decided, I told my wife. I was 242 wins away from 4,000 wins, and I'd worked hard to get to that point, and I said, "You know what?" (I had to lose thirty-two pounds.) And I said, "I can do this." While I was getting the weight off, the HBO special followed me around, and I got down naturally to about 125 stripped. And that was my point, on the HBO special, to try to come back to the weight and do it naturally. But then when I got to 125 I couldn't bring it down further without getting in the hot box.

Then I started heaving again, and getting into the box, and I got it down. In my mind I was going to win enough races to get to 4,000, and I was going to retire. But then I landed with the big outfits that I was riding for—I landed those again, Nick Zito and Steve Asmussen—and my career went back to where it was before. I started winning the big races again. I rode the colt favored in the Kentucky Derby last year, and then there I was on top again. I got to that point where I was successful, making money again. I had put away money, but we take home less than twenty cents on the dollar. After paying the agents thirty-something cents, and the valet is five cents, with Uncle Sam you're in the 40-percent bracket. You have to buy your saddles, this and that, and so again we don't take home but a fraction of what we make. So I had managed to save money, but being off for two years I had no way of making a living. I have no education, I can make minimum wage and that's all I can do. So when I started making $25,000 to $40,000 a week again, I said, "I'm going to do this again until I make sure that when I walk away the next time I don't have to work again." So it got back down to surviving in my life once more. My family got used to living a certain life style and I didn't want for them not to have that life style. It was like being that fifteen-year-old kid again! I had to support my mom and dad, and I did that role until today.

When it stopped was a year ago, when a young kid fell in West Virginia. His name was Gary Burson, and there were only five states that had riders covered under workmen's comp. I was riding in New York at Saratoga at the time, and New York is a workmen's comp state. Well, West Virginia wasn't. It's like in the other states that don't have workmen's comp, the racetrack covers you $100,000. It's called track coverage. This kid was in a wheelchair. He went through $100,000 in a week, and his bills were over a million dollars. He was being turned away from rehab centers because he didn't have the money. In other words, he was going to be in debt for the rest of his life, and in a wheelchair with no way to make a living. It hit me hard. I thought about my family in these terms, and two weeks later I was coming back to Kentucky to ride—which is my base, and in Kentucky we didn't have workmen's comp, only that $100,000 policy—and I looked at my wife and said, "I'm riding for Nick Zito. I rode the favorite in the Kentucky Derby. I'm riding for Steve. I'm riding for the two best trainers in the country. If I fall and have only that insurance, and if I'm in a wheelchair and my bill is a million dollars, I'm going to lose most of my kids' future." And I made a decision. I said, "I'm quitting."

I didn't retire, but as of last August I told everyone that would listen in the industry about the changes that are overdue for respecting riders. Other riders said, "You're crazy; you're at the top of your game," and I said, "I have to make a conscious decision for my family. If it would be just me and I was single, I love riding so much that I'd take those chances, but if I fall and lose my kids' future it would be on my conscience for the rest of my life." I couldn't have lived with that, so I told them I was quitting until we get better insurance. And then we went to fighting for Tony D'Amico, who fell two months later, whose bills went rapidly over $100,000. We went to raise money for him. Then some other riders said, "We can't do it. We need the insurance." We ended up with eighteen riders who refused to ride. The governor of Kentucky stepped in and instead of $100,000 they now have a million-dollar policy. And the change spread out to many tracks, which had to bring the rider's policy up to a million, too. And now it's going to go on and on.

From that point I was pretty much blackballed. They hauled me off in handcuffs at Churchill Downs because they thought I was a threat, that I orchestrated the walkout. In fact it was those other riders who stood in front of the track five days before the Derby with picket signs. I didn't do anything but stand up and be a voice and tell the people. But I said from that point I'd never ride a racehorse again. I'd made my money and now I was going to help my sport and hope I saw the day it was fair for the riders. And I wasn't afraid to lose any mounts. I wasn't afraid to stand up to Churchill Downs or any other racetrack.

The stances I've made have cost me. I'll never be in the Hall of Fame because of them. Jerry Bailey, one of the world's leading jockeys, told me at the dinner the night before the Derby last year, "Shane, I told my wife in '97 I beat the lead rider at Gulf Stream. I told her that you were the best rider in the country—'The only thing that will hurt him is his mouth. If he'd just play the politics of the game.' There's no doubt in my mind you are the best rider in the country."

It hit me: "Golly, that's coming from Jerry Bailey, he don't never compliment." We were very tight and what he said was true. Between my speaking out about weights and the riders' health and the insurance I was getting to be political. As Bailey said, if I'd just played the politics of the game I'd have had it easy. I won 4,000 races and over one hundred million in purses by going against the grain. What do you think would have happened if I'd just played the game? But I never did. Having said that, I looked to myself and realized a different direction I was beginning to go. So I quit riding, and I weigh about 150 pounds, and I'd do it again.

The riding career's over. I'm not jockey-weight. God, I just feel like a new person. When I was riding, I was depressed all the time. Some days I couldn't get off the sofa; I was just in this dead-feeling state. I didn't know the cause of it. Every day you'd have to wake up and look at that scale, and know you went to bed with nothing in your stomach. You'd wake up and you couldn't put nothin' in your stomach, and if you did you'd have to throw it up. And then on top of that you'd have to go in and pull four or five pounds of water and then go and ride. Mentally it just destroyed me. It's a brutal choice you'd make. Gary Stevens, when he retired, said, "I just can't get in that hot box no more. I can't do it no more."

But instead of these guys standing up and fighting, and telling people they have a problem, they're listing their weight as 116 and riding at 124, and they're paying the clerk of scales. I did it for the last ten years. I wasn't going to kill myself to drop down more. I thought, "If that guy's going to let me ride three, four, five pounds over, I'm going to do it." And every place I went in the country I did it. I wouldn't pay him off but I'd buy him dinner. I wouldn't look at the scale. I would do my best—I heaved everything, I got into the box, but I wouldn't go and pull five or six pounds, I'd go and pull one or two pounds. Then I'd get on the scale and I'd grab my saddle and look so I didn't see the number. But I knew I was heavy . . . Man, I'd look at the other guys when they got on, and everywhere I rode in the country that's what would happen.

And in New York this year the state stepped in to prosecute Robby Alvarado and Jose Santos. I saved their asses again. They wanted to prosecute the riders and the clerk of scales. And I told them, "If you grant me immunity I'll go and I'll talk." And they did, and I went in front of the grand jury, and I came to tears as I told them what we do for a living. I said, "It's not our fault; it's not the clerk of scales' fault. It's the State's and the industry's fault for not raising the weights. We're dying, you know."

And they didn't prosecute the riders, but I'm sorry to say they're prosecuting the clerk of scales, Braulio Baeza, one of the best riders that ever sat in a saddle, because the riders didn't want to testify. Robby Alvarado, for example, told them, "I didn't know I was overweight. I wouldn't look at the scales." And that's what riders have constantly done.

After the HBO special I was in the box with two top riders, Mark Guidry and Robby Alvarado, and I'll never forget it. I said, "I'm coming back to ride. I lost twenty-seven pounds." I said, "I'm putting 116 down." And I knew I couldn't do sixteen. But I knew I could get away with doing sixteen with the clerk of scales. So I told him. I said, "Men, let's all do sixteen and then what are they going to do?" I went out there and put sixteen down, and you know what they put? Thirteen. You know what they were doing? Twenty-two. They were doing the same thing as me. But they figure to get an edge. But they were cutting my throat. I don't feel bad about doing it. Again, I didn't really know what weight I was doing, 'cause I wouldn't look at the scales. I knew I was over, and I knew the others were over, 'cause I was looking at what they were doing, you know. But at least I was fighting to change the regulations. That's why my conscience is clear. And I was winning. We were all winning. We were in the rank of leading riders all over. As for those couple of extra pounds, it wasn't hurting the horses.

Now, weighing close to 150, I look back at photographs of me, and it makes me sick. I can't imagine. My little boy is thirteen years old. Clothes that I had in my closet he's wearing. I was going to throw a lot of them away—suits and jackets that I had. I mean, I had expensive clothes and I can't put them on. My thirteen-year-old son is wearing them. He asked three days ago permission to wear them, and I was just holding on until—'cause I never in my heart said goodbye to the sport. I cried many days when I realized I had finally said goodbye, but I just gave all those clothes to my kid, and I look at him fitting them and, I mean, he's thirteen years old!

When I look in the mirror, I see a man and not a boy. I'm comfortable physically. I fell off my roof and injured my ankles, which meant three months of crutches, so I'm having to get into shape. I work out. I still weigh myself but not every day. One hundred forty-two pounds would be my natural weight, and healthy and in shape. When I rode you could say I was physically in shape but at the same time I was cannibalizing my body, so that makes me sad to recollect.

When I came back to riding, I couldn't ride without pain pills. I got addicted, and when I stopped riding I checked myself into rehab. The first day I went they took blood, and I didn't know they test for your liver, kidneys, and everything else. It took weeks for my tests to come back, and I was scared to death. I knew what I did to my body, and thank God my tests came back pretty good. Not great, but pretty good. They told me, "You can't do this again. You can't do these things to your body to keep the weight, especially not at your age. You're thirty-eight years old." And it scared me. The first thing I thought about was a friend of mine, a rider, Randy Romero, how he damaged his liver, and doesn't have any kidneys. He's dying. He's living off machines. That wasn't a choice to do what jockeys do. Riding was his livelihood, he belonged to the sport, and he did what he had to do. It scared me 'cause I knew how long we went on ruining our insides.

Again, I look at my pictures downstairs and in a way I thank God I fell off that roof and have plates in my heels and can never ride again. I look at the riders today and say to myself, "Shane, I know if you could get the weight down, you could still ride with these kids." There's no doubt in my mind. But I really thought about my course of action and believe there's a reason why I fell off that roof. God said, "Shane, I gave you two chances. I'm not going to look after you again."

Then I began to reflect beyond my own self, and found myself angry at the game, at the industry that allows these kids to die. When is the government going to step in? You're never going to see twelve horses coming out of the gate with no riders on their backs. It's never going to happen. But having said that, are you going to allow more deaths or bring sanity in? You know they're dying; you're putting heaving bowls in the damn jocks' rooms for them.

Racetracks are promoting bulimia. The industry needs to be held accountable or to change the system. Why wouldn't they change it? It would be good for everybody if they did.

The role I see for myself now is to help enact this kind of legislation and change. I've been doing it for two years. I'm committed to doing it until they lay me in the ground. My speaking out has begun to spur some action. If you look at the weights now, at the bottoms, the least you see a horse is with sixteen, seventeen, eighteen. In Chicago they upped the top to twenty-four; the bottom is seventeen. Before, you could see a horse come in with eleven, or nine, so I did make a difference around the country, and I'm very proud of that. Before that HBO special, people didn't know that there was a problem with riders making weight. Now it's a known fact.

As I say, the solution is not just raising the weight. You have to have a governing board in the industry that protects these kids from killing themselves. When I was a kid there was nobody who was going to caution me not to do it, because I had nowhere to go, man! I had my mom and daddy; I had my family to support. And this has been the situation of almost every other rider. Look at the history of horse racing. How many riders have a high school education? A hundred years ago it was a different society. Now the new riders aren't U.S. born; they are Hispanic kids mostly, who come from third-world countries. The nutrition is not what it is in the U.S. Look at basketball and football players thirty years ago. Oh gee they're much bigger, a normal human being is bigger. I see the Little Leaguers. One pitcher is eight and weighed 160 pounds. Come on, are you going to tell me that a twenty-five-year-old man can be 113 pounds naturally? You're going every once in a while to find one, like Pat Day or Willie Shoemaker. Those greats. Ron Turcotte said when he started riding he weighed 135 pounds at sixteen years. He fought like hell to get his weight down. The guy ended up riding Secretariat.

You have maybe ten percent of people who can naturally make the current weight. And you know who they are? You have the most women riders that you've ever seen in the history of horse racing. Why? Because they can make the weight. Otherwise the majority are Spanish-speaking, or come from third-world countries. American men cannot do it. So either let's ban American guys from riding, or raise the weights. But, as Pat Day said, I'm not against raising the weights; I'm against raising the weights without a stipulation, because—and it's the truth—otherwise it will continue like a vicious cycle; you're still going to have somebody trying to get down.

I applaud wrestling for finding a way, after those three kids died, to save the sport and make it healthy. Every state has horseracing, and taxpayers as well as people who love the sport have benefits from horseracing. One day the government is going to step in and say, "Okay, time out, eh? Kids are dying here." I'm working for that day and I'll never stop until they put me in my grave. I have nothing to lose.

*I grow lean
in loneliness
like a water lily
gnawed by a beetle.*

—Kaccipettu Nannakaiyar,
third-century Tamil poet

Elisa Donovan
(actor)

THE MOUNTAIN DOESN'T GO to Mohammad, and we didn't antici-
pate that celebrities would offer to come to us. Elisa Donovan, who
lives in Beverly Hills, agreed to an interview in New York, and two
days before the set date she e-mailed her coordinates. She planned
a noon checkout from the Soho Grand Hotel, then she would be
available for the interview, hang out in Greenwich Village, and end
up staying overnight with friends in Brooklyn. She planned to
travel to North Carolina the next day, then fly to Hollywood
to shoot a movie. The note ended: "So how long is the train ride
to where you are in Connecticut? (You may feel more comfortable
in your space.) I leave for San Francisco in an hour or so. Talk to
you soon! Elisa."

Needless to say, we met in New York. Heads turned as this daz-
zling actress came into the Washington Square cafe. With her intense green eyes, carefree wavy red hair, outdoor-girl fresh coloring
and freckles, Elisa might have been a graduate student in the arts at
New York University, except her clothes were slightly California

123

Carnaby. Suddenly the intensity lifted as Elisa gave the people staring our way a big smile.

Her enthusiasm was sustained throughout the interview until the moment she dashed away, long spangled scarf flying. "It was so nice to meet with you and share!" she shouted back. "It is fantastic and so important to get to meet and experience inspiring women, women on their journeys. I am happy to be a part."

Born in Poughkeepsie, New York, Elisa grew up on Long Island. She was a cheerleader at Northport High School—an all-American girl who flirted briefly with gothic chic. She attended college at the New School for Social Research in Manhattan and did theatrical work while supporting herself as a waitress. She was a regular on the soap opera *Loving* and the sitcom *Blossom*, appeared as Amber in *Clueless* (both the movie and the TV series), starred in the E! movie *Best Actress*, and has appeared in numerous other films. She is currently starring in two indie features, *The Bliss* and *Kiss Me Again*. Her current favorite off-time pursuits are painting, kickboxing, and driving race cars.

—J.M.

My becoming anorectic was perverse. I had a supportive family and a wonderful circle of friends and as a young teen had set sail on a sea of activities. Yet with every chance for self-expression, the reality was I was learning to squelch my own feelings. The nosedive—and this is my best explanation—was like a misapplication of the same discipline and perseverance that's central to who I am: the traits of personality which I'd relied on and which brought me early success.

I've been known to try most anything. For instance lately I've dabbled in race car driving. A couple of friends pulled me into it. The first race was the Grand Prix of Long Beach. I figured I'd get into this sleek little car, turn the key in the ignition and race out onto the track. But when my friends took me to the car I said, "Are all these cars stick shift?" Everyone was dying laughing: "Of course." It hadn't occurred to me that race cars are stick shift, but I wasn't going to back down. They taught me to shift as well as the other techniques of driving a race car. It was wonderful, so exhilarating, and great fun. My persistence generally serves me well, but not when it came to exerting self-discipline over my dieting. That's what led me to anorexia, where I executed a perfect downward spiral. You can see where going with grit and resolve into something and being very competitive can spell trouble for a girl on a diet.

Even as a child and all through my teenage years I was a performer. I was acting at seven. Soon I was competing in gymnastics, horseback riding, and dance as well. I was hugely energetic and strove to obtain perfection in all the areas of my life. Everything I did was for a live audience, and I felt I had to be perfect for them.

In junior high and high school I was very active. I loved everything artistic; for a while I was gothic punk. I took photographs and painted and spoke forth about my ideas—but soon I was this person who became successful but wasn't really present. I couldn't enjoy these fortunate circumstances. I couldn't go anywhere because I was confronted everywhere by food and normal attitudes about eating, which I scorned yet secretly envied. I did everything with a manic energy.

Why did I sacrifice my opportunities to be skinny? What was the trigger? Growing up, my identity was bound up with excelling as a gymnast and dancer. When I started to get a little bit taller and go through puberty I wasn't as good at gymnastics, and my body had changed. I was never able to manipulate my body, or starve myself, or over-exercise, to stay the body type and weight that was most desired. I simply wouldn't twist myself up over it in high school. Instead of sports and dance I switched my interest to speech, drama, and experimental theater. I remember one time when I was thirteen my father made a joke. He said, "Don't eat those crackers before dinner." I was like, "Why not?" He said, "You're going to get fat." He was making a total joke but it registered differently with me, and I went, "Oh."

That's when I understood that what you eat has a corresponding effect on how your body looks. It sank in, and I went "Whoa!" I just sort of clocked that information and left it in my head. Then when I was in high school I got into this health kick with—and it's funny because now I am very holistic and organic with the foods I eat, but for very different reasons—a selection of sort of magic natural foods. I ate bran muffins and drank a lot of water, things like that, and I started to try to eat less and eat low-fat foods, but I never really could do it.

After high school in Long Island I moved to New York City. I wanted to take a year off before college, and I attended Michael Chekhov's acting studio full time. I moved into an apartment on Bleecker Street with a woman who was an actress, much older than I, probably thirty-something, which seemed so much older. I felt isolated and alone. And coming from an intense, very active life, being a big fish in my little pond of Northport High School, when I moved to New York—even though I loved it and had always come into the city when my parents would let me, on weekends and at night—it got scary. And that was the only time I gained a little weight. I wasn't overweight, but I was using food as a mechanism of comfort. With abundant free time, being in acting school, which has its own rigors, and working at a series of restaurants, my life became sort of crazy. There came a moment when I was really down about my prospects. I was sitting with a friend at a place in Soho and explaining to her my frustration over not getting an acting job. I had an agent after I had done this off-Broadway show that I co-wrote with another woman, and we did it at La MaMa. I had a good agent but was still not getting work. I was auditioning and doing classes but my confidence was faltering. Also I felt I was getting old! That's something that happens in Hollywood and in life too. I remember being nineteen and feeling over the hill, that it was too late for me. Now I realize that if I felt that way turning twenty, I clearly don't have a good sense of a lot of things, and that it's the career that's unstable, so let it go! And now I'm completely happy to let it go!

So, as we ate lunch, I literally took the plate, as if I was wrought up and couldn't articulate why I was upset, and pushed the plate away! When I did it I felt this power and a sensation of, "Oh, this is the first time."

Not everything do I remember with that total recall, but I distinctly remember this gesture that proved so decisive. I went "Whooah" and experienced the control. A question arose in my mind that this was a power I sought, but could I keep it? It really was control that formed the hook as I see it now. Because I was getting into a career where there is zero amount of stability, and where your success is not necessarily based on merit or talent. It's really overwhelming for anyone, and I was an inexperienced nineteen.

So that kicked in: I would be anywhere where good food was in abundance, and I would go "Noooo." I would just push it away. When I would be with people and not touch food, I realized "Oh, this is a whole new thing I can do." Not eating might have been a new course or sport! I was already disciplined in other aspects of life. Gymnastics especially is so disciplined and meant practicing four hours a day after school as well as competing. I switched it right over to what I consumed, and that was the beginning of the whole tailspin.

And very quickly my body began to change. Willing to eat next to nothing began in the spring of 1993. By the time I moved to Los Angeles in 1994 I'd been doing it for a year—eating much lighter, but still eating. Then I just moved much, much further and further along.

After a couple of months, people noticed I'd lost a lot of weight. In the beginning they complimented me, except for one friend of mine who is an actor with whom I'd become close working in theater in New York. He had tried to help me get a one-woman show off the ground there, which I actually did years later in L.A. His girlfriend of many, many years—this is another thing that helped my demise. She had been anorexic for many years and is a very successful person, intelligent and vivacious. I always thought, "How does she get to look that thin? How does it happen?" I'd not said anything to her about how her body looked until I said, "Is that all you eat?" She was eating a carrot at a function. She went, "Huh? Well, you know." She wasn't cagey about it. It was clear she had issues with bulimia or anorexia. And her boyfriend chimed in, "Yeah, we're dealing with that." So I said, "Oh, so she does not eat." My reasoning was that a person could look like that if this was what she did.

Clearly I don't blame her or other poor role models. It was another nudge in the wrong direction, a key that opened the wrong door, the suggestion that it was possible to exert this kind of control over the surface of oneself.

I had really solidified my way. I had lost a significant amount of weight to the point where people were saying, "You look a little thin." People were drawing attention to it. The only person I knew in L.A. when I arrived was my friend Jennifer. She was a playwright from New York. I had been in the productions of several of her plays, so I stayed with her initially when I went out there. Jennifer saw me and said, "Lisa!"—which was my name then—"Oh my God! You're so thin! What are you doing? What happened?" To which I immediately said, "What do you mean?" and I immediately translated that in my mind to "She's just jealous."

That's what I would do. I would interpret people's concern or shock or just gawking at skinny me as "They're just envious of how I look," or "I'm almost where I want to be, so I'll ignore them." All those things that people say to wake you up do not help. To hear you're skinny or too thin or just getting more attention is feeding the fire of the problem. At that point when I saw people who knew me for a long time they'd ask, "What are you doing?"

It's funny because I have a big head. So when I would lose weight, being big-boned, my head would look unduly large—disproportionately so. Eventually I asked people, "Why can't I get any thinner?" and they went, "Because your bones are large! You can't shrink your bones!"

I suppose I could have. There's so much sick humor in the insanity of this behavior. It's unbelievably painful also. I had no inkling I was at a dangerous point. I didn't realize how far gone I was. I knew my body was thinner, and that only made me happy. I didn't realize the deterioration of my personality. My friends would say, "You're not yourself." I'd return to New York and hear, "You aren't fun anymore. Do you see what you're doing?"

If you have anorexia you can't even go to dinner anymore. Think about the actor's life and how much socializing is over meals. I'd meet friends but then I'd have to leave and meet them later. They'd say, "So what is going on with you?" And I couldn't see how it had affected my livelihood and personality.

I don't know the source of that except to say that when I was doing the movie *Clueless,* if I had a six o'clock call in the morning I would either work out before that or work out after twelve or fifteen hours of working, and honestly I was living on seedless grapes. That's all I was eating. And somehow the body has a miraculous ability to survive. It utilizes food with incredible efficiency. I would pass out places from time to time, but I only remember one time distinctly of seriously blacking out for several seconds in the bathroom of a restaurant. So I would be wavering and fuzzy a lot of the time—which also blunted my emotions and made it easier to live. The shutting off and the condition of not feeling anything: neither sadness, grief, nor really feeling joy either. No feeling anger, certainly. You are listless, and that protects you from frustration as well. All those human emotions die right off.

People ask, "How did you do it?" I think about the character that I played that was the first big-name film role that I did. She was a memorable character, which I feel blessed and happy about. On the other hand, looking at her I think it's preposterous and near miraculous that I even did it. I don't know how I persevered. Only there's the record to prove that I did— the character's there on screen. It's uncanny how I recall every day on the set, operating on automatic and being half-dead. Since the work was often all day there was all this food around, and I would be just staring at it . . . walking disembodied through the making of a film. Yet the wardrobe people were happy because I could fit into all the clothing. We had fittings, obviously, before we started shooting, but by the time I would wear the clothing it was too big. They would have to take it in as I was actively losing weight still. Even the spiral down isn't smooth because at some point you can't really lose anymore. It suddenly goes into starvation mode. That realization, as it clicks into your warped thinking, causes more anxiety.

I got into recovery in the middle of the movie *Clueless,* so by the rough-cut screening I was in recovery, but very early on and uneasy. We went to the test screening and most of the actors were there, and I brought a friend with me. As we watched the movie—first of all I knew it was going to be a big success, and I looked skin and bones and I thought, "You're going to be famous and you're going to be imprinted on people's minds like that," and I wondered why I had gone on becoming not-me. My friend Justin said as I was walking down the stairs in front of him, "You're like a bone, you are like this little child."

Something was clicking at that exact moment I saw my image in the movie. I was still struggling with the idea of recovery and I asked myself, "Well, that's what you get, isn't it? If you want to be the skinniest, that's what you get—to be the skinniest. You don't get the best part in the movie, the most glory, or friends, or money. You don't get anything else. You get to be the skinniest. I get to be the little bone who's walking down the steps with everybody taking care not to jostle me."

And that night a very good friend, Jorge, who was visiting from New York, told me, "You have to help yourself." I told him, "I'm in recovery," and he said, "Well, I don't see it because you still seem crazy, and you're still really skinny." He may have been a little more diplomatic about it. I'd been to the doctor and acknowledged my problem and was willing to take lengths to get better. Still, something changed after the screening. I turned a corner. That objective look at myself, at what I'd been reduced to, motivated me to want to get healthy. The spell was broken. I saw that "this is all you get." We can create this whole mythology of what it's about, an entire history. The stark reality is, all you get is to be skinny!

There are flashes where you wonder if your view is a little askew—until the flashes of reality, with luck, add up. If you are going to have a good life, you are not going to be living on air.

My publicist at the time I was coming back to life knew about my problem. When we first started working together, and the work was coming in fast, he said, "You've got to tell me everything. Whatever your skeletons are, because people are going to know. And what's your story?"

So I admitted that I had been anorexic and was still very much in the beginning of recovery. "Well," he said, "you can go two ways. You can wait for people to find out and ask you about it. Or you can speak about it and tell your story."

Looking back on this, it's funny because I was so in the beginning of my recovery that it's almost as if talking about it was a wingless flight. It heals you when you are communicating with people about it, and I always tell the truth of the thing. When approached by the media, talking to a teen magazine reporter, or writing my experience for *Chicken Soup for the Teenage Soul,* I was looking upward at a platform where I aspired to be. I was aspiring to be in a better place about the sickness than I actually was. Recovery is a long process. When you're close to the old behavior you're tender, and I was not distant from it, as I am now when I was asked to speak about it. In the account I did for *Chicken Soup,* for instance, I can see I was wrestling with one aspect of my history that is bound up with the anorexia—perfectionism—but was still re-finding my identity, which an anorextic kind of mislays along the way.

For me, therapy has been the single most important part of recovery. I'm such an emotional person, but also very intellectual and analytical. Therapy is so important because you verbalize the jumble of emotions, but there's a trick in it as well. I noticed from the beginning that I could talk my way through or in and out of seemingly anything. I could completely manipulate my first therapist to the point where I was actually setting the rules and she was a player in my game. After a month or so of sessions, I gained two pounds and completely freaked out. I had a nutritionist, too, and I went through the roof and blamed them both.

They were out to get me! The direction of increased weight was terrifying. Having no concept of normal, functional eating anymore, I calculated that if I gained so much weight per week over the next couple of years I'd be too fat to stand up! That's where you go if you're anorexic. My therapist at that time was wonderful, but this wasn't especially her area. So she focused on quelling my fears to calm me down. She said, "Well, I'll talk to your nutritionist, and we'll figure out how to maintain where you are." Yet the whole point was to gain. I had manipulated her into trying to help me to lose weight again, or resist weight gain. Even sick as I was, I recognized she wasn't the person to help me. Because when treating this disease you cannot say that; you cannot say, "Like, okay, we'll get you to lose it again"! You can't say anything like that to an anorexic. But then I changed to a different therapist, the woman I see now. She herself went through a bout of these problems and the therapy has helped me tremendously. I think it was a combination of that, of the desire to get healthy and the desire to have a normal life. You see, my life had become extremely tiny!

I was told as far as diets go, that's a word to take forever out of my vocabulary. My therapist suffered from anorexia and bulimia for years. She was very much in recovery. She gave me a list of foods the first day I went to see her. You could mark on the sheet "safe," "unsafe," "not sure," "like it," "don't know if I like it." I check-marked the whole thing: every food on the list was unsafe. I wrote unsafe, unsafe, unsafe—except for grapes.

And I would eat sashimi from time to time, go to a sushi bar and take out the fish from between the rice in sushi. The therapist got me from that to eating rice like a normal person now. But that took a long time. So what we did was, we sort of made agreements. The deal was three meals a day and snacks, and I had to write down my food. At first I was eating a bowl of cereal for breakfast. She would ask where I would go for breakfast or where I would eat, and what makes me the most comfortable. And I would have two cappuccinos because of the milk. She wanted me to have lattes— but I was not ready for lattes—and two pieces of toast and a bowl of fruit. For a year I ate that. A fruit bowl without bananas, without stuff that I knew had more calories. And I would wind up having one piece of toast, or with daring, one and a half. Lunch would be all based on protein and carbohydrates, and each meal had to include a protein. At that time milk was the sketchy protein. I was moving out from safety and testing my nerve.

The objective wasn't just to put on weight but to reestablish comfort and balance the foods, as I was trying to get better across the board. We worked like that and I could call the therapist at any time and tell her if I felt crazy. She would weigh me weekly, which was a whole debate; I didn't want to know. She said, "I have to do this. I'll only tell you if you gain or lose more than three pounds." And I said, "Okay, that's fine."

So the time went by, and I gained three and a half pounds, and that's when I really went through the roof. I had a whole episode where I was seized with terror. She was supportive and clear. She would break the mirage in me, the crazy idea that I had constructed in my head about what food was about. I had bizarre ideas of food properties. For instance the grapes that kept me alive. In my mind they imparted life and were safe. Why?

Grapes are mostly sugar and hardly a complete meal. On the other hand, I wouldn't touch vegetables that seemed more substantial. In recovery I admitted that if I ate a bucket of vegetables it would be not many calories, and that the body uses up calories: it doesn't turn them instantly to fat.

Even as I internalized the truth about nutrition, for a year I ate the same things, and would always try to hold off the meal. Particularly on Sundays I would not have breakfast until one or two. Then I'd get away with only having dinner and skipping lunch. Then dinner would be a roll of sushi. I'd never eaten a grain of the rice, but eventually, in therapy, I had to eat half the rice. She'd break down the actions that required me to move along. We'd go over the most minute measurements. She'd say, "There's really only a quarter cup of rice in this." The therapist was amazing in how she dealt with me. She knew the ins and outs of this sickness. For me the biggest fear was, if I started eating I was never going to stop eating. I definitely was stringing along my own little story, so there was a period when I was obsessive with foods I hadn't eaten before, and had to "eat through it," as my therapist and I called it. (Being able to laugh at yourself helps.) Okay, if I needed to eat a certain sugared cereal every day, that was what I was going to have to do, and I'd tell her.

That first year of recovery was crazy. One day I went to a salad bar: my therapist wanted me to try something new. I was in this place and I thought, "What do I do with this? I don't know the sizes of things." I was overwhelmed because I was trying to eat something different, but my method was about compartmentalizing. I picked out two kidney beans and a few forkfuls of sprouts and things, and I wrote it all down on my little sheet and left. My therapist said, "That's not a meal." We went over it and I started to see how strong this reality was I had created in my head—about what I should be eating, what's normal, what's right and what's not. When the therapist told me that the average person eats so many calories per day, I said, "I can't. That's absurd." I simply didn't believe her. And she took my notebook and said, "No, this is what people eat on a weight-reducing diet." She got through to me. I trusted her because she came to me via someone who is now one of my closest friends, who is also anorexic and helped me and brought me to her. Even though I didn't trust anybody, I knew I could trust her.

Initially it was grapes on one side and all other foods on the other, so I was able to see my progress when I did not feel anymore like Alice looking at something that said, "Eat me."

Even now there's always that element: if I try that cake, not only is it going to make me instantly fat—which I'm not now but was then convinced it would—but it will bring along a nightmare where maybe I'll eat it forever. Controlling and compartmentalizing ended up creating an insanity.

It's an inversion: that as my career began to take off and my life got for all tangible purposes bigger, I just got smaller and smaller, to the point where I didn't go out—and I'm such a social person. I love people and I love communicating. Of course I didn't realize what was happening, but if I wasn't working I was either at the gym or at home or I was walking around. In L.A., where nobody else was! I couldn't go to dinner because what was I going to eat? And it is not just that I wouldn't put food in my mouth. I couldn't go to a restaurant because the whole environment made me feel desperate. And then people would ask me, "Why are you not eating?" When you look hungry, as I did, this is hard to dodge! I remember going to a birthday dinner with someone that I was kind of dating, which you can't even imagine I knew how to do at that time. He kind of didn't know what to do with me, and we went to this birthday party for a friend of his, and it was sort of at the end and we didn't even have to eat, but just as we came in everyone was being served cake. And so I said, "No, no, no, I don't want any cake." And then someone said, "No, you have to have cake. It's a birthday cake. If you don't have some it's bad luck." And I said, "No, I don't want the cake!" He insisted: "Just have a bite." I went, "I don't want the cake!" And this was an L.A. party where people are laid back.

The thing was, I was murder to be around. My close friends who had known me for years felt this door had been shut in their face. We talk about it now all the time. At the height of my problem and for years afterwards when I was still very sensitive, they said, "It was so impossible to be around you. And you didn't realize it."

It was as if I'd literally suck the energy out of the room. You don't realize how it permeates everything around you. Your misery in the confines of your body makes everyone acutely uncomfortable. Nobody knows what to do to bring you back into the fold, plus this manic energy that I had would twist things up and make people feel wretched. My sickness certainly affected my family. They were baffled how to handle me, and worried. We're not a very verbally communicative family. It's an Irish-German-French heritage and our motto is, if it's unpleasant don't deal with it or don't bring it into the light. In this regard therapy has been a great help to me, because I've been able to not only express my feelings but stop overvaluing the withholding of them. I have taken the time to think through matters of an emotional and psychological nature that we never talk about in my family. Because so much of this type of disorder is about stuffing your voice: that's what I realize from the process of recovery. I had got myself to the point where I was just a hollow shell. All of my personality and assets and qualities that made me an individual, I had lost. It's ironic, because kind of the initial intention is to be special in some way, whether it's blatant or just one of the elements. Yet you become utterly bland and the same because you have nothing to offer.

Now I see women who are doing as I did—their avoidance, the secrets. I've gone through stages. If I saw them in my work, or just on the street, they used to make me unbelievably uncomfortable. I did not want to be around the disease. Sometimes, still, if I'm in a particularly emotional place it upsets me. However, now I have compassion for them and think, "I know the pain that you are in and what's going on inside your thoughts," and it makes me terribly sad. And it also makes me grateful because I feel as if I escaped, and the majority of people don't.

It's possible to escape your pretend world. You can't model after other people because they have an innate clock called simple, natural appetite, and yours when you start recovery is busted. No, you have to be reborn slowly, and while the new body and new emotional fibers grow, and the new habits form, you hold onto the truth that you will get better. Sometimes I'm in a mood where I have a sudden awareness of the state I was in. It's like a shadow passing. Overwhelmingly, though, I feel that perfectionist person that fell on life's sidewalk just crumbled away. Not that it had to happen, but it was a part and stage of my past.

It's a very Twelve Step thing to say that you'll always have this problem: don't let yourself slide. I understand that mentality, and I've been to overeaters' support groups many times. Initially, when I got into recovery, I couldn't go there because I felt that everyone just talked about food and their bodies and it made me crazy. Then a couple of years down the line I responded more to the Steps and spirituality, and I've gotten a tremendous amount of healing from the program. Yet if I speak at meetings I always say that the eating disorder I had is not something that defines me. I don't believe in saying that it will never go away, because it's my opinion that we manifest what we want. And the spoken word is very powerful.

There's a period of time when you need to acknowledge it. First to yourself, then to others. In the beginning of recovery I didn't acknowledge it. I was telling doctors, "If you can tell me how to be anorexic or the psychology of being skinny I'll be happy." I was insulted they were telling me that I was already. I'd counter with "You really think I'm fat." However, as the place the disorder occupies in your mind shrinks, as it clears out of the cells of your body, if you are saying on a daily basis that you have this problem, establishing it with your word, you're putting that energy into the world. You're stating "This is who I am," and I think that's unwise.

After you pull out of it there's a very tricky line of acknowledging and knowing that you have these tendencies and not defining yourself by it. Because that could become a crutch. It's as though you always will have this disabling thing and walk around with this cloud over your head. I didn't get better, I didn't get into recovery so that I could feel beholden to this horrible thing or feel miserable all the time. I'd rather be miserable and skinny—fashionably emaciated! So why resist it? I got better so I could be happy and enjoy my life . . . .

When I talk in meetings it can be tricky. I'm a believer in the notion of acknowledging your insides and mistakes, your issues and all of that to get rid of it all and take responsibility for it. But I'm not such a believer in every day saying, "I got this problem." As a personality changes, some central problems or dilemmas fade away or become tangential.

A lot of people have a sense of anxiety and shame and fear of "Oh my God, it could happen again. I tremble that I could go there again." I so believe in sharing your experience and learning from it, and showing by your life that you can recover from this in a positive, meaningful way. More than half of this disease, or problem or whatever you want to term the behaviors it takes, is about hiding. Obliterate the secrets. Part of it was always for me, "This is something I'm going to be better at than anybody else." Obviously I was not consciously thinking that, but it was like doing a very small part perfectly—all about performing.

When you're anorexic, your eating becomes this cloak-and-dagger thing. I was dating someone when I first moved to LA and he was only semi-conscious I had the problems I did. He wanted to help me, but there was nothing he could do. I kept my emotions in check and on the surface had this model, if very tight, behavior. When I first got into recovery the disorder affected my relationships a lot more. Because then things were coming to the surface. I was dealing with how I felt. For one thing I felt absolutely enormous, so fat I couldn't be close to a man. I realized at the same time how much I'd been shutting all feeling down.

Once I went to a play with a couple of male friends. One of them was the guy I'd been dating at my low point, and I had to stand up and walk in front of them, as our seats were in a row. I just couldn't! I didn't want to be looked at but I had to pass by them as I was going to the ladies' room. It took everything in me. I was talking to myself in this manner. "Go, just do it, just walk in front of them!" Several months later one of those men said to me, "Do you remember when we were at the play?" I thought, "Oh God, he's going to say how fat I am," because I'd just shared with him what was going down. Instead he said, "I remember thinking that she's so skinny, I wish she'd just eat something." And I was like, "Are you kidding me?" And I thought, "Wow, there was a whole different story going on in my head." He said, "I was thinking, 'If she gained a little weight she'd be so—' because you're so beautiful and great but . . ." Meanwhile I was imagining that the men thought, "Here comes the cow walking across the row."

That preoccupation with tiny fluctuations in weight and body, and pathology of control, are the anorexic's cross to bear. You have to want to change your life to get out of it—that's the bottom line. I won't tell you that I don't sometimes still feel uncomfortable in my body, but honestly I would say those moment are few and far between. When I do have them I know it's not about what it appears to be, it's about some feeling that I don't want to feel, always.

There's also my grand theory of how I just can't go there anymore, how it's not an option any longer. So the disorder doesn't occupy the state it did. It occupied every thought of my being, every waking moment and probably my sleeping moments as well. That's over and done. As you value your life and champion it, the self-mutilating thoughts disappear. They have no place and you let them go. This does not get pretty when you're older, and how much easier it is to change it when you're young.

I have been a beggar with a begging bowl.
I have been a queen with a golden crown.
I have been so hungry I ate my soul,
But never outcast and never thrown down
Since I was alive
And able to give.

But never the beggar and never the queen
Could live without hope behind a closed door,
And the hungry poor never felt this pain,
In the place where I could not give of my store,
Not a crown of glory
Nor a beggar's story.

—May Sarton, "Beggar, Queen, and Ghost"

Cynthia French
(singer, songwriter, music publisher)

CYNTHIA FRENCH'S SPEAKING VOICE is a liquid gold drawl, her smile is broad and fetching, and her hair cascades in loose curls down her shoulders. Her attire and her demeanor are businesslike yet feminine, glamorous, and distinctly Southern, suggesting a professional singer or maybe a mover and shaker in the entertainment business—and she is both.

Oklahoman Cynthia French has had a multi-faceted career as a country and pop singer and music publisher. In 1995 she founded the Harry Max Music Publishing Company in Nashville, which has represented many notable songwriters. Cynthia has since expanded and renamed the company Harry Max Entertainment, now encompassing music publishing, production, management, public relations, and bookings.

She has also been a successful singer and background vocalist, contributing vocals to the albums of artists such as Reba McIntyre,

Mindy McCready, and Andy Griggs. She has performed around the world, solo and with REO Speedwagon and Billy Joel, and at the Grand Ole Opry.

Cynthia received her formal education in business, earning bachelor's and master's degrees from Oklahoma State University. Numerous charitable organizations count her on their committees and boards, and she is a nationally renowned speaker who has toured the country speaking about her life experiences.

The derailing effects of an eating disorder, and the factors that can help lift a life back on track, are the subject of Cynthia's successful novel *Humanville,* which is based on her career as a professional singer.

—J.M.

I was raised in a somewhat controlling environment with very loving parents, but parents that lived in a conservative setting and dealt with their lives in a very simple, codified way. We didn't have a lot of freedom in childhood. I had a creative spirit and independent streak, and experienced a lot of frustrations not being able to express myself.

It was a very typical environment. I had an older sister who turned a little wild when she became a teenager, and I watched her really upset the family structure. So I decided I'd be perfect to make up for it. I also had a mother who—bless her heart, love her dearly, and she is in a very healthy place at this point in life—but who when she was younger was insecure, and if you were close to her she talked about her weight all the time. So I kind of took on her burden and just wanted to fix everything and everybody, so I headed into anorexia.

When I became fourteen I started playing varsity sports for the first time, so all of a sudden I had an exercise routine that I never had before. It started innocently enough, with a bet with another girlfriend who was playing ball, as to who could lose ten pounds faster. So being the competitive person I was, I took it on and won. That was the first time I success-fully lost weight. As a younger person I had always felt that I was a little overweight, and so the victory was awesome. And I thought, "Well, I can lose ten, why can't I lose fifteen?" And that started my fall into anorexia, and before I knew it I had lost about twenty-five pounds. And it felt great.

This happened in the seventies when nobody understood what anorexia was. I didn't even know I was anorectic. I just thought that I had conquered the battle that so many people my age can't conquer, and if any-body said anything to me I thought they were jealous.

It got worse in college. I took up running and ended up doing nine to twelve miles a day for years and years, and that was the essence of my life. And eating five to six hundred calories a day, and feeling like I was on top of the world because I had won the battle that nobody else wins. Every-body else would gain ten pounds. I lost ten pounds in my freshman year.

I was very much stuck in that life and in that mindset until my senior year, when I set a trap for myself, as every anorectic does. When you make your body have that much of an energy output and you don't give your body very much fuel, it adjusts accordingly. So, high energy output, low fuel intake, the second that you slow down at all your body's going to start gain-ing weight, because it's accustomed to operating on five hundred or three hundred calories a day. . . So that happened to me my senior year. I became anemic, and I stress-fractured my foot. I was still running five miles a day on the stress fracture, but I wasn't running nine to twelve!

When I started gaining weight, the panic set in. My body was just so thrilled that it was getting some weight on it that I felt out of control. My senior year I gained probably twenty pounds, which put me in the normal range, but I felt like a failure! That's when I headed into bulimia, in a panic state. I was appalled at bulimia at first, but it seemed to fix my problem and that lasted about fourteen years.

I allowed the diseases to be bigger than I was. I didn't understand that I had the power to choose not to partake in the diseases, to take the power away from them. I was in my mid-thirties before I was able to touch into that part of me, what I call the higher self, that God within. And through almost losing my life, I was able to tap into that inner voice that helped me start the process of turning my life around and understanding the power of choice.

I was a successful singer, and I was living in Los Angeles with my fabulous, perfect boyfriend, and had to start working in Nashville. I had a management, production, and publishing deal: I was well on my way, but scared to death, and insecure about it. Eventually my boyfriend and I broke up because the long-distance relationship wasn't working—to be here one month, there one month, and there were other issues, obviously. So we broke up and I moved to Nashville, and I was in shock because I hated it. And I hated leaving the place I loved, which was Los Angeles, and I was miserable and I was a martyr and felt so sorry for Cynthia, and was falling more and more into bulimia, and was really in a state of depression.

Then I lost my publishing deal because my manager had been Michael Jackson's manager, and Michael Jackson fired him—fired the business manager who was in partnership with my deal. So when they were fired the situation fell apart, and so I was literally in a place I hated with no job, no income, no boyfriend, and so I hit rock bottom. I was driving back from visiting my folks in Texas, having had a horrible experience with them because I was being such a bitch, basically, and I just couldn't take it anymore. My eating was out of control. My life was in the gutter. I had nothing positive to hold onto, and I really wanted to end it. I really wanted to drive off the road, and was ready to do that. I had been so depressed and angry and lost.

My message is a spiritual message, which is why the book I wrote in recovery is a fable. It takes a character who is loosely based on me, and walks her through the same process that I went through, with that same kind of pivotal moment. It takes place in a fictional city that is based on money, power, greed, and image, on what you drive, where you live, who you know. It's her story of finding out that those aren't the important things in life, that love and the powers of choice and service are what give us the ability to live a healthy and balanced life.

Certainly I was angry at God at that time—if there was a God; I didn't buy that there was any sort of higher spirit. I had beaten the sensitivity to divine power out of myself. Because my life sucked. I was going to kill myself or presumed I was, and thought, "If I am to do this, maybe just to make sure I should figure out how I feel about this whole God thing, on the outside chance that there is a God out there and I go through with it and I'm screwed!" I needed to come to peace with the meaning of my life before I ended it.

That was my warped place. So I turned on the radio and started to really get out of my own way, to get to some decisions about how I felt about God. Probably it was the first time in my life that I wasn't afraid, because I knew it was over and there was no reason to shield myself or be afraid, because I was done. And since I was able to get out of my own way, I was able to have an experience of hearing that inner voice clearly. And it freaked me out. I thought, "What the hell is that? Because how could I have ended up in the family I'm in? I am an alien in my family. They are traditional, God-fearing people. They don't understand me; I don't understand them." And in this low moment of complete honesty, I heard this little answer that said, "Gene pool." And then I heard it a little better, and it said, "Your parents possessed all the qualities that I need you to have, to do what I need you to do while you're here." And I thought, "Whoa, okay, that was weird!" And I thought to myself, "But they don't get me; they don't understand me." And then I heard the same sort of answer that said, "Well, the word is 'understand.' You don't understand them either. They can't fathom you and your lifestyle because they've never been exposed to it. You've been in the entertainment business, you lived in Los Angeles, traveled all over the world, and you expect them to relate to that? So you are judging them more than they are judging you."

I'd never considered that before, because I'd been so self-centered and self-absorbed with poor me that it didn't dawn on me that they felt alienated from me, too. So this experience that lasted five or six hours on my drive to Nashville changed my life. It didn't cure the bulimia overnight, but what happened was I had found out that I could tune into a part of me that was what I call the God within, the higher self. However you want to describe that part that is love-based. And over the next six months I learned how to trust that voice, and trust the love voice, not the negative voice, and understand that the negative voice is fear, and understand what fear is, and put it into the proper perspective.

Now I began to learn how to differentiate and take enough time to work through the fears. For instance, in my novel the character goes through the same experiences where her feelings are hurt by others. She used to react to words of injury by burying her pain through bingeing and purging. After she had this life-changing experience she saw that sometimes the insult or offending words came from the other people's pain. They were hurting and it had nothing to do with her. The fault did not lie with her and she wasn't a bad person. She learns to take time and process these situations and slights before she goes and hurts herself. She realizes that 99 percent of the times she would blame herself because she got her feelings hurt, it wasn't about her: that person had a bad day and was taking his feelings out on her. Learning that process is how she grows up. Because anorectics or bulimics take everything on themselves; they blame themselves for everything. They want to punish themselves because they are so worthless.

Where do we learn that? There are so many influences and everybody has a different story, but in my case what I had to learn is "It's not all about me." I had to get out of myself and understand that other people around me are in some pain and have trials too, and look at them from a loving perspective instead of a fear-based perspective.

This process took years; it didn't happen in a blink of an eye. It has been a process of holding onto that power, and then implementing it into my daily life. I was able eventually to live 99 percent of the time in that good place instead of the fear-based place. I decided I was so blessed by this turn in my life. Obviously, living in that perspective helps in all aspects of life, because being in the entertainment business can be rough riding. When someone didn't like my song, my writing or voice, I learned to understand that it was not I was a horrible person but that what I was offering wasn't fitting their needs at that time. This is basic 101 stuff, but for somebody who comes from a background of anorexia and bulimia it was like a miracle to see that.

When I came out of the twenty or twenty-five years of living with these diseases, I felt so blessed that I came out unscathed that I decided to try to give something back. And that's how the novel *Humanville* came about. I wanted to explore the subject without making it threatening to someone who has anorexia. Because bulimics know they're bulimic—I mean, that's an action that you have to do, but I didn't know I was anorectic. I wanted a young girl, young or middle-aged woman, or young man, whoever—to pick up this novel and be able to read without being threatened by it. That's why I set it in an esoteric environment.

These days my relationship with food is just about as healthy as it can be. I eat when I'm hungry. The other thing is I learned is how to listen to my body. It tells me when it's hungry or tired, and when it's full, and I trust it now. That was a big victory, because we screw up so much of our bodies, when we are living out either of these diseases, that it's hard to find the natural drives again. Although when we do, they will tell us our needs loud and clear. For instance, I found my natural weight. I didn't know, all the years of trying to deny it, that I am naturally a pretty thin person. I wouldn't allow myself just to be normal. So I fought myself.

I don't focus on food anymore. I'll eat anything. I'll eat when I'm hungry and I don't eat when I'm not. It's not based on emotions, and by not focusing on it I've been given this well-balanced life.

Sometimes I laugh at myself because holidays like Thanksgiving or Christmas used to involve the most frightening experiences for me. To have to sit down to Thanksgiving dinner was a source of the worst dread during my bulimic years. Now I don't have to think about it. When I was speaking nationally about *Humanville,* it did bring the subject matter to the surface a lot more. I naively didn't realize when I spoke in public about this that it would return to the forefront of my life. It didn't dawn on me. But it was an exciting experience to be candid about this time in my life, and not have the disorders creep back in, or to become afraid of them. I'm not afraid of food anymore—that's the bottom line.

When I was pursuing my artistic career, up until the time when the bottom fell out in Nashville, I was constantly insecure. I lived with this grim secret and was aware I was hiding part of my reality from everyone. I did it even though it affected my voice. I persevered but I listen to the recordings I did right at the beginning of the bulimic years, and my voice was much stronger than in the middle of those years. But mostly what I hear is the absence of self-confidence and assurance that I am thankful to have now.

If you don't break your ropes while you're alive
do you think
ghosts will do it after?

—Kabir, "Think While You Are Alive"

Uri Geller
(paranormalist)

CAN THIS STRIKING YOUNG MAN with the bony features and wiry, athletic build be sixty? Even in a photograph, one senses something uncanny about Uri Geller. And indeed, he has led an extraordinary life. Today he lives in England and is invited on peace missions all over the world. But Geller's roots are in Israel and Cyprus, where he grew up as the son of Hungarian and Austrian parents, related to Sigmund Freud on his mother's side.

At the age of four, while playing in a garden near his house, Uri had a mysterious encounter with a sphere of light—an event he now sees as life-changing. He became aware of his paranormal abilities when he was five. One day at the dinner table, Uri's spoon curled up in his hand and broke, although he had applied no pressure to it. Year by year he discovered more strange powers. He could move a compass needle or fix a broken watch or appliance with his mere thoughts.

As a teenager he lived in Cyprus. Geller then served as a paratrooper in the Israeli army and was wounded in the Six-Day War of 1967. Later he worked briefly as a model. Not until his early twenties did Geller begin to demonstrate his powers of telepathy and psychokinesis to audiences. Soon he became famous throughout Israel. Then–prime minister Golda Meir, when asked on a national radio program what future she predicted for Israel, replied, "Don't ask me, ask Uri Geller!"

He left Israel for Europe in 1972 and began performing public feats such as halting a cable car in midair and stopping the hands of Big Ben. When physicians asked him to test his powers in controlled experiments, he did so willingly, wanting to understand them better himself.

During my research for this book I was surprised to see Geller's name on a list of famous people with eating disorders. A slim, handsome celebrity known for his mental powers didn't seem a likely candidate. When I sent an e-mail request to meet with him, he answered immediately: "Sure, I'll be happy to give you an interview." He had just returned from Geneva, where he was helping negotiate an agreement between the Red Cross, the Palestinian Red Crescent, and Israel's national emergency medical service, Magen David Adom.

What the hell is a spoon bender doing negotiating an international treaty? I wondered. When I finally reached Geller on the phone to arrange the interview, he told me he would be in Washington soon for a meeting with secretary of state Condoleezza Rice. He said he often consults with government officials about various political matters. According to Swiss foreign minister Micheline Calmy-Rey, "Uri plays a pivotal role in helping people focus on the main objective, and overcoming differences over secondary details."

Again I thought, *A spoon bender consulting with government officials?* It sounded pretty crazy to me, but I remembered that Mary Todd Lincoln used to hold séances in the White House. And didn't Ronald and Nancy Reagan regularly consult with an astrologer? Didn't Arthur Conan Doyle commune with spiritualists? I guessed that Condi's meeting with Uri was no more implausible.

As we discussed his eating disorder, I was surprised by its influence in his life—how a man possessed of such mental power could have been affected so dramatically. But unlike many contributors to this book, once Geller recognized that he was in the grip of a true disorder, he immediately called upon his superior mind power to overcome it. No surrender or treatment program for him. I think what most impressed me about Geller, aside from his willingness to talk about his problem, was his amazing focus during the interview.

—G.S.

In the early seventies, when I left Israel, I was basically broke. But I knew I had the determination, the motivation, and the inspiration to make it, to succeed in the world. I was taken out of Israel by American scientists. It was a government decision to test my abilities, so they started at the Stanford Research Institute, then Lawrence Livermore National Laboratory, then the American Naval Service Weapons Center, and at least another dozen institutions and laboratories. And obviously that put me under tremendous pressure.

One side of me wanted show business. I wanted to be on Johnny Carson. The other side was pulling me towards acquiring credibility. Then there were those who tried to attack me. Skeptics and cynics, who said, "Uri Geller is just a magician." Then came the bookings. Hundreds of shows at universities, television shows around the world, and so on. So basically what happened to me was I couldn't handle my success. Money came too quickly towards me. I started finding oil fields and gold mines. So in a very short time, from being a kid from Israel with no money whatsoever, success fell upon me.

Strangely enough, my eating disorder started when I met a producer, who was also manager of the Bee Gees, named Robert Stigwood. He later on produced the musical *Evita,* and the film *Saturday Night Fever* with John Travolta. I was now circulating with these people—Travolta, Madonna, Elton John. John Lennon became my closest friend in New York. He actually changed my life.

Around 1975 or 1976, Robert Stigwood wanted to produce a movie based on my life story, which he never did produce. He paid me a lot of money for an option, and bizarrely, many years later there was a movie, which Ken Russell directed. It was hard for me to believe that here was this big, huge mega-producer wanting to do the Uri Geller story. And he looked at me and he said, "You know, you should lose a little weight." I was never fat, of course. I was never even chubby, but I was heavy. And those words sort of zoomed into my mind, in a panic, and I didn't realize that, "Hey, maybe I'm overweight."

But because of the turmoil I was in, it was almost like a whirlpool. I did not want to give up my luxuries. I was rather shallow then, and basically I was on an ego trip. All I cared about was fame and fortune. I'd walk into Bloomingdale's and instead of buying five silk shirts I'd buy one hundred shirts. I would exaggerate in everything. I would not buy one Rolex, I'd buy four Rolex watches. It was an obsession.

I did not want to give up my food either. I would go into a restaurant and order ten desserts instead of just one dessert, and I would taste each one of them. What Robert Stigwood told me had such an impact on me, that I one day simply excused myself from the table, walked to the toilet, and vomited. I had absolutely no idea what bulimia was; I had never even heard the word. I just reflected back to what the Romans used to do. They used to binge and then they'd stick a feather down their throats. And then go back and eat, and I did the same thing. And it overpowered me and it became addictive to such an extent that my finger wouldn't do the job anymore. I would stick toothbrushes down my throat. I had a limo and I'd carry vomit bags in it, which I would collect from the back of seats on airplanes. So I could even vomit in my own car.

This thing lasted for a year. I went to a doctor, and the doctor looked at me and said, "Look, Mr. Geller, if you continue this you'll be dead. Very, very soon." And somehow I managed to awaken my willpower and what I call my power of human potential. And that day I stopped. I stopped cold. It was on Fifty-seventh Street and First Avenue. The chauffeur opened the door of my car and I could barely get out. I had to actually grab the roof of my car and pull myself out. As I stumbled towards the canopy of my apartment building I simply screamed out, "Stop, I've got to stop this." I went up to my apartment and I've never, ever vomited again.

That's why I believe in positive thinking and human potential. This is why I do motivational lectures today.

There's no doubt that all eating disorders manifest themselves partly because of your character. The mood you're in, your surroundings, the pressure you're under, the "control freak factor." And I was a control freak at that time. I wanted to control everything, and therefore I did control everything, even what I ate. I didn't want to get fat so I controlled the manner of getting rid of it.

Now I've totally changed. I'm quite amazed that I was able to change my character from Type A to basically a person who is relaxed and has peace of mind. It's interesting. It was John Lennon who pushed me to do it. One day he told me about spirituality. And I said, "What is spirituality?" And he said to me, "Go and find it yourself." Yoko told me that the best place to find it is in Japan. So I actually practically gave away my apartment in Manhattan, my house in Connecticut, and I got all my family on a plane. (My kids were small then.) My son was four and my daughter was three. My wife, myself, my mother, and my brother-in-law—we flew to Japan, hired a van, drove to Mount Fuji, disappeared into a forest at the foot of Mount Fuji, and stayed there for one year. And that was the major changing point in my life.

My father was a military person. He was very Germanic and pedantic in his mannerisms. Because I discovered my abilities at a very young age, my mother had a very tough time accepting them. She immediately attached them to Sigmund Freud, because I'm related to Freud. That was an escape hatch for her. So I had something so thoroughly unique in my childhood, knowing that no one else could do what I do. All the other kids drew, played sports, but no one could bend spoons, and no one could move the hands of a watch. So I found myself very isolated. I tried to build a powerful identity around me, and later on in my life I learned how to re-invent myself, by dipping into other talents that I have. I'm a painter. I used to paint when I was a child. I did work with Salvador Dali and Andy Warhol in New York. I helped people like Basquiat. So I started painting and exhibiting. I started motivating people. These are all things that have nothing to do with spoon bending, but they have a placebo effect. When I remind people what made me famous, that gives them an in, an opening to the powers of the mind.

I'm finishing my seventeenth book now. My last one was published by Reader's Digest, called *Life Signs*. I do very major things. I negotiated for the American government last week in Geneva with the Palestinians. I was there with the head of the Israeli foreign ministry. I do this for free because it's a positive thing. I often do negotiations for governments. I have many outlets. I help young artists. Financially I have nothing to worry about. Therefore I'm free to do what I want. I've learned how to use money to help others. Money is a positive tool if you know how to use it.

I think that if I did not have bulimia, if I did not have panic attacks and anxiety attacks—which by the way went along with it—I wouldn't be who I am today. I stopped all three conditions at the same time: the bulimia and the panic and anxiety attacks. Sometimes I even think that it could have been something supernatural or paranormal that I managed to stop. My bulimia, panic, and anxiety attacks all ceased at the same time.

I'm a vegetarian, not a vegan. I'm against killing animals. I do not wear fur coats. I'm against that as well. I'm a member of PETA. I'm a vegetarian because I do not want to kill animals. It also, obviously, is a healthy diet. I eat a Mediterranean diet. My wife does likewise. We exercise, we take care in what foods we buy. We look for additives. We don't buy food with additives, preservatives, artificial colorings, and so on.

You know, the most important thing in life is health, and no amount of money will buy that. It also won't buy happiness or peace of mind. If you have peace of mind around you, if you can manage that, you don't have to be wealthy. If you can create that peace, your life will definitely be better. And if you have faith—and this is something that was scientifically validated—your life will be better. The British educational authorities came out with a staggering report saying that people who go to a synagogue to pray, or to a church or to a mosque, live longer, have less disease, and are happier people.

Nowadays I do what I think I should to keep my body fit and my mind fit. You know: mind, body, and soul. People who exercise regularly definitely need to do it in order to connect to that chemical in the brain. But there are degrees of obsession and addiction to exercise. While I was ill in New York I was addicted to exercise. I would run around Central Park three times. In hotels I would run up and down staircases if there were no exercise rooms. Today I basically do a half-hour of aerobics. I take my dogs out for a good walk, but it's not an obsession any longer. For instance, in Geneva when I was negotiating, I was with all these government people who were trim and lean, and I asked them whether they exercised. They all said they had a regime of exercise, but now that we were all together in Geneva they had no time for it. So it was no big deal, and I didn't exercise for four days. That would have been awful in the seventies if I didn't have an outlet to exercise.

Pink: "Stupid Girls"

The first song on Pink's fifth album, downloaded by 8.6 million people as soon as it was available on the Internet, is "Stupid Girls." Along with its attention-grabbing mockery of several Hollywood starlets, the song makes important points about healthy self-image for girls—and about the devastating effects of bulimia. Shortly after the video for the song was released, the International Association of Eating Disorders issued a statement noting that the song "highlights the culture's relentless and unrealistic pursuit of thinness and unattainable drive for physical beauty."

Against her label's wishes, Alecia Moore (Pink) fought for the song's first position on the album, *I'm Not Dead*. In retrospect she seems to us a hero. The song and its video carry shock value throughout, including a brief scene in which two girls puke in tandem over the sinks of a public bathroom.

Pink is a bold creative artist who sparks dialogue for laudable reasons. In an MTV interview she voiced her satisfaction that the song has inspired controversy and raised consciousness. Nor is she an outsider passing judgment on others' problems. She admitted she has "fat days" when she doesn't feel pretty enough, when she is obsessed by image over substance. When Pink tells the listener to make something of herself, "Stupid Girls" is her weapon of protest and inspiration. For years to come this will be recalled as a seminal song about an epidemic problem. Pink says she is "a work in progress" and we honor her.

continued

Stupid Girls

Stupid girl, stupid girls, stupid girls
Baby if I act like that, that guy will call me back
What a paparazzi girl, I don't wanna be a stupid girl

Go to Fred Segal, you'll find them there
Laughing loud so all the little people stare
Looking for a daddy to pay for the champagne
(Drop a name)
What happened to the dreams of a girl president?
She's dancing in the video next to 50 Cent
They travel in packs of two or three
With their itsy bitsy doggies and their teeny-weeny tees
Where, oh where, have the smart people gone?
Oh where, oh where could they be?

Maybe if I act like that, that guy will call me back
What a paparazzi girl, I don't wanna be a stupid girl
Baby if I act like that, flipping my blonde hair back
Push up my bra like that, I don't wanna be a stupid girl

(Break it down now)
Disease's growing, it's epidemic
I'm scared that there ain't a cure
The world believes it and I'm going crazy
I cannot take any more
I'm so glad that I'll never fit in
That will never be me
Outcasts and girls with ambition

That's what I wanna see
Disasters all around
World despaired
Their only concern
Will they **** up my hair?

Baby if I act like that, that guy will call me back
What a paparazzi girl, I don't wanna be a stupid girl
Baby if I act like that, flipping my blonde hair back
Push up my bra like that, I don't wanna be a stupid girl

Oh my god you guys, I totally had more than 300 calories
That was so not sexy, no
Good one, can I borrow that?
[Vomits]

I WILL BE SKINNY

(Do ya thing, do ya thing, do ya thing)
(I like this, like this, like this)
Pretty will you **** me girl, silly as a lucky girl
Pull my head and suck it girl, stupid girl!
Pretty would you **** me girl, silly as a lucky girl
Pull my head and suck it girl, stupid girl!

Baby if I act like that, that guy will call me back
What a paparazzi girl, I don't wanna be a stupid girl
Baby if I act like that, flipping my blonde hair back
Push up my bra like that, I don't wanna be a stupid girl

> *It was a carnal knife that let*
> *Red Riding Hood out like a poppy,*
> *Quite alive from the kingdom of the belly.*
> *And grandmother too*
> *Still waiting for cakes and wine.*
> *The wolf, they decided, was too mean*
> *To be simply shot so they filled his belly*
> *With large stones and sewed him up.*
> *He was as heavy as a cemetery*
> *And when he woke up and tried to run off*
> *He fell over dead. Killed by his own weight.*
> *Many a deception ends on such a note.*
>
> —Anne Sexton, "Red Riding Hood"

Joyce Maynard
(writer)

JOYCE MAYNARD IS A VERY recognizable person to her readers: the big doe eyes, the heavy, blunt-cut hair and bangs, the pixie face. The gamine poses that she takes, entirely naturally, suggest a young yoga instructor.

Originally from New Hampshire, Joyce now makes her homes in Mill Valley, California, where she raised her son and daughter, and Lake Atitlán, Guatemala. A journalist and fiction writer for more than thirty years, she has been a beacon for younger writers and a serious commentator, especially on her generation, and also a mischievous *enfant terrible* of the literary scene.

She began her career while in high school, writing for *Seventeen,* and came to national attention with the publication of her 1973 *New York Times Magazine* cover story, "An Eighteen-Year-Old Looks Back on Life." She was a sensation with her memoir, *At Home in the World,* written when she was a tender twenty, and again over twenty-five years later when she revealed her nine-month love affair with the writer J.D. Salinger, the most mysterious and iconic of all living American literary lions. He was fifty-three at the time; she was eighteen.

Joyce has been a reporter and columnist (*Hers* and *Lives*) for the *New York Times,* a syndicated newspaper columnist, and regular contributor to NPR's *All Things Considered,* as well as to national magazines such as *O, More, Redbook,* and *Parenting.*

Her five novels for young people include *The Usual Rules,* a story about mothers and daughters and loss, which was chosen by the American Library Association as one of the ten best books of 2003 for young readers, and *To Die For,* written in response to the 9/11 terror attacks.

In addition to her writing career, Joyce participates as a frequent performer with The Moth, a New York–based storytelling collective, and speaks to corporate groups on the value of storytelling—and truth-telling.

—J.M.

As many stories of mine that I've told, I never fully told this one. Maybe because it never fully ended.

I'm one of two sisters, and our family was split down the middle in so many different ways. I had one Jewish parent, one not-Jewish parent. There was the parent who got drunk and the parent who was sober. There was the younger daughter and the older daughter. There was the good girl and the difficult girl. I was the happy, easy, smiling younger daughter, who would bring happiness and joy to my parents, two brilliant people of vast gifts, who had known enormous disappointment and frustration in their lives. Even as a very young child, I recognized my job in life was to lay at their feet the acknowledgment and success that had eluded them. I would be successful. I would be artistically fulfilled. I would go to the big city, New York, and become rich and famous there.

And a couple more things: I would be happy, and thin. My mother used to put her fingers into the corners of my mouth and turn my mouth into a smile. She was a dramatic, exotic beauty of a woman who always struggled with her weight. Really she had a lovely, voluptuous body, but it was not a slim body. I became the designated skinny person in the family.

It's so interesting that these roles that are assigned to us fly in the face of physical reality. In the family mythology, my sister was the plump one. I was the skinny one. Actually my sister was the tiny one of the two of us. A petite woman, and I was really not this frail waif but was cast as the frail waif. My mother took great delight in that. The person to whom I was compared and with whom I identified was Audrey Hepburn. It's odd. My ex-husband and I named my daughter Audrey, though never consciously acknowledging, when we did that, any connection to the movie star I had loved, growing up. I guess you could say, "God, she hasn't dealt with a few things."

I was always a skinny kid and it was always easy for me to be a skinny kid because I was a notoriously picky eater. It's hard to know which came first, but I really didn't eat and there was a huge focus on me to make sure I got enough to eat. I was sort of naturally thin and I believe my mother took enormous pride and pleasure in that. She would show me off in little waif dresses at the age when people might not be wearing waif dresses anymore.

And then in my teens, like so many other girls my age, I wasn't a skinny waif anymore. I wasn't overweight. I just had a body that was filling out in a womanly way. My mother was deeply concerned. As I had done all my life, I took onto my shoulders the responsibility for my parents' disappointments, and attended to them the best I could. This happened in the fall of my senior year of high school, when I probably weighed 120 pounds.

I began to go to a gym. This was in the days before it had become a part of normal routine for young, healthy people to visit gyms. My mother and I went together to the Elaine Powers Figure Salon. Though I was going to Phillips Exeter, and applying to college, and taking exciting courses, suddenly my life revolved around this gym, and eating as little as I possibly could, so by the time I graduated from Exeter I weighed eighty-eight pounds.

There are so many things that could make my mother seem like a terrible person, and I have to defend her. I have to say, "She did not know." Some of this was a function of the times, too. The disease of anorexia went largely unnamed at that time. Certainly my mother was blinded by her longing to be "the thin person," so she was "the mother of the thin person."

So anyway by the time I graduated from high school I was very, very thin, and nobody ever said, "This is a problem." I actually took a lot of delight in that. That summer I took a job in Boston writing copy for a mail-order catalog and I was down to eating one apple and one ice cream cone a day. And that was pretty much the state I was in when I went off to Yale.

At Yale, I was suddenly surrounded by high-achieving young women with their own troubled family stories, no doubt, and they were all doing the same thing. There was actually a line waiting to stand on the bathroom scale, sometimes. Of the girls on my floor in Vanderbilt Hall in the fall of 1971, I'd say that most of us were either starving ourselves or stuffing ourselves. I think that almost none of the young women I knew in that particular entryway were free of food and eating issues. And many of us were so competitive with each other. One of the things that makes me saddest about this—as a woman who has learned over the years to treasure friendship and sisterhood with my fellow women—that instead of supporting and nurturing each other, we were checking to see who was the thinnest. And of course it makes me sad to think how much of my time and energy it took away from more interesting and important things I could have been doing, to count calories and do sit-ups.

I was at this wonderful university surrounded by really thrilling, brilliant people, and I was thinking a lot about my calorie intake. And that's my shame and regret. Going to a dining hall was a big struggle. Eating in public, finding a place to set down my tray, these were huge issues for me.

In the midst of that struggle a rather large challenge came into my life, in the form of my sudden and rather dramatic so-called overnight success as a writer. In the spring of what turned out to be my one and only year at Yale, a story written by me was published in the *New York Times Magazine* section, with a picture of me on the cover of the magazine, looking very skinny and waiflike. It was my piece, "An Eighteen-Year-Old Looks Back on Life," and within a couple of days there were three huge sacks of mail sitting on the step outside my room. Here was the fame and fortune I'd been working to achieve all my life, for my parents.

The sacks included all sorts of offers to come and talk to publishers, magazine editors—invitations to pose for *Mademoiselle* and have lunch at the Palm Court with some movie producer. I was actually invited to, and did read for, the Linda Blair part in *The Exorcist*. There were all these offers. Everything that I had been seeking for all of my eighteen years of life. And now it was there.

But so too was another letter; sort of eerily knowing and wise. A letter that said to me, "You're probably sitting in your college dormitory room right now, surrounded by letters from book and magazine editors and people who want to take you out to lunch at the Palm Court, and have you model for *Mademoiselle*, and fly out to Los Angeles and try out for movies," and all the things that were in fact happening at that very moment. The writer went on to say that he deeply admired my piece in the *New York Times*. That he felt I was a real writer and—here was the ironic part, given what ultimately transpired—to warn me that I might so easily be exploited. He urged me to be wary and move slowly. Two things that were just about impossible for an eighteen-year-old girl growing up in a small New Hampshire truck town, dreaming of New York City and success and fame and acknowledgment for all those years, and suddenly given a big possibility of achieving that.

That was my first letter from J.D. Salinger. I would have been more impressed if John Lennon or Bob Dylan had written to me, actually. So it wasn't even the fame of Salinger or the fact that he had written *Catcher in the Rye* that really spoke to me, as it might have to a lot of girls at Yale, because I had never even read *Catcher in the Rye,* and I wasn't really a reader.

What spoke to me in that letter had far less to do with Salinger's fame than with what he said to me, and the sense I got from his letter that for the first time, ever, I had encountered someone on the planet who actually understood me, which is, of course, exactly what people who are passionate about *Catcher in the Rye* always say about that book and the man who wrote it. This writer seemed to know them, understand them as nobody else ever had. I think that's fairly irresistible to anybody, but in particular to a girl who feels so misunderstood, so alone and alienated. It was a huge gift. Indescribable joy, and I paid virtually no attention to the fact that he was thirty-five years older than me. He was my friend, my *landsman*. That was the word he used. It's a Yiddish word, meaning a person who comes from the same village you came from, in the old country.

So of course I wrote him back and embarked on a correspondence with Jerry Salinger that overtook my world, and it obliterated all of my previous concerns with college, and friends, my schoolwork, the play I was acting in, the papers I was writing, and even, to a surprising degree, the flurry of attention and success I was receiving. I did go into New York, and I did meet with those editors, and did in fact sign a book contract for a book that was to be hastily delivered before I became "too old."

But by far my most intense and joyful attention that spring was the hour and the day when the mail would be delivered to the Yale post office, and I would go pick up my letter from Jerry. So it was no big surprise that when school let out in June, the first thing I did was to get myself up to Cornish, New Hampshire, to meet him. And I should say that my mother sewed me a dress for that visit—a dress that was made out of children's drapery material, with the ABCs on it. It was an A-line shift, very short, with no darts, and two buttons at the shoulders. You sort of stuck your hands up in the air and pulled it over your head, and that's all that was necessary. That dress had two giant pockets, one with the letter A appliquéd, the other with the letter Z on it. Not all that different from the dress I wore to my first day of first grade, actually. And this was the dress that I wore to meet Jerry Salinger.

It's only in retrospect that I realized the strangeness and sadness of that. It fell within the range of what my mother used to call costumes. Costume was my mother's name for whatever getups we wore. And the uncanny appropriateness of that for him! Somehow my mother sensed that this was just the dress that he would want. I was, in fact, eighteen years old, but I was a particular kind of eighteen-year-old. I was an eighteen-year-old who looked twelve.

I spent the weekend with him and didn't want to leave. I thought, "This is where I belong." In fact I had been given an astonishing job at the *New York Times*. I was brought in to write editorials for the summer, and somebody had offered me the use of a four-story townhouse on Central Park West to live in. I quit that job within a few weeks of taking it and left

New York City and the townhouse and moved in with Salinger. I withdrew from Yale where I had a virtually full scholarship, and I disappeared from the world.

Almost from the day I moved in, with my little wardrobe of alphabet dress and equivalent outfits, the same things that delighted Jerry about me on paper were very troublesome and annoying to him. He said to me the very day I moved in that I was behaving like a teenager, which of course I was.

I must say that for a young woman with already well-established eating problems this was a disastrous destination. This was a man who, for a very different set of reasons, subscribed to an austere, limiting, and rigid diet. It involved no food cooked over 110 degrees, all sorts of rules about combinations of things, and very meager food, and no sugar.

Of course I was always from my earliest days the good girl whose job was to please. Here I was yet again in the presence of someone I loved desperately, and I use that word advisedly. That's how I loved him . . . desperately. And I desperately wanted to please him, make him happy, make sure he kept loving me. So naturally I tried to eat the way he ate, but in doing so I inhabited a state of almost constant deprivation and longing for other foods. Sometimes I would go off and sneak foods. The food was really symbolic of all the other things I wasn't getting too. It was a very austere life that we lived together.

Then, into this already very restricted and unhealthy eating environment came a new habit. Jerry did break the rules when his son Matthew, who was then twelve, was staying with him. He loved Matthew so much, and he wanted him to have a happy, normal life, so when Matthew was with us we would go out and get pizza. And when Matthew went home to his mother, or would go to bed, Jerry said to me, "You know, we shouldn't have eaten that pizza—it's putrefying and we need to get rid of it."

That was the word he used. There was a book he gave me to read called *Food Is Your Best Medicine* by Henry Bieler. Anyway, he said, "That dinner was putrefying, and we need to get rid of it," and he showed me how to throw up, which he did as well. And once I learned that trick, I was off to the races.

So that is how I lived when I was with him. Living on raw food and nuts, and sometimes sneaking off to have ice cream and making myself throw up afterwards. I was hungry all the time. Not just for food, of course: I was hungry for the world.

In the spring of 1973, three weeks before the publication of my book *Looking Back* (a project for which he had utter contempt), Jerry told me to go away. He had no more use for me. As much love and adoration as he had showered on me the year before, that was the degree of his contempt and weariness with me, now. On a trip with him and his children, to Florida, he stuck a fifty-dollar bill in my hand and put me in a cab and told me to move my things out of the house and be gone before he returned home. It was March in New Hampshire with snow on the ground—cold, gray, and bleak—when my mother came to take me back home.

Looking back on this event now, I can recognize Salinger's behavior as unspeakably cruel, but at the time I thought I was just unworthy. The man I admired more than anyone in the world told me I was worthless. I believed him.

And then I began to eat. I didn't know how to eat anymore. So I began to eat and began to throw up. The concept of a normal, regular meal was not in my memory, so I had no idea how to control my eating, and I couldn't do it. Before long, I wasn't a skinny waif anymore.

This was three weeks before my book was published. The great moment that I had been building up to since I was probably eight years old. And the book actually got an enormous amount of attention, and I was going to be sent on a book tour, and I was on the *Today* show and lots of things like that. But I could do almost none of it. I was really incapacitated. The one thing that I did do—one of the very few things I was able to do, and this spoke to my vanity, of course—was that *Vogue* magazine selected me as one of their "Women of the Year," and each of them was to have their portrait done by Richard Avedon. I associated the Avedon portraits with those beautiful models. So I kind of thought that Avedon would make me look like that. I actually thought about Jerry seeing that picture.

So I did go to New York to have Avedon take my picture. It's funny. I've thought about this many times over the years. As part of the deal I was supposed to get a print of my portrait, and when the magazine came out with my portrait in it, which I now recognize to be a brilliant portrait: it did absolutely capture my grief. Everything that had happened to me in the preceding eighteen years was on my face. So needless to say, I looked nothing like a *Vogue* model. I didn't recognize that, I just thought that this is not a pretty picture. It is the picture of a girl with puffy eyes and a haunted look in her eyes, a hungry girl, and a heartbroken one. It's a photograph that reveals, to an extraordinary degree, in fact, a great deal of what was going on in my life at the time, but I hated it. I never even pursued the fact that I didn't receive my Avedon print. To this day I don't own a copy of the photograph. It's interesting to me because it looks so much like my daughter Audrey, except that my daughter Audrey is happy.

I really couldn't function in the world after that. I didn't know how to be with people after that. I couldn't imagine going back to Yale. I did actually know how to continue writing and I never stopped working. I had a small sum of money from the sale of that book and I did a thing that I thought Salinger would respect. I bought a house in the country and went to live there by myself. I was still longing for his approval. I was longing for his friendship. I know now that it was not a love affair. I had never experienced a love affair or a major boyfriend. That was a category that Jerry put it into, or that the world did later, but he was my guide, my teacher. So I lived by myself in that house, and once again, obviously, it was a most difficult place for a person with food problems to solve them. There is some comedy to this, though. I was at this point sort of the anointed expert on young people. Living on yogurt and popcorn. Throwing up a couple of times a day. The Youth Spokesperson of America, 1973.

And of course, there was my book *Looking Back* on the marketplace for sale: a 160-page volume that purported to be the story of my life. With not a mention on any of those 160 pages of my having grown up in an alcoholic family, having dropped out of my Ivy League university to be with a man thirty-five years older than me, or the fact that this man was J.D. Salinger, and certainly not that while I was composing that book I was making myself throw up every day. But in my "youth spokesperson" young girl writer-about-town mode, I would drive into New York City periodically to meet with editors and get assignments and earn money to pay the mortgage on my house.

I recall one time going in to talk to the editors of *McCall's* magazine. I always had a little notebook where I'd pitch one idea after another. And one of the ideas that I cleverly camouflaged with a whole lot of other ideas too was that I said, "You know, there is a phenomenon that some girls in America are experiencing called anorexia." They really had not heard that word yet. This was 1973 and I thought I would write about that. The editor, Bob Stein, an exceedingly nice guy, said, "Oh, I don't think our readers would care about anorexia. That's pretty bizarre and specialized." I didn't get that assignment. I went on to write a profile on Mary Tyler Moore (a woman I admired for a whole lot of reasons, her skinniness among them), and something called "My Parents Are My Best Friends." I never got to do the anorexia piece for them. I continued to live alone in the house in the country for a surprisingly long time. However, I did have a recognition that I had a problem, and I really wanted so badly to be well.

In what would have been the spring of my senior year at Yale had I stayed there—by this time I had been out of college for three years, I was twenty-one, and there had been no man in my life—I was living in a very solitary way. My dear friend Graff, whom I had known for many years, not as a sweetheart ever but as a best friend, invited me to come back to Yale and act in a play. He did this amazing thing. He got me a room in the dorm as if I were a regular student, and a meal ticket in the dining hall. When I think back to Yale that spring I remember less about being in the play. It was *A Little Night Music* and I was playing a child, a little girl, because I was still mostly skinny. But really what I remember that spring was reentering the world of normal life, and going to that dining hall, and trying very hard to behave in a regular way. And I actually had a regular boyfriend. He was a young guy who grew up in New York City in a family that loved restaurants and food. He had plenty of money and he used to take me to restaurants . . . I hadn't eaten food in years! I could almost say "never." There were really basic foods that I had never tasted. I think I connect the reentry into the world of eating with the entry into the world of healthy sexual activity, both of which occurred that spring.

That, of course, wasn't "happily ever after." He left and went on to other things. He attended medical school and there I was back in my house in New Hampshire, hardly living a typical girl's life. I was twenty-one years old, paying a mortgage, writing magazine articles, but not belonging to the world of young people. Again I think I recognized that I needed to get out so I rented my house and moved to New York City. I would have taken a waitress's job at Chock full o'Nuts just to be out in the world again, but what I ended up doing was getting a job at the *New York Times* and I became a general assignment reporter there.

I don't want to suggest that my problems were behind me. It was extremely difficult for me to have what you might call "a healthy relationship with food." Or a healthy relationship with a man, come to think of it. And maybe there was a connection.

What I had done for years was to periodically stop eating altogether. Just sequestered myself somewhere. Then I'd go off to some yoga retreat or something and eat nonstop for ten days, two weeks, whatever. However, it became very hard to indulge those secret habits in the stressful, high-pressured world of a reporter for the *New York Times.*

When I was twenty-three, I met Steve—a man I'd known briefly when I was eighteen, back before the *New York Times* and Salinger and all the rest of it. The night we met, he suggested that we should get married and have babies, and I loved that idea, and I loved the idea of having what sounded to me like a normal, regular life. I said yes.

Steve was very athletic, a fit person who had none of my kind of food and body issues ever. He was a very disciplined person too. Very early on— when I told him about my problem—he said to me, "Eat everything I eat; do everything I do." Looking back I think that this model didn't bode well for our relationship. However, at the time that was most comforting. I thought, "Okay, I'll copy Steve and it will be fine."

But very soon there was something I was doing that he wasn't, and that was having a baby. Once again, all my usual measures of where I stood were gone. After all those years of depriving myself, now I ate, and I was hungry all the time. I was loving being safe and cozy and normal, and so I was baking a whole lot and was freezing things obsessively. There was a picture I made my husband take of me from that winter with all the pies and cakes and brownies I had put in our freezer. We were also totally broke and I was panicked about money and security, so I would bake things without letting Steve eat them. I would just stash them in the freezer. I became a squirrel.

I gained about seventy pounds during that pregnancy. For me, the trauma was not labor and delivery. It was waking up the next day and discovering to my horror that as a woman who had gained seventy pounds during the last nine months, and had given birth to a seven-pound baby, I still had sixty-three pounds to lose. For someone who had once panicked if the scale indicated a weight gain of a few ounces, let me tell you, this was horrifying.

Eventually I did lose that weight, but it was excruciating. Just devastating. And I wasn't ever a waif again.

I had two more children, but I never let that happen again. My daughter is twenty-eight now, the younger two are twenty-four and twenty-two, and I'm fifty-two. What I would say now is that I'm certainly not cured, that it's not all done and over. It's not like somebody gets cured of cancer or some other disease. Instead I can say that I have learned to live at a certain level of vigilance and tolerance. I have an intensified awareness of all things to do with food, weight, eating, body, which will never go away. In the same way that a person who is sober, but once had a problem with getting drunk speaks of herself as "a recovering alcoholic," I am a person in recovery from food and eating issues, and though I look normal, and I have a pretty good acceptance of my body now, I will be that all my life, I know.

A helpful element now—and this has come with age—is the embracing of good health. When I was younger I would have guzzled arsenic if it promised to make me thin. I remember actually the first thought that would pass through my mind if I got sick, which I hardly ever do, was, "Oh good, I'm probably going to lose weight." As I've grown older I've come more and more to appreciate and value health and strength over skinniness. I really desire to be strong, and I am strong.

One of the healthier experiences in my life has been working out in a gym in a very different way than with my mother, when it was all about getting thin, no thought to building muscle, just burning calories. Over the years, I've developed a love of being outdoors: swimming, riding a bicycle. This was after my divorce. I was really sad, but I took the sadness to a healthier place, which was the pool and the gym. I worked out in a kind of way that I never had done before. Somebody said to me, "What competition are you training for?" There was still of course the obsessive quality I've always possessed, but at least I was applying my obsessiveness in a more healthy way. I was in terrific muscular shape, and I wasn't skinny. I began to feel that I could like that. I probably put on weight—I'm sure I did, because muscle is heavier—but I felt really good about my body.

In my relentless effort to find redemption, I now find it in my children. I was most worried that I would transfer my own enormously distracting and sometimes even debilitating set of obsessions to my daughter. At one point in Audrey's life when her father and I split up—she was about eleven—she put on a bunch of weight. I worried terribly about that and then worried terribly about worrying. I remember seeing her take a container of ice cream out of the freezer and start to eat it right out of that container, and I was so not wanting her to do that, that I started eating the ice cream so she wouldn't eat the ice cream. And as the daughter of a woman who had herself lost touch with where the mother ended and the child began (as my mother had, when she herself half fell in love with J.D. Salinger), I was terrified of doing that to my own darling child. I had to look very hard at the question: "Where does the mother stop and the daughter begin?"

But thank God, Audrey is a healthy, integrated person. I don't take credit for that. I think she saw what she didn't want to become in me—a woman who had wasted too much precious energy worrying about how she looked. She is a lot better than I was as a young person: at treasuring her own self, instead of looking for some man to tell her she's good enough. Or not good enough.

So my daughter has a lovely, naturally curvy body that she's very accepting of, as she should be, and that is everything that I would want for her. I didn't hand my troubles on to her. And as much as I may have taught her over the years, she has taught me some of that acceptance for my own life—and not a moment too soon, given that every day I'm one day older, and one day further away from being that waiflike ingenue once pictured on the cover of the *New York Times Magazine*. And it's really okay that I'm not that person anymore.

> *You don't put them in, they can't stay in:*
> *calories I mean: you don't put them in, you*
> *don't have to get them out: you can sit all*
> *day at the TV, a couch potato, and shrivel up like*
> *a stale french fry: you won't have to exercise*
> *a bit, pretty soon a skeleton would look fat to you.*

—A.R. Ammons, "Slacking Off"

Catherine Hickland
(actor)

WHEN YOU LEARN THAT Catherine Hickland, a longtime leading lady of daytime TV, is married to fellow actor Michael E. Knightly, who is "Tad" in *All My Children,* and that "Michael Knightly" was the fictional character her first real-life husband David Hasselhoff played on the soap opera *Knight Rider,* you know that life imitates art.

For twenty-eight years, Catherine Hickland has been perfectly beautiful on television. Her first professional job was in a commercial, playing a flight attendant in National Airlines' "Fly Me" campaign. She broke into the soap opera scene in *Texas,* playing Dr. Courtney Marshall. She also played dual roles in *Capitol* and had leading roles in *General Hospital, Loving,* and *The City* before joining the cast of *One Life to Live* in 1998, playing the manipulative but charming Lindsay Rappaport.

"Cat," as her friends call her, also appeared onstage as Fantine in the Broadway production of *Les Misérables,* and recently portrayed part of her own life story in the much-heralded off-Broadway play *Pieces of Ass.*

175

The sickness of a culture that is crazy over thinness is obvious in Cat's account of her struggle to stay slender for the camera. Cat is loved for her fresh beauty and direct, unaffected style of acting. But the down side was that she took to heart the beauty masters' critiques—before reinventing her sense of self. Today she also runs a successful cosmetics company, but Cat's message to women is that a body is not a costume to be altered at will, but part of an identity to be treasured and burnished.

—J.M.

I grew up very directed, very sure of where my path lay. We lived in Florida and my parents divorced early but my siblings and I were close. I have a brother, Robert, and a sister, Kim. I grew up in Fort Lauderdale, Florida. I knew from the time I was five I would be in the arts. I would be an entertainer or actress. I knew it and my parents knew it. There was no doubt about it, which is why it happened. No matter how much doubt someone wanted to inject in my mind, I had already accepted from an early age that this was how it was going to be.

I had always struggled with my weight, from my teens. It would go up and it would go down. It seemed that with my weight if I didn't watch it, that it was easy for me to get pudgy. But when I moved to Los Angeles I was really a young girl feeling fine, and a very strong-willed person. I had a very strong sense of self. Where I got it from, believe me, I didn't know, because it sure wasn't anything that was put in me as a child. Of course, looking in the rearview mirror now, it's clear to me that God made me that way, and I am just blessed enough to see it.

My idol was the singer Karen Carpenter. I learned how to sing to her records. She, to me, was the most outstanding singer of her generation. I was absolutely blown away by her, so this is what happened . . . This was 1978 and I was in California studying acting and whatnot, and I was invited to a big political fundraiser. John Wayne was there, and every other big star in Hollywood that you could imagine. It was just wow! But the one person there I wanted to meet was Karen Carpenter. The person I went to the fundraiser with knew her, so I said, "Please take me and introduce me." So he brought her over. She put her hand out and I saw her arms. They were like sticks and her hand looked like a bird's talon.

I remember my overwhelming love for her was being confounded by what I was seeing. "What's wrong with her? What's happening?" Because we didn't know anything back then about anorexia. It was just coming into knowledge or awareness, and was not in-your-face prevalent as it is today. So I remember being torn by my absolute thrill of meeting her and my absolute bewilderment of what was wrong with her. Because it was clear to me she was way too thin, she was skeletal, although her sensitive face, her eyes through which you could stare at her soul, that was still there. So was her warmth, love, and graciousness at meeting this unknown admirer, and believe me I've met many celebrities since then and they don't all have this gentle warmth. And Karen Carpenter was a superstar, so in that sense it was a great experience for me. But the idea lodged in me that you could fall to that point where she had fallen.

The next year, 1979, I was cast in my first soap opera, called *Texas,* in New York. I was kind of pudgy but not fat, more soft or zaftig—I'm trying to think of a word that would describe me. By today's standards I would have been twenty pounds overweight for a Hollywood actress, fifteen to twenty, because they really want you to be skinny today. So I'd screen-tested and gone to New York. If I'm not mistaken my screen test was in a bathing suit, which is a nightmare because nobody wants to be in a bathing suit unless they look like a Playboy Playmate airbrushed on the page. You don't want to be made that self-conscious when you act. So I get the part and move to New York. Now this little girl had barely settled in L.A. and all of a sudden she's in New York and making really good money, and living in a breathtaking penthouse apartment . . . I'm on my own and I'm Marlo Thomas in *That Girl,* except I have a job. It was great but the pressure that I wasn't aware of—so many things happen to us subconsciously—was how much thinner and in shape everybody around me was. This was below the level of awareness—no one ever said a word to me during the show, but discontent had already sunk in. When I was in Hollywood prior to getting that job I'd lost weight because they'd say, "You know, if you could just lose some weight." I'd heard that a lot before I got this part. So that was pulsing in my subconscious. Whether I recalled it, it was in the hard drive. I'd literally lost parts many times because I wasn't perfect. I would be perfect to some people but I wasn't according to the criteria for a girl to make it in Hollywood at that time—and now it's even more so.

So here I am in New York and I'm on a television show and my personal life is kind of disastrous, because I'm hooked up with my young romance from my hometown in Florida, and he was wonderful but very jealous. He didn't understand my job, that I had to fall in love with and kiss people on camera. He wasn't an actor and his disapproval put increasing pressure on me, and my life began to feel like it was spinning out of control. But again, you don't know this when you're in the middle of it. You just know things are falling apart. You feel bad without knowing why.

The out-of-control feeling is what propels the disorder. Because you're looking to control any little thing you can, and you don't even know you're doing it. This is what's fascinating. You're in denial with no insight into your actions or state of mind. And then I lost some weight—ten or twelve pounds, because I got sick; I had a little bout of pneumonia. Everyone said, "Wow, you look fantastic!" Well, that went into the hard drive, also! So all the things that I'd been collecting were all now in this head, floating around, and I thought, "Okay, I lost that weight, now I just need to find a way to keep it off and lose some more, because if people think I look good like that, wait until they see me like this!"

So now I just wanted to lose some weight, but somewhere in there all that loss of control in my personal life was spinning. I was in a very stressful relationship, which had turned codependent beyond belief, and so what happened was I lost the weight and then people went, "Go, Cat, go! You're really looking great." I looked at how I'd altered myself and loved their praise. "Oh, no," I thought, "no one's ever said that in my life. I look great? I'm beautiful, I'm skinny?" And then that control thing happens where you feel like you're removed from everything around you and you're exerting control where you can. What doesn't go into your mouth is a form of control. You hang onto that. Even now, what doesn't go in that mouth, believe it or not, that's a form of control for me!

And then people started to become alarmed. "Oh my God, you've lost too much weight, Cat!" Well, that's hilarious to a person who's gone from being overweight. That's the best thing you could say to them! Now I'm down to ninety-five or something—my lowest weight was eighty-nine. I have a picture of that; I only saved one. It's so horrible.

It was one of those things where I'd go out to dinner, and I had just learned how to rearrange my food and get people to eat off my plate to the point where they wouldn't even know I hadn't eaten anything. It's the same basis of disease as other addictions. The base of it is fooling everybody. If you're in denial you get very crafty. You want people to stop saying these things because now it's become annoying, so you learn deceit—like an alcoholic hides the bottles; it's the same thing. You learn to get creative and make people think you've eaten so they get off your ass and you can achieve your not eating for the day. Then the Ex-Lax, the laxatives, anything you can do to keep from gaining. Because believe me, you're either putting on the same pair of jeans to make sure you haven't gained an ounce, or you're getting on a scale because now you're obsessing about staying that way. And how it actually gets to you—you're destroying yourself if it does—is very individual.

What happened was, the producer of the show called me into his office. I said, "Okay, I wonder what this is about." And I went upstairs thinking I never looked better than this in my life. Now I'm maybe eighty-nine or ninety pounds. So he asked me to sit down. He played my screen test for me. And I'm horrified because that fat girl in the bathing suit comes on. I just can't stand it . . . "Please make it stop! Take it off. Turn it off! How could you hire me? Look how fat I was." And he says, "I don't know what's going on, but that's the girl I hired, and that's not the girl sitting in my office."

You know what? He didn't have any filters. He was saying what he needed to say and wanted me either to get some help, to determine what was wrong, or to call it to my attention. It was embarrassing, but I didn't know what he was objecting to. I said, "What are you talking about? That girl's fat!" He said, "That girl is healthy." So he was really in my face. That was 1980, and I'd been on *Texas* for about a year.

So my family began saying things to me. If enough people call you a horse, you really have to buy a saddle. Especially when everyone's pushing you to do so, and my job was on the line. The producer made that clear. If I wasn't going for help he'd get rid of me by recasting.

I started going to therapy and I didn't like it, and I didn't like gaining weight. It's a nightmare because you feel you're losing all your beauty and all the hard work, and you're also giving up your control, and that's really hard. Then I went to the extreme opposite. I gained without paying heed. That year I met David Hasselhoff. I was not over the disorder, certainly not. It would come to haunt me many times in the following years. I was either overweight or way too skinny, bones sticking out of my back. And whatever was going on in my life you could tell, because when I was in distress the weight would plummet. I would just stop eating. I didn't mean to; that was just my response to having circumstances fly—like into an electric fan. I'd just go right back to that unhappy place.

I scarcely went to therapy. I had all this survival behavior going on, developed from issues in my childhood. I'd been the adult when my parents were complete drunks. For sure I'm not blaming anybody. They did the best they could, and it's up to you to take care of yourself and stop the madness, and self-actualize, and get help, and grow up. But I just didn't for a long time. I didn't know how. I went for many years recreating all this chaos in my life via the weight fluctuations and secondarily in relationships. I still find myself reverting to it if I'm not staying in that state of self-awareness. It's so in there that until you learn how to read the feelings and behavior, it will come back and come back. So you constantly fortify yourself. I'm grateful for this moment. I've had a great life so far and expect to continue to do so, but that eating disorder is a foe I fight.

It didn't isolate me as it does some people. I had a normal life and normal relationships. I never dropped to eighty pounds again, never got that far. But I remember I went into the gym in Los Angeles, right close to my divorce from David, and of course my life fell spiraling out of control and I was skinny as a whip, so skinny. And of course I didn't see it. I thought I was fat. So I walked in—this was well into the 1980s, and I walked in and asked if I could please speak with a personal trainer. And the personal trainer came out and said, "What can I do for you?" And I said, "I really have to lose some weight." And he didn't say it but he took me on because he thought, "I've got to help this girl." He said that when he interviewed me his thought that minute was, "Oh my God, girl, you need to get a hamburger! Lose weight? There's something wrong with her. I'll take her on because I want to help her." And he did.

It's accurately called body dysmorphic disorder. I can't tell you how prevalent it is today. I know this from talking to teenagers. I'm in touch with them all the time because in connection with my company I teach seminars and workshops all over the country. Makeovers from the inside out. These girls come to me, and they're beautiful, and they don't see it at all, and I understand them completely. I see the mothers banging their heads against the wall and I think, "You'll have to let it go because they won't listen to you, they'll listen to someone else." If you're the mother, if you're the wife—our husbands don't listen to us; it's the weirdest thing. Your husband can fail to hear you say something, while another person, anybody but his wife, will say the same thing, and he'll hear it. You'll say, "Well, I said the same thing," and he'll say, "Well, you said it differently." "All right, no I didn't. . ." but this is the way it goes, and girls don't listen to their mothers about their appearance. They think, "Oh, my mom loves me. She thinks I'm pretty because she loves me and I'm her daughter."

There's a lot of that in there which is natural. But I see in such extreme cases as body dysmorphia, that people develop obsessive compulsive behavior over flaws that aren't even there. Again it's about everything happening from top to bottom, from the neck up. What we do is create the very thing we fear. We create the screwed-up body we fear. When I see a woman walking down the street now, and she has that skeletal kind of physique, my heart breaks.

I eat normally. I know what it is to be broken, but I have the sense of being healed. Yet it's sitting there waiting for me all the time. The disorder is always waiting. There's a seat right next to me with my name on it and anorexia underneath. And there's another seat on the other side of it that says "Fatso." So it's constant work. I would think that it's like taking an alcoholic into a bar. It's not that it's on your mind every day, but I still get that same clutch sometimes. If I gain three or four pounds because I went on a great vacation, I feel panicked. When we get home and my pants are tight, I know I'm going to do one of two things if I don't get a hold of it. Either I'm going to lose ten pounds or gain ten, from despair either way. I'm either going to punish myself one way or the other. Or my better choice is to say, "That's all right. That's three pounds I didn't need to gain, or four pounds, and I can get that off. I know how, and how to do that healthy. Here are my choices." It's a matter of how much you're going to let that mind roam free. I have a good long history with making the right choice—but the issue's waiting for me, always.

What I'll do is go right to therapy and talk about it with my therapist. I never involve my husband in it. Those who love and care for you are just going to get alarmed, worried for you—all kinds of things that will just add to your stress. You just have to get a grip. I certainly talk about it in *Pieces,* but the people who live with me day in and day out would not be really aware that I possess these thoughts. Because I choose to go down the road that's the best road, which is, "Oh, I've gained three pounds and didn't need to. Clothes are tight now. Think I'll lose three pounds in a healthy way. Maybe I'll cut out the sugar and treats that are not good for me anyway." I won't go down that other road. I started to go down it about eight months ago and lost a lot of weight, because I had a certain stress around me again that was creating a desperate feeling. My weight plummeted—I wasn't even conscious how quickly, and I couldn't seem to put it back on. At first everyone was "Wow, you look great" and then they started doing the "Aw, Jeez, you're looking a little too—your face looks drawn, Cat." Now I know that means something. It means "Stop!" People aren't lying to you; they're telling you the truth from a place of love. You don't see it because you're entering into the dysmorphic disorder, you're falling into a ditch but you can get out. I haven't owned a scale in at least ten years on purpose. Now I know if enough people call you a horse that you need to buy a saddle!

You need to channel your energies in the most positive way. When I galvanize myself to stay healthy, it's totally the same energy I draw on for acting. It's a person's drive. I do have a strong will, which works for somebody to the good and to the bad. I've learned to channel everything into positive mental energy. And I'm not afraid anymore. That's the biggest thing. I'm in control of me and me only, so I don't try to control events outside of me, or the outcome of things. I can work toward a goal, and that's the best I can do, and all my control is just what kind of job I'll do on my way there. The outcome rests uncertain and outside my actions. I can envision and believe it, but I stopped trying to control things except my part. That helps. Some people never get it, that the beauty of life is that it can change today. I think about me that all the signs are she's much better and not a horse anymore.

For actresses our looks are like our instruments; we are hyperaware of appearance, weight, and beauty. Usually women get somewhat over their hyperawareness of looks after their teen years, but no sooner are they in that comfort zone than they hit another area of confusion and self-doubt—men. Self-doubt about finding happiness in their relationships, and a poor relationship as a trigger for general misery about themselves. Why, when there's somebody for everybody in this world? If you can just imagine how the man you want looks, and how he treats you. "What does he look like and how do I feel when I'm with him? How does he feel when he's with me?" People say that's fantasy, and yes it is, and you better start fantasizing right now! Start co-creating and you will get it, and you will also get something else if you don't. It's like that with a life problem. You prepare, you do your best, and it can lift off.

I've been cast in some strong woman roles. In daytime TV a lot of the female characters are strong while their men are invalids or drunks. We used to have a joke for a new actor who came on the set. One of us would look upward. "What's that hanging on the ceiling?" she'd say. He'd look up too, and then she'd say, "Must be those balls you checked in when you came on the set."

I don't think I'm an extreme or self-critical person, but it was being in show business that set the switch off on my eating disorder. I wouldn't have thought it was smart if I'd never had anybody say, "You know, you'd be such a beautiful girl if you lost a few pounds," or "You're too overweight for this part," or "You should lose some weight, you're such a pretty girl." I can put it in a million different ways, what was said to me. It doesn't matter how strong your spirit is—when you're just a young girl and you're out on your own, you may think, "That's just their opinion," but everything critical that's said to us is stored in the hard drive. If you don't believe that, you're foolish. So you have to deal with the feeling of something when it's happening.

I've learned to see where I'm at by what I'm craving to eat. When I crave sweets all the time—and sugar's my Achilles' heel because I would really rather have that than food—when I crave cakes and candies and that's all I want to eat, then I need to stop and check what's going on with me. I'm quite objective about it. When I've got a wicked sweet tooth I think, "Uhh, what's going on? What's making me like this? Am I getting disassociated from myself?"

That split is self-destructive. You know if you have the disorder what it's going to lead to. You're going to gain weight and feel crummy about yourself. You're at a perfect weight now. You feel well. Everyone thinks you look good. You're not the skinniest girl in the room but you're in great shape, and you know what it takes to stay here. It's not a lot of work, it's just not flipping out, so think why you crave that candy. I've learned to monitor myself by what I want to eat. Because so much about eating goes on subconsciously. If people need to lose weight but can't it's the same thing: it's all emotional baggage. A weight issue is emotional baggage, end of story. It's how you feel about yourself. When I meet women at my workshops who are overweight, I'm very conscious of their sensitivity and how they're treated and dealt with in public. And they get very defensive and say, "I love myself just the way I am." And you know what? If that's true it's great. Loving yourself as you are is the biggest gift you could ever give yourself. But it's very rarely so. When we start to talk, and they feel in a safe environment, that we're all there for the same cause, to evolve, feel our innateness, learn how to make that happen on the outside too, they all break down.

The worst age in the world for painful emotions toward food and weight is between thirteen and seventeen, when you doubt everything about yourself. Classmates seem so mean, and the boys are saying offensive things, and you take so much in. There's no class in high school like Life 101, or Tell Them to Fuck Off 101, or None of Your Business 101, or How to Love Myself 101. There isn't that. A book like *The Gift of Fear* by Gavin De Becker, about how your intuition can save you, should be required reading in high school. Teach them confidence. Teach them that they're meaningful and don't ever have to put up with anybody's shit. I'm being vulgar because I feel so strongly about it. This is a very strong subject.

I wish I'd retorted with what I felt to those people who told me I'd be gorgeous if I just lost weight. I wish I'd done it at that point. If a casting director told me, "You'd be perfect for this role if you were more slender," I could say, "Yes, well, that's probably true, but this is the weight I am at today, and if you don't want to give me the part today because of that, then that's up to you. But I am happy with the weight I am right now. I feel good."

Wouldn't that have been a healthy answer? And then I could have walked out and decided whether I wanted to lose a few pounds. Maybe I would have said, "Are you going to give me the part? Because if you are, I'm going to lose a few pounds."

I also like the technique of telling people, "When you say, I feel." For instance, "When you say things like my cheeks look full or things about my weight, I don't feel I'm beautiful. You don't see who I am." All you are saying is how you feel. What are they going to say to that? They're going to say something, aren't they? I always say whatever they reply is the right answer because you'll know what to do from there. Each person is valued and no one has to take criticism that can erode you. Instead of sitting around thinking, "Wow, doesn't he see me for the person I am?" the mind will go to assumption-land pretty quickly and that's not going to take you anywhere good! So I'm all about saying how I feel, because it's not attacking anybody, and we're entitled to our feelings.

Everybody comes with something. If you can't live with somebody's stuff you need to bless them and be on your way. Actors have a certain amount of baggage as we all do, but we don't have a harder time in relationships just because of that. Careers don't make marriages—career schmareer! Fifty percent of marriages end in divorce no matter what you do. If you marry someone in the same business it can be nice. I've tried to date civilians and it doesn't work very well. I don't think the business has anything to do with your capacity for intimacy, though. It's deciding how you'll treat each other. It's also this sense of aligning yourself with someone who's willing to communicate completely. I would go so far as calling it full disclosure, meaning you talk about things as they are happening, to the end of it, and then get to the love again. This is something I'm learning how to do right now. It's hard. Silence is death to a relationship, that's what I've learned in my life. You don't have to create distractions or contain your feelings. If you don't like the man you're with, you don't have to stay with him either. You can just go home and get that paper out and start writing down your ideal man. What would he look like, sound like, feel like? How would he speak to me and how would I feel with him? Oh yeah, he loves and respects me. He sees that I take care of myself. And he thinks, "She's the most beautiful woman I've ever seen." Why not?

If you're an actress, unless you get extraordinarily lucky or have someone taking care of you, you have to regulate a life with the steepest sort of ups and downs. Extreme fame will take you to a level of losing your independence about taking care of yourself, looking after yourself in the normal, natural, realistic-world kind of way. That turns out to be really sad because most famous people live beyond their means, and anything can happen. Learning to readjust to live in the world and to take care of yourself is a problem. With the super-famous, everyone is making sure they're okay so they're very fortunate. And in my field generally everyone is making sure the men are okay. But for most of us who are actresses, as women we're the caretakers and who's going to take care of us if we're not taking care of ourselves? We have to. You can't expect that other people are going to look after you. But if you're working from your divine self and are at one with your source, you're going to have a very strong need to be connected and be living in reality and peace.

When I was in Los Angeles I noticed that most everyone was on one or another drug—antidepressants, anti-anxiety medications, anti-everything. Yes, certain people need them, but a lot of people don't. And when you don't need them and you take them, you lose your ability to learn how to cope. People are making a mess by getting a quick fix when they aren't able to cope with their struggles. For two solid years I was on antidepressants and anti-anxiety pills, which I didn't need to be on. I needed them briefly, but then the time came when I knew I just needed to learn coping skills. I expressed this to the doctor who put me on these drugs, who was seeing me every two months and making three hundred dollars each time he saw me. So one day I decided I was going to stop taking them. Stopping abruptly might not have been the most prudent thing to do because I suffered for two weeks: horrific feelings, endless crying. I didn't understand I was going through withdrawal. But once I got through it I didn't take any of those drugs anymore. I began to understand about the need to align with the universe and source, which for me is God, and that my problems were circumstantial and my peace would come from within. I could shore up my own reality, not go on in a condition removed from reality.

I've been so grateful to be out of the fog! Being on drugs did help me for a time to get through the circumstances I was fending. It dulled the anxiety of prolonging a marriage that was past saving. But sometimes in a crisis is where you connect with yourself. If you can get to that clarity you won't need anything artificial. How do I co-create with the universe? By thinking through this in a very personal way I came across an unbelievable benefit. Coming from despair and battling my troubles, I found a joy that transcends the circumstances. If you find that, you can apply it to many things that are bothering you in life.

Now I record my inspirations on a Web site for my cosmetics company. The first of each month, in their e-mail boxes, my client base of 60,000 women get the inspiration for the month. I love writing these thoughts, and the women's responses will often make my day. I've come to believe that I was put here to heal people and help them on a journey. I know that's why I've been given this platform of a career. The soap operas I've done are built on examining feelings and relationships. People who watch them ponder their own acts and emotions while following a story. I think sometimes women need to make more conscious what they already know to grasp their lives better. Surfacing what I know to help myself and others makes me feel life has more meaning than "What's it all about, Alfie?" Because I've been on television for twenty-seven years: I've spent my whole life there so far. What's it for? Not to see my picture in a magazine, it can't be that; that's not all there is. It's been an evolution in myself, a journey to "Ah!"

There is a show called *Pieces* that I was in off-Broadway. It's monologues about what being a beautiful woman does to your life, about the good, the bad, and the ugly—great stories, and funny, sad, and scary stuff. It's ten women's revelations and it's an amazing show. They asked me to be in the show. To be in it you had to write your life story and then craft your monologues off that. The result is a revelation for the audience and also for the performers.

I was told, "If you're going to do this you can't sugarcoat it. It has to be interesting, and for that you have to tell the truth." And I thought, "Okay, I'm ready for it," and I mean things went into that show I hadn't told my husband or anyone in this world. I talked about being molested by the family doctor. I talked about growing up surrounded by alcoholics and surviving the chaos of it all. (It's a bizarre disease. It's funny how codependents and alcoholics find each other in this world like magnets.) And about the codependency I had to break from in my relations with men. I stood on the stage and people I'd known all my life were finding out things about me for the first time. It was really scary but also incredibly liberating.

It's a multimedia show and you see yourself on big screens that go with your storyline, so the monologue has to be crafted and learned, which takes considerable skill. I talk about my anorexia and soon I found that people would wait for me after the show every night not because of any other reason except they wanted to tell me, "Me too, me too," and "I never told anybody." And I thought, "My God, this is it. To help other women is why I'm here."

Men love *Pieces* too. It's very insightful for them because they have no idea how we're wired. They think it's like peeking through the window of a slumber party to see this show. They don't know how they affect us. The way their judgments and behavior make us feel. The whole show is all about that.

I had reached a point where I could stretch out and live new dreams. This self-revealing role in *Pieces* is a dream come true, and I love being involved in the cosmetics business for the same reason. I like relating to other women and they tell me that my willingness to acknowledge my struggles helps them—sparks their thinking and spurs them, if they've stumbled, to get up and forge ahead. It was an enviable chance to play a piece of my life; doing *Pieces* showed me I'd come far enough. I was equipped to do it, to speak out about the anorexia and heartaches or traumas without getting pulled down.

One thing about running my company that I love is I'm knee-deep in women constantly. And I've discovered that as different as we are, we're alike in our sameness. We all want to be seen, heard, loved, respected, and valued.

I don't have a problem with the effects of aging. In my mind I've accepted that I'm just getting better and better. Like I said, everything that happens from the head down really happens from the neck up. If it's in your mind that aging is scary, and you don't want to get old, then what do you think is going to happen? You are what you think. You can control your weight, your face, your everything with that mind. It's incredible what this mind can do. I'm always telling people, "Be careful what you think."

Even when I was slender, I was fat.

—Judith Moore, *Fat Girl*

My father catered Bruce's bar mitzvah and conceivably Vilanch could hold my father responsible for any eating disorder he might admit to ever having.

—Richard Lewis, in an e-mail to Gary Stromberg

Bruce Vilanch
(comedy writer, actor)

HE'S JEWISH, GAY, AND BLOND, and he's written for some of the biggest names in entertainment. Richard Pryor, Lily Tomlin, Joan Rivers, and Bette Midler have all benefited from his writing talent. He's also the comedic mind behind many Oscar, Tony, Grammy, and Emmy awards productions. But with all of these great comedy credits, Bruce Vilanch is probably most remembered as the wild "center square" on TV's legendary *Hollywood Squares.*

Bruce is also known for something else . . . being outrageously fat. Does anyone else carry heft with such aplomb? It's not a subject he talks about much, though. Not that he shies away from it, but other people usually tiptoe around the topic. It's much easier to discuss his homosexuality or his burgeoning career.

I've known Bruce for more than twenty years. We wrote a treatment together for a movie that never got made, we had the same Hollywood agent for a while, and we often ran into each other at show business functions. I've always been fond of him, as I'm certain he is of me. It's been an easy friendship, peppered always by his comic flirtations. I've never been hit on by a man as often as Bruce has teasingly hit on me.

So, it was natural that when my partner Jane and I started to plan this book, Bruce came immediately to mind. As luck would have it, he was just beginning a starring role in the Broadway show *Hairspray* when I e-mailed him with my request. A lunch was soon arranged, and Jane and I headed out from our Connecticut digs to meet him in the Big A. What transpired was a pleasant enough conversation, but one that contained a big surprise. While readily admitting being grossly overweight, Bruce denies having an eating disorder. Read for yourself his unique explanation.

—G.S.

I was a fat kid! I was always a fat kid, but I look at pictures of myself now as a kid and I don't think I look that fat. But when I was a kid I felt very fat. In comparison to other kids, I think I *was* fat. I was also awkward, I was clumsy, I was ungainly, and I was never any good at sports.

My family wasn't fat. At least I didn't think so. As my mother has gotten older, I've noticed that she has a constant battle with weight, but she's certainly not obese. She's never been heavy; she's just not thin. Not the thin I think that she would like to be, but on the other hand, I think she's at peace with how she looks. I was adopted, so I have no idea what gene pool influenced my physical development, and my father didn't have a weight problem at all.

From the time I was a kid I just remember being big, and my mother was very afraid for my health. She wanted me to lose weight because she was afraid that if I stayed heavy it would lead to all kinds of health problems later on. Also, I think, she wanted me to look a certain way. She had certain standards, and I was never going to be able to live up to them. I was never going to look the way she wanted me to look. When you're a fat kid and they force you into real clothing—jackets and ties, et cetera—you're never comfortable. They never build them the right size for you, or at least they didn't in those days.

I was never a binge eater, and I never actively sought comfort in food, until I was older and became aware I was in some kind of pain. I think that when I was in college I would seek out pizzas because they were very comforting. I would hear friends' stories about binge eating and how they would eat seven pizzas. I would have a few slices and that was okay for me. That was enough comfort.

I went through my entire life knowing that I was bigger and that I wasn't going to get any thinner. Even if I did get thinner, I wouldn't turn out to be who I wanted to be anyway. I would never be Brad Pitt, even if I lost a ton of weight. I would look in the mirror and it would still be me. My struggle was all about the way I looked, not about eating. I still, to this day, don't eat that much. I'm just a big person.

I remember I went to an OA [Overeaters Anonymous] meeting to see what it was all about. I had wanted to lose weight at one point, about twenty years ago, so I said, "Let me see if I can; let me go on a food plan and see if that will help me lose weight." Eventually I went to Weight Watchers, and I did lose weight, because I was counting calories and measuring my food and doing all that stuff, and I enjoyed it.

But I never did any bingeing or purging, the stuff I heard about at OA. OA was also full of a lot of people who were using food the way they used alcohol and drugs. I didn't use anything to a level of abuse. I was just a big guy who never exercised. When I started exercising, I would lose some weight, but I would never "act out" with food. I had a friend who really did. I was staying with her here in New York. She worked in an office in midtown and the apartment was on the Upper West Side. She would walk home at night by way of every doughnut shop. I would find her sitting in the lobby of her building with powdered sugar covering her breasts! She was too stoned to come upstairs, from all the binge eating she had done. I never had that kind of frenzy.

As I got older I became diabetic, so I changed the way I eat, but it didn't make me any thinner. I just changed the way I was handling sugar.

During my OA period I heard stories about people who would totally abuse food, using it the way they abused substances. It just wasn't me. Sometimes I would look at them and see girls who were ten pounds over-weight. Especially in Hollywood. They were going through the agonies of the soul over these ten pounds. Bingeing and purging, bingeing and purg-ing, and they all *looked* fine. And I thought, "This is not my room! I don't have this disease. I have something else. I don't know what it is." I guess it's called "big-bone-itis." I had a doctor who told me, "Some people are just meant to be big." I would work out; I would diet; and basically my frame didn't change.

So now that I'm an internationally famous raconteur, superstar and sex object, I've been offered a TV series called *Celebrity Fit Club* on VH-1. To me, it's the absolute nadir of reality. They are getting a team of twelve fat celebrities together and putting us on a weight-loss regimen. They are pay-ing us a fortune. One of us will win even more money. But that's not why I'm doing this. I'm doing it because I may as well do something for myself. I've done enough jokes about being fat. Now I can actually do a TV series about being fat and get paid for it. I may end up losing weight. I may not wind up losing weight. My guess is I'll be in better shape when I end up, but I'll never be Arnold Schwarzenegger. No matter what I do. Now I'm fifty-eight years old, and the reality has finally sunk in. I'm who I am, and I'm not going to jump through hoops trying to change that. I am what I am, not that gorgeous leading man hiding out in the closet, but a fabulously large flamboyant homosexual, and making a handsome living at it.

I don't want to make light of it because it is a serious disorder, and I have lots of friends that are afflicted with it. In those OA rooms many years ago, I was investigating. I had a roommate, a woman who was an alcoholic, and because I loved her, I was going to Al-Anon, which is an organization of people who sleep with alcoholics. I wanted to be able to deal with her disease. Because I am a "big boy" I was immediately pounced upon by the members and sent to an OA meeting. "Clearly, you're cross-addicted," they told me.

Years ago, I was going to AA meetings a lot, because I have another friend who's an alcoholic. I was kind of a fixture there. I was telling another friend about the meetings, how fabulous they were, and what a plan for life this program has, when he said, "Well, I'd love to go," so I said, "I'll take you. Come sometime." He said, "Won't all the people there who know me think I'm there spying on them and be uncomfortable?" I said, "No—they'll think you're an alcoholic." He never went!

I think the Twelve Step programs are fabulous, and I read their books all the time, but in my particular case, I don't think I have a disease. I remember someone at one of those meetings saying to me, "How can you be over three hundred pounds and not have an eating disorder?" I said, "I just don't agree with you." A lot of times people in a program like that will take an offensive attitude because it makes them feel better about their own problem. "You're here, dammit, you can't live in denial." I'm not denying I'm a big, fat person, but I am denying that it's a problem. I don't eat twenty-two cupcakes at a time because I have a disease. I just don't.

My mother keeps saying to me, "You eat so much fish, why aren't you thinner?" And I don't know the answer to that. I do know that when I ate right I lost a bit, but I never had a cataclysmic weight loss.

I heard wonderful stuff at OA meetings twenty years ago that I carry around with me today. Like if I'm really tired and I think, "I'd like a big bowl of spaghetti," I say to myself, "No, don't do that." I remember that someone at OA said that the difference between AA and OA is that a food disorder is like having a tiger in a cage. Three times a day you let the tiger out to feed it, and you hope the tiger comes back. You can never be sure the tiger will come back, because it's a tiger. And that's what an abstinence plan really is: A hope that when you sit down to eat, you'll eat in an orderly fashion and return to the cage. Occasionally that will come to me when I'm thinking, "Maybe I should have that chocolate mousse soufflé." But then I think, "I just don't need it. I'm not hungry and I don't have a craving for it, so I don't."

I've become a big customer for food delivery services here in New York, only because I don't cook a lot for myself, and if I do cook, I'll make the wrong stuff. This way, I know I'll have a refrigerator full of food that is good for me. That doesn't come from working a program; that comes from my own inner sense of what's right for me. If I had to work a program to do that, I would, but I don't.

Yet, with all that knowledge, I sit here large!

You know, I've been doing the play *Hairspray* on Broadway for over two years now, based on John Waters's movie. It's all about tolerance and acceptance: accepting people for who they are and accepting yourself for who you are. Including your weight level. The play teaches a powerful message of loving yourself for who you are. I've always felt that, barring some hideous misfortune, you're living the life you want to live. If you don't want to live it, change it. Most people live in denial of that fact. "They're doing this to get ready for that." It's usually bullshit. Ultimately you have to say, "I'm doing what I want to do." And if you're not, then change it. I learned that a while ago during the AIDS epidemic. Losing hundreds and hundreds of people in the third and fourth decades of their lives. When that happened, I learned that "I better be doing what I want to do, because there clearly ain't much time for anybody." These people are gone and I'm still around, and if I'm not happy, it's my own doing. It's unfortunate that I had to learn that watching so many people die. Many felt they hadn't done what they wanted to do yet, and they were taken away by the disease.

I've been asked if I could be the same person if I were thin and I remember that Jerry Seinfeld said, "Ten pounds either way and you lose your funny." But Jerry Seinfeld never had a weight problem. He's a good-looking Jewish kid whose comedy never depended on his looks.

To be visible all the time—to live
In a swarm of eyes—
Surely that leaves its mark on the face.
Features overlaid with clay . . .
I have to be myself
Ten minutes every morning,
Ten minutes every night,
—and nothing to be done!

—Tomas Tranströmer, "Solitude"

Magali Amadei
(supermodel)

MAGALI AMADEI'S CAREER began in 1992, when the seventeen-year-old from the French Riviera made an uncommonly quick ascent to supermodeldom. She was signed to come to the United States by a New York modeling agent who literally discovered her on the beach. Soon everyone recognized her, although few knew her name. Dark, bewitching, with a tall frame, olive skin, and slanted eyes, she was the model compared to Ava Gardner and Sophia Loren.

Magali has graced the covers of *Vogue, Elle, Marie Claire, Cosmopolitan,* and *Harper's Bazaar.* She earned top modeling fees while avoiding overexposure and household-name status. Who could pronounce it? But let's try—*Mah-ya-lee,* an ancient name from the sonorous language of Provencal.

Segueing into acting, Magali starred in two off-Broadway plays, *A Matter of Dispute* and *Fiesta Wear,* before moving into film work. Along the way she went public with her seven-year battle with bulimia. In a stroke of irony, for the Jennifer Lopez–Matthew

McConnaughy vehicle *The Wedding Planner,* she donned a fat suit for her role as a pregnant woman.

The first top model to admit to an eating disorder, she has appeared on *20/20, Entertainment Tonight,* and *Good Morning America* to speak about the disease. To the surprise of some of her glossy magazine clients, Magali received great admiration for talking about conquering her demons, and has since soared ahead in her life and career.

—J.M.

I grew up in Nice, in the south of France. It's a real big mystery to me why people develop an eating disorder. There's no black-and-white reason. It's an agglomerate of circumstances that make a person veer off this way. Even where I lived had something to do with it. The south of France is very much like California—you're half naked the whole year round, and you compare yourself to others a lot.

I'm looking at my six-week-old daughter right now and thinking what will be instilled in her. A friend came by and said, "Oh, she's going to be gorgeous," and my first reaction was, "Well, I hope she's a nice person," because I remember from growing up that the focus on looks over everything can be really damaging. And then I thought, "Well, there you go, it starts that little."

If I had a son, I'm not sure I'd say, "Oh, you're so handsome, you're so gorgeous." And I'm not so sure my friend would have said, "Oh, he's going to grow up to be a knockout." Because I don't think we put that much emphasis on beauty for men as we do for women, even though valuing men's looks is on an upswing too. But we pre-prepare a woman's brain by saying those things: "She's going to be gorgeous" or "Look how cute she is." All these compliments that are lovely to hear—and my friend didn't mean any harm saying what she said—I appreciated her complimenting, but it just made it clear to me that the distortion starts so young.

I was also a ballerina. Even though by the time my eating disorder started, at fourteen, I had figured out I would not dance professionally, being in ballet school I was hyperaware of weight. Growing up I was a high achiever who felt all the pressures that can go with that sort of activity.

And definitely my personality is a perfectionist's. I think that has a lot to do with the disorder, too. Growing up I did everything just right, positively no slip-ups. As a teenager you realize you can't be perfect, and you have to peck out of that shell or you carry it and live under the constant pressure.

And the fact that I come from a family of Italian background has something to do with it, because, though I don't want to make big, wide judgments, my family was very secretive. Some cultures are more like that than others—the members subsumed under the unit of family, which is on top. There were many subjects we did not or would not touch on. That was an element that led to my hiding my eating disorder, so when it started it just got worse. I can't say this is why, but to me it's another factor that's part of the reason.

Then my brother, my all-beloved older brother, whom I looked up to so much as a little girl because he was a big man to me, got into a motorcycle accident, which I was really freaked out about. He basically got taken for dead when he was on a motorcycle and met with a truck. And of course the family didn't speak about it. We dealt with it shut up like clams. My father would just sit at the dinner table wearing dark glasses, and cry underneath them. My mother was busy at the hospital, and at the same time we were all trying to figure out if my brother was going to live. And I was sort of left there to figure out whether I was going to have a brother or not.

This was part of it. My brother lost his kidney, not his life. He survived, but the disruption to the family lasted a long time. And I revered him so much that there was such an emotional shock that never came out anywhere. I carried it within me.

Then one day I was at school—and it sounds very banal, but I think this is how big things start in life—someone at school told me, "Oh my God, you are fat!" Of course I was fourteen, and I wasn't, but I was going through puberty so my body was definitely changing. I think that's what that kid meant, and I can't stress enough when I talk to children that you really have to be nice to each other and mind the power of your words, which of course we don't realize when we're that young.

Basically that's all it took: someone to say, "Mon Dieu, you're fat!" It sounds simplistic. But puberty, to me and a lot of others, is very confusing. That period of time, in and of itself, with attraction to men, with seeing your body change—that also was a big part of it.

My eating disorder started with a girlfriend at school. Funnily enough we found each other. She was of Jewish background and as I said I'm Italian, and I would go to her house for food, and she would come to mine, for Italian. And we both started holding each other's bathroom doors, and bingeing together, and then throwing up, and then after a while she was like, "Are you still doing this?" And I was like, "No, I'm not," and she was like, "No, I'm not either." But we both were. So what happens is that after a while an eating disorder develops, where you're not in control of it. It's in control of you, and you aren't aware of it, and you start keeping secrets.

So I continued. It's really easy. It was a problem right away, but of course I didn't think it was. I thought it was just something we did. I said to myself, "Oh yeah, this isn't important." I split it off from myself and everything else I was doing.

Then a modeling agent discovered me. I was seventeen and had graduated from high school. She said, "Oh, why don't you come to New York for the holidays?" So I did, and the second I arrived in that city my eating disorder became something that I did maybe not every night but something that I lived by. It became part of my family, and then all of it.

When I started modeling I was very successful right away. From the outside I didn't have a reason in the world to be miserable, but I was. I was terribly lonely. I think that's what's so powerful about an eating disorder, how alone you feel and how completely ashamed you feel of yourself. And it's strange to be on the covers of magazines and be that lonely. Because it appeared I had everything that every woman could dream of. But I was completely miserable.

That went on for a while and, as the story goes, I'm not sure if you start with a depression and then develop an eating disorder, or if it's the reverse—the chicken or the egg. But nonetheless my depression became so deep that after a few years it came to a point where I couldn't even get out of bed. And that was my low, low point, where I decided to write a letter to my boyfriend at the time, and I handed it to him, and went running to the bathroom and locked the door. I was crying so much that I thought, "Sure enough, I am going to extinguish myself." You know, I felt I was going to disappear.

That didn't happen, though. I'd said, "I think I have a problem: I make myself throw up." Of course I didn't use the word eating disorder, or the words bulimic or bulimia. That took years to utter. And I told my boyfriend how I felt and why—what I understood of why. And it was amazing because when I came out of the bathroom, after his knocking on the door for I don't know how long, he just gave me a hug. It was the first time that I felt relief.

And that, I guess, was the moment when I started recovery. Which took a long time because it's not something that you just recover from by the snap of a finger. Recognizing you have a problem is the first moment when you can start helping yourself and getting up.

It was like coming up from a haunted place of all my secrets. When I told my boyfriend I let in fresh air and sunlight, all the more so because to me it was always really hard to express feelings. I would experience an action and then I would have the reaction of bingeing and throwing up, purging. But I didn't know what the feeling was attached to it. Let's say I was in Italy doing the shows, and a designer would say, "Oh, her belly is fat in this dress!" That would be the action that made me go around the corner, buy an armload of *panini,* and then purge. Instead of expressing anger or shame, I just reacted through my eating disorder. Now, after the feeling of depression I would go very low.

However, like the other boyfriends he soon passed out from my life. I cheated on all my boyfriends—I hope they're not going to buy this book! Yeah, I was a terrible person to be in a relationship with, because, as I said, my eating disorder was my boyfriend, my family, my everything, so I didn't have room to have another boyfriend. I belittled myself, and them, by making sure that I didn't give them the importance that they had in my heart. This is why I cheated on them all. It was a terrible repeating thing.

And of course—this is the key of an eating disorder—up until that letter to my boyfriend, none of them knew how much I was suffering. You know you have a problem, because you spend so much time and effort thinking about planning food that it sucks the entire energy out of your life.

I had no power over it, no choice, or so I thought, which is, you know, so classic when you're addicted. You swirl downwards in this spiral and you slip into chaos.

Eventually a few things happened chemically, regarding the bodily functions. My periods were few and far apart. Eleven caps, seven root canals, two bridges, and two implants because my teeth got rotted by my stomach acids. My hair became really brittle. I had dark circles—which of course everyone put under the factor that I was constantly traveling around the world. Those were the actual physical signs, and if you binge and purge, there's the aftermath where I would sort of go through major shakes. My body was deprived of essential electrolytes, and that was just the shock of it. That was a chemical reaction, a consequence I could expect, that was waiting to attack the system and the nerves.

And no one noticed because I had two personalities. The Magali who was working outside and was happy and everything was fine. I always had this bright smile on my face, and was just a people pleaser. Nothing fazed me and I was really alert to other people's needs. And then there was Magali when I closed the door and went back home—which was basically my hotel room—who was really lonely, really sad, who didn't talk to people and had no friends. Because for years my friend was my eating disorder. It was my friend, my family, my everything.

I compare it to scuba diving: when you scuba dive you have the oxygen tank on your back, and you're in this world. Well, my eating disorder was kind of like my tank. In order to recover, first of all you have to be aware that there's another world, and you have to find that world, because it is not visible once you are scuba diving, where up and down are not obvious. Then you have to surface, and surfacing you still have the tank on your back, and you're walking around and breathing that tank air. And then the idea comes, "Oh, maybe I can live without the tank." So you take it off . . . But then you put it on again, because you despair—"Oh my God!"

Then, slowly but surely, you get to live with the normal people at the surface without the tank.

That's really what it feels like. It's really hard to explain to people what an eating disorder feels like. Because it's an addiction, and an addiction is hard to explain. But unfortunately it's not like drugs or alcohol where you can abstain and be sober. That's the difference with eating disorders and why they are so deadly. Someone with an eating disorder can't just abstain from food. The key to getting healthy is learning to be aware of your appetite, to eat consciously, nourish your body, and avoid using food to deal with emotions.

My rock-bottom moment was at a photo shoot in Paris. I've told this before but I don't have to think to make it fresh. Despite throwing up as many as seven times a day, I hadn't revealed this problem to anyone. Sometimes I wished a plane would crash and end it, and with this thought would come a little relief. I remember walking on the cobblestones in the back of this alley going into the studio. Basically I'd started taking laxatives. It wasn't that every day I woke up and said, "Suppose I take twenty laxatives," it was where I gradually worked my way up—if I can say that word "up" regarding this. And the night before I took twenty or more. What I didn't realize is there's a threshold that your body can take. And that was my threshold. I was shooting happily and everything was well, and then I felt crampy and not well. I went into the bathroom and basically I saw my death. It was a terrible, terrifying feeling. I swayed and fell and everything blacked out. I found myself curled up on the tile floor, shaking, sweating, and unable to move from the cramps. I was in so much pain that I thought, "Please just let me die now. I just want it to be over." The physical pain and being trapped there in the studio where I was working was unforgettable. Then the pain passed.

That was my wake-up call where I thought, "Oh my Lord, I could die doing this. It has become really serious." Because in my mind it just wasn't. I didn't even acknowledge I was ill. But that moment was when I thought, "Oh this is serious." It was not much time before I told my boyfriend. After that I was recovering, and recovering takes time. Luckily, besides having spent an entire fortune on my teeth, I don't have other complications that have stayed with me. Many people have consequences that are much more serious than mine, and thankfully I was even able to have a child.

When I started recovering, I didn't have a therapist. That's why I went on this quest, this journey, getting the word out that there are therapists, because in Europe generally the attitude is that you've got to be nuts to go to a shrink. Then again, the shame factor was so huge that I didn't investigate sources of help. Maybe had I known there were specialized therapists for eating disorders, I would have gone.

What I don't want is a recovery of fear. That's oftentimes how someone stays away from the addiction: you give up your own power to let the abstinence take you over. A lot of countries are ruled by fear and it really wields power. If that works for you it's a wonderful way, but it isn't going to solve a food addiction. We can't be afraid of food because then we'd stumble into anorexia, and just develop another, new eating disorder. Addictions involving food are just there on a daily basis. You have to deal with them. Everyone finds a different way, and the best is not to restrict. To me the basis of any eating disorder is "I can't have this, therefore I'll have that." Restriction is a big part of our daily life, and part of the brainwashing is when we turn on the television. "Buy fat-free cookies!" And what happens? Instead of having one lovely full-of-chocolate, full-of-butter, gorgeous full-of-crumbly-sugar cookie, we'll have the fat-free kind, and end up eating the whole box!

I completely stay away from that attitude of fear and denial. For example, I don't eat anything that claims to be fat-free, because I do not identify with this whole guilt-free culture. If you run to the gym twice a day, and buy the latest cream to stay young, you start to become this consumer junkie. What profits is not the individual but the beauty industry, racking up ninety billion dollars a year because we're all made to believe if we look a certain way we're going to feel fabulous. Being a model I am very much a part of that message.

I consider myself an actor now, because I don't model much anymore, but I love modeling and despite my aversion to the superficial culture I don't at all knock modeling—I lived it my whole life. It's much fun and a great, fantastic world full of fantasy, sparkle, and glitter. But if it's taken seriously it's a dangerous world. I don't think it's a world people have much information about. Women don't realize that every cover they look at, every picture on the cover is retouched. If you have played with Photoshop you know the power of it. My advice to everyone is to buy Photoshop for Christmas and become your perfect person. Retouch yourself and see how you look, and then get bored with it, like Adonis did.

Any business where everyone is brainwashed to want a certain look is the same. One day I was given a movie and then it was taken back, which often happens. I asked my agent to find out why. To get into a movie there are all these steps where you are seen by the casting director, then the producer, and then you do a test with the actor and all that. The agent called me back and said, "Well, it's because you don't look good in the test." There was this blank on the phone and I said, "Come again?" He said, "Well, yeah, you don't look good enough, that's what they said." I said, "What do I do for a living?" He said, "You're an actress." And I said, "What did I do before?" "You were a model," he said. "And what does that mean to you?" "Look," he said, "they just didn't think you looked great on film." I said, "Maybe I don't fit the role but, honey, I *know* I look good on film. My God, that's my job, that's what I do for a living. For ten years I've been paid to look good on film. Call back and ask them why the hell they didn't give me the job!"

My point is that if you haven't been a model you are more likely to have doubts. Even a very good actress may not know how she looks on film. So you're going to believe him, and try and find your physical flaws. He'll say you didn't get the role, it's your nose. Or he'll say your hair is too dark, because his girlfriend is a blonde. And you'll say, "Fantastic, I'll lighten it." But what does he know?! Sometimes there's just no reason why a man doesn't respond to your looks or you don't get the job. In any job you deal with rejection, and in modeling and acting it's your physical body that is in a way rejected, so you have to deal with it. Ask yourself, "What do they look like, these ghost people who are the wanted ones?"

I'm not a shrink, but eating disorders to me are about feelings that aren't expressed. About trying to fit in. About hating yourself and being hard on yourself. Ultimately it's about wanting to be in control and feeling completely out of control, and food is the easiest thing to control. And the world we live in bombards us with that message that if you look a certain way you will feel a certain way and your insecurities will disappear. And of course that doesn't happen. So we keep trying and failing, because there's no way to measure up to an unattainable idea!

I think that if you have an understanding of the world we live in that it can help. For example, I was fascinated that the second you get pregnant, it's all about numbers. How many months are you, how much weight did you gain, how old is your baby—everything is about a number. When you go to the gynecologist, he doesn't say, "How do you feel?" he says, "You've gained this much weight and you're this many weeks." It's just a numbers game! Then when the baby is born it's even more so; everything revolves around numbers. It's my pet peeve! I think all of us who recover find our own path of feeling good, and mine has been on purpose not to weigh myself. Because of course I used to weigh myself a million times a day. I don't own a scale. It used to affect me that if I weighed a certain number I would feel a certain way. But when you're pregnant everyone has to ask you every minute the weight as well as how many weeks and when I answered, "Hmm, I don't know how much I gained," everybody looks at you with the most fabulous eyes. It was so delightful to be pregnant and answer that question with "I don't know."

And afterwards typically people say, "Oh, you look good, you lost so much weight." Who the hell cares? Ask me how I am and how my child is. Don't, please don't compliment me on my weight!

A few years after being recovered or in recovery—two schools of thought on that—I was chatting with a girlfriend when she broke down and said she had suffered from an eating disorder for many years. Now she had taken that step: it was wonderful, and having taken it myself I knew how hard it was. Then other people in my life started coming out of the woodwork. I realized that everyone in my life either knew someone with an eating disorder, or they had an eating disorder themselves. All I needed to do was talk about it for this positive effect. And I found a few things that were curious and definitely piqued my interest. If you are at the dinner table and people talk about a drug addiction, they're "Oh my God, what happened?" Or if it's alcohol, "Oh, I'm so sorry!" Talk about an eating disorder and peoples' stark reaction, even if not vocalized, is "Ugh!" They shrug and look away. They feel disgusted because it's gross, and the message to you is to please not talk about this. My agent, whom I love, when I told him that I had an eating disorder and wanted to talk about it said, "Ewww, that's disgusting!" God bless him: he's so honest. That told me that I needed to bring it into the open, that it's a shame that for me it went so far. Some of my clients threatened me not to mention it, which is a shame too. When I heard that I was like, "Please, now I really have to! Let me call CNN!"

So that's what I did, I talked about it. Claire Mysko and I created a forum. Claire is an eating disorder specialist, and we became best friends when I approached her about telling my story publicly. Several beauty product companies sponsored us, and we spent a year planning the approach we wanted. In 1999 we went on a tour across the country, speaking at colleges, auditoriums, and in classrooms. We created an open place where people—girl-people and guy-people—can come and share what they know, hear, or feel in their life about food, disorder, images, and mothers and fathers. In Georgia—I remember where because I called them "my peaches"—there were three hundred girls, and the principal came up and shared about his daughters. And at the end there were a hundred and fifty who had something to share. It was a wonderful but terrible thing. Wonderful to see that these girls were in an environment where they were supported, but terrible to know that so many of them were dealing with these issues.

Not that the problems are limited to one region. Claire and I made sure to go to very urban localities and also suburban. We went across the board. We found out after doing the tour that it really didn't matter. It didn't matter your background, economic status, race, or age. We were flying across the country and flight attendants would come and say, "Oh, I saw you on *20/20* and let me tell you something." And sure enough it would come out. Or the cab driver would be driving and pour it all out. Or the television interviewer would say during the break, "Oh, you know when I was little I threw up . . . and now back to your story." With some people it would take five margaritas for them to come out with it, while others would blurt the story out. And again, background, ethnicity, or bank account didn't seem to be factors.

When we planned the tour I knew I wanted it to have a purpose. I wanted to talk about my experience without the focus being "I, me, me, me, I." And the purpose was to direct people to avenues of help and to therapy. We came up with the idea to travel and be met in each locality by a therapist, which proved a good idea because once someone did get very upset, and the therapist was able to give the proper care.

We found a lot of people who didn't even have the vocabulary to know what it is that they were doing. Personally if you had told me "You're bulimic," I would have been, "I'm not." I wouldn't have known. Also people tend to use the words flippantly in our culture, saying "She's so bulimic" or "She's an anorexic." They don't understand that a bulimic is a person who purges not necessarily by vomiting but other ways, like exercise. Are people aware of that? Some might be bulimic by exercise and think, "Oh, I exercise a lot and that's fine." Meanwhile they're obsessed with food and think about their weight incessantly. That to me says you have a problem, maybe not at the level of a diagnosable disorder but it's certainly eating disordered behavior.

The antidote to its being hidden and disguised is not hiding from yourself or others. A friend of mine has developed a huge drug addiction. Before that she was anorexic. It went untreated for years, and then it developed into a drug addiction. That's very common. I toyed with the idea when I was recovering. I thought, "What the hell? What am I going to do? I need to substitute something. Surely I can't be normal, so what shall I do?" I thought maybe I could become a cocaine addict—"That will be great. It will control my weight." That's how the mind works! Consciously I also thought, "Shall I be an alcoholic?" That didn't work out either. You have no markers, nothing familiar, what we call in French *repère*. So I toyed with the idea but it didn't really work out for me.

Being normal is so frightening! The disorder says, "Surely you must find something else to replace me." Overall it's still very acceptable to say "Oh my God, I have a drug addiction." But how shameful to say "I have an eating disorder." None of us wants to stick her neck out, or stand out for this, but when Claire and I went on our tour we did stand out. Altogether this was the best thing I've ever done with my life, after having a child.

Freedom. It isn't once, to walk out
under the Milky Way, feeling the rivers
of light, the fields of dark—
freedom is daily, prose-bound, routine
remembering. Putting together, inch by inch
the starry worlds.

—Adrienne Rich, "For Memory"

Andrea Gruber
(opera star)

LINCOLN CENTER IS NOT the Baths of Caracala—no elephants or cast of thousands marched onto stage of the Metropolitan Opera for Verdi's *Aida*—but the set was spectacular, and was matched by the performance of native New Yorker Andrea Gruber as the exquisite Ethiopian slave girl.

Critics praise Andrea for the dramatic power of her voice and the lasting impressions of her operatic interpretations. Her singing has an ethereal sweetness and mystery punctuated by bursts of boundless power. A soprano, she hits the gorgeous high notes with an air of ease, and without a trace of haughtiness, as though she is having a great time. The audience is spellbound as the wonderful fusion of role and performer occurs, and we tune in not to the musical phrases but to the heart and soul of Verdi's creation.

Andrea has made a comeback after a recovery from multiple addictions, a journey as remarkable as her rise to stardom was meteoric. She was an international star in her twenties, making her Metropolitan Opera debut in 1990 in *Götterdämmerung*. Then, in

1995, when her longtime drug addiction became impossible to cover up, she was banished from the Met. Ironically, I am seeing her perform this same role at the Met a decade later.

This season she was also heard as Minne in *La Fanciulla del West* at Covent Garden, Leonora in *La Forza del Destino* with the San Francisco Opera, *Turandot* in Trieste, and Odabella in *Attila* in Naples. In concert she has sung Verdi's *Requiem* with the Atlanta Symphony at Carnegie Hall and in Atlanta.

My meeting with Andrea was at the Manhattan Deli on Broadway and 77th Street, around the corner from her apartment, and from the Ladder Co. 25 firehouse, where she is honored as a figurehead. At a low point in her life, Andrea often meandered home high on drugs, and the firefighters saw her safely into her building. Seven of those firefighters lost their lives in the 9/11 terror attacks. Andrea was very much involved in helping out at the firehouse then, and in 2002 the firefighters honored her with a medal.

The Manhattan Deli is busy day and night, and I was concerned about conducting an interview there. I was seated, however, at a table in an unusually spacious nook at the rear, which I later learned is reserved for Andrea when she is in town between engagements.

What a stark contrast! On Monday I saw a dusky Aida wrapped in a seductive white dress with a profusion of black braids. Mid-afternoon Tuesday, a very hip short-haired Upper West Sider with an ebullient air entered the deli and made her way to me. It took a while. The staff responded like an ensemble. She waved and gave a big smile, she chatted and laughed, then she admired a baby and said hello to a woman I recognized as Dr. Ruth Westheimer. It is a phenomenon dear to New Yorkers that stars are treated as regular customers in their habitual cafés and restaurants.

As we spoke, my impression was confirmed that Andrea's "big personality" was exactly that, a big personality without any element of pretension. She was funny and warm and smart. She had a bright speaking voice with a touch of a New York accent. There was a slight enjambment between her sentences, but her voice was natural and expressive, not theatrical. In fact what seemed "over the top" wasn't the voice but the scintillating dark eyes that glitter like diamonds.

As a great American opera star, Andrea is creating a unique legacy. She is as lovable as the gritty, urbane version of the girl next door. She has found a path of genius yet stays in touch with the rest of us. Her triumphs over long and dreadful struggles connect us to her.

—J.M.

＊

Ten years ago Halloween, which is kind of creepy—October 31, 1995—I sang my last Aida on stage at the Metropolitan Opera. I got fired because I was so stoned I could barely stand up. It was eight months more before I got sober. Since then I've had a lot of big successes at the Met like *Nabucco* and *Turandot,* but this is the first time I've sung Aida again.

I'm not a nervous singer. I'm grateful to be alive and singing for joy, but last Thursday I was really nervous because I had all kinds of weird sense memory. I had flashbacks where I was sitting on that same rock as the Aida at the Metropolitan Opera. So it was really strange. This is just one of these things: I needed to sing these five performances—and then never to do it again, you know. *Aida* is not my favorite opera to sing in the whole world at this point anymore. But I needed to get back on the horse on that opera, in that opera house. I was just grateful to have been able to go up and do it.

I just turned forty on November 28. I'm proud of every second of my life now. I had a long history with addictions of one kind or other and got sober for the first time when I was nineteen.

I grew up on the Upper West Side of New York. I started getting high when I was eleven. I was pretty troubled from the beginning. There was police involvement the first time I got high. I smoked pot and passed out. It happened when I was on the phone with a friend of mine's mother. She had called the house where I was with some people and she was looking for one of them, and I passed out. And she freaked out and called the police. That was my first run-in with the law. And so from then on it was pretty much more of the same for many, many years. There was constantly, always alcohol. That was not my drug of choice, but I did my share of drinking.

And before drugs I had an obsession with food. There was a very great control issue in my family about food. I remember going to a friend's as a child and seeing in her bedroom candy bars and sweets on the counter, and I just about fell over. It was like going into a fairyland. I said, "You're allowed to have those?" She said, "What are you talking about?" Because in my house sweets were hidden from me, literally in locked closets. I don't know why they did that. It wasn't the luxury aspect. I didn't know whether my father was just into denying me things, whether he feared I'd be fat, though I was slim until I got fat when I was stealing money from him to buy candy. You take something from a kid and they're going to want it badly. It was unusual, this kind of denial. They used to hide Pepperidge Farm cookies in a cabinet behind all the pots of plants, and then I found them and used to eat them. There is absolutely no reason that I would have been fat had I not been set up to have this relationship with food that was all about having to sneak things out to get them. If they'd just given me the damn cookie, I wouldn't have eaten a whole bag. I don't eat a whole bag now because I can eat whatever I want. If it's okay, it's no big deal. When you know someone's holding something from you, it's forbidden and you're going to want it, especially if you're a kid. I still, when I see a pack of Pepperidge Farm cookies, view it like a bag of dope, because I recall what it felt like when I used to sneak into the cabinet to steal the bag of cookies, growing up.

It was a lot of craziness. My first treatment came when I was nineteen. I went to inpatient with a lot of guys. I was the only woman in treatment. This was 1985 so it was basically boot camp for sobriety. They would kick your ass and beat you up about it, and I'd had enough humiliation in my life at home and elsewhere, so this wasn't a very helpful approach for me. The real problem there was that they told me I wasn't an alcoholic, that I was a drug addict. So when I graduated I was given drinking privileges, which in those days was quite common. They would segregate you as a drug addict from the alcoholics. In reality the addictions overlap. I'm an alcoholic, I'm a drug addict, and I'm sorry if at a recovery meeting it offends anybody to discuss them as one addiction. I say that I'm here at a meeting because I need to stay clean and sober to stay alive. I have a problem with segregating those who suffer from different types of addiction because I'm a hard-core drug addict, and a twelve-step recovery program saved my life.

The singing was just an accident in that music was always a huge part of my life. I played the flute from the time I was very young. I thought that was what I was going to do professionally, except that I was really gifted but I hated to practice because I was more interested in getting high. So from the time I was twelve my musical gift for playing the flute was very great, and my willingness to work was very minimal. Somebody suggested that I study voice at a music conservatory in the summer. I was playing the flute, and I auditioned for the singing stuff just for fun, and the woman who ran the voice program said, "Oh, you have an incredible instrument, you should start to study."

I was in secondary school in Vermont at the Putney School, so when I was sixteen—this was my junior year there—I went to the Manhattan School of Music, and I started to study voice. From there I went to the Met, to the Young Artist program. Singing was an accident, and I had a gift. There is pressure in singing as a vocation, and it affected me a lot when I was getting high. I imagined it my responsibility, because I had a gift, to pursue singing intensely as a career. I have come to realize you don't have to pursue a gift. You do so only if it makes you happy. I loved singing but, you know, my whole life I felt like a fraud. More than anything else, in every facet of life, I felt like a fraud.

This part does go back to my family. You know, my whole life I wasn't good enough. I was always told that I didn't measure up. And so suddenly when I was a teenager I rebelled, and always tried to please my father but never succeeded. My father is Austrian, and he fled with his parents from

Hitler in 1939. He was twelve. He came from a well-to-do-family. My grandmother was Catholic but converted to Judaism to marry my grandfather. And when they fled from the Nazis they came to the States, basically with a hundred dollars among the four of them. And I think one of two things can often happen to you when you are torn from your world and immigrate like that. You can either become a great humanitarian or a little Hitler. And you can figure out for yourself which of the two my father became.

So, beginning with the food obsession and the drugs, I was trying to prove something that was unprovable. When I became a famous opera star, then he wanted back in my life, of course. I stopped seeing my father a number of years ago when I got sober, but the *New York Times* did a big piece on me last year, detailing my singing career and my struggles with addiction, and I heard through the grapevine that my father said, "Really, she shouldn't have done that. That's going to ruin her career." And I thought, "Oh, you just don't get it." So basically my whole life was spent trying to prove to an abusive person that I was worth something.

I was lucky. I certainly could have had opposition, yet no one objected to my being a musician. My parents were both history professors and had an appreciation of culture, so I don't fault them; it's not that. But I grew up not being good enough for them.

So I go to the Metropolitan Opera at twenty-one years old, two years out of treatment, already starting to take pills, feeling the world's greatest fraud, and having one of the world's greatest conductors telling me that everything he'd learned he'd learned for me, because he was waiting for me to come along. You know, that expectation and I'm a kid and I'm a junkie.

So I really felt very much like a fraud, and the drugs just continued numbing me out from any feelings that I had, as they had for my whole life. The feelings may have been different but I was numb, and it was all the same to me. I certainly wasn't equipped to deal with any of that pressure, but it was the same idea as what happened to me in treatment. One day I went in there, and I was a piece of shit, and the next day people were saying I was a role model. Then they said, "Out, your time to go—out the door! Andrea, your time is up. You're a role model. Live and be an example!"

Everybody has a different path of recovery and mine is that my big step to sobriety came when I was kicked out of a treatment center. I went there because I had almost died in Vienna from a blood clot due to an overdose. My best friend and my manager, as well as other people, were trying to get me home; they were afraid I would die in Vienna, and they wanted to get me back into the hospital. When I got there I was very, very sick, and I was detoxing very badly from the morphine, and I was up to a hundred Percocet a day then. I really was sick. And because of my extensive history—I'd been in and out of rehab, different facilities, three times. I'd also been in and out of detox, and now I was very sick and they wanted me to go into long-term treatment. And I said I wouldn't go, and they said if I wouldn't go then I'd have to leave.

My wish to leave had nothing to do with my work. On the property of the rehab was a lake. My dorm overlooked the lake, and then there was a huge hill and up the hill was a tall tree and a bench. Now I had this blood clot in my leg, and I was about a hundred pounds heavier than I am now. My leg was taped from my toes to the crotch. I was huge, I was sweaty, it was summer, and I was gross. They presented me with this option for long-term treatment. I toured the facility and then I proceeded to literally half walk, half crawl up that hill to go sit on the bench and think about it. And I was detoxing, I was sick and it was a nightmare, and I sat on that bench and—you hear people talk about this all the time in recovery—I had this moment of clarity which was . . . I had been in and out of treatment since I was nineteen, yet all of the friends I had were clean and sober. At this point I was going to meetings while still getting high. Meanwhile all of my friends, the people in my life, were in recovery and didn't have drugs and alcohol in their lives. So I had this moment of clarity. "Maybe if I just do what they do, and listen to what they say, and really give it a try, I can actually do this. I have all this information, I have had all of this support, why don't I go home and try it?" My reasoning had nothing to do with singing. I didn't care if I ever sang again.

So I stumbled down the hill, and I told them that I wasn't going to stay. And they said, "You have to leave." I'd been there only sixteen days and it was a twenty-eight-day program and I was very sick and detoxing terribly.

I called home. My friends, I'll never forget my assistant saying, "You're going to die. I'm not going to stand this." They were so worried for me. It took them so much to get me there. But my primary care physician agreed to detox me at home, to give me the medicine that I required—which was unbelievable. I came home. My friends dragged me around—detoxing, sick, fat, disgusting, pathetic—took me everywhere. I counted my days. I went to recovery meetings. And I've been sober ever since. And it was just that I had this moment of clarity. It wasn't I knew I'd never get high again, because I don't feel that sitting here today: that's not what being sober is about. But I had a window of opportunity, and after all of those years of fighting and struggling I thought—I didn't know what I felt—this sort of moment of hope. And I just went with it. I didn't know what the hell I was doing. I just went with it.

So after the rehab ejected me I stayed in touch with my counselors and one year later I went back to treatment, and I got to speak with the whole community, and I got the commemorative coin they would have presented to me had I actually graduated appropriately, and it was just the coolest thing. So now when I sing, I sing with all my coins in my bra, or if the costume is worn without a bra, I have them sew a little pocket in so I can have my coins in my costume. Very cool!

There are a couple of causalities for my addiction to drugs and food. As a kid, as any other addict will tell you, I didn't fit it. I was extremely sensitive. I felt too much. I was like one big raw nerve, and I felt everybody's pain, as a small child. That's not normal for small children. And when I talk to other addicts, whether they're rock stars or teachers or construction workers or whatever, they all share that experience. That just has to do with some kind of wiring.

Then there's the home stuff, and, you know, people have very different experiences with that. Some people I know had wonderful, lovely, supportive environments. Mine was not like that. I think that I was a prime candidate to be a drug addict. I don't know about the history of alcoholism in my family. There's a whole lot of denial on so many levels in my family, on so many things, that it may be a while before I can get a handle on it all, and frankly I don't much care. I know a lot of people who feel the need, perhaps, to know if it's a biological thing. To me it's irrelevant because one way or the other I'm a junkie. Whether I was born that way or whether I became that way it doesn't matter, it's who I am. It's as much of who I am as anything else. It defines everything that I do. In some ways I'm very lucky to be in a business where it isn't something that I have to hide. Because I have friends whose relatives don't even know that they're recovering alcoholics. They haven't had a drink in ten years. People may have noticed it but they don't know that they're sober.

I think also there's a piece of being young and being a junkie where you think that you're invincible. And then there's the death wish part where you just don't care. For me it was more that than anything else. I thought I'd be dead before I was twenty, and I didn't care. I truly didn't. I was not one of those people who thought I was invincible, like I would live forever no matter what I did. It wasn't like that. I was not a happy-go-lucky or fun party person. You know, you see kids all the time who go out and love to party. That was not me at all. I was more the fatalist. I totally identified my sickness with Janis Joplin, who is still my idol. I identified with her in so many ways. I identified with her being ostracized at school, for her gift, for being addicted, for all of that—and with the level of abandon that she had in her music and her self-destruction. When you think about what she could have done had she gotten sober!

It's a classic problem of many artists and writers. I checked myself in twice. Once when I was sober, because I cut myself up badly with a razor blade when I was two years sober and had a bad patch. There's a lot more to getting sober than not drinking and drugging. And for me when I tried to kill myself was when I truly realized that the work that I had to do came when the choice was made: "Okay, I'm not going to pick up, I think I want to die." And I have to take that next step. And so I sliced myself open and my best friend took me to the hospital. I don't know that I would have died, but I hurt myself pretty badly. I was in a suicide watch for a couple of days, and then they took me by ambulance up to a place upstate where I stayed for a month, something like that. It was twenty-eight days, probably. And I took a year—eight or nine months, something like that. I was up in New York state at Shady Pines, as my assistant loves to call it. (He has called all of my treatment periods "Shady Pines.") It was a real interesting place. There were people there getting sober, there were people there who were bipolar, there were people who were out of their fucking minds, and then there was me, who was sober but who had tried to kill herself. And I was there to heal. While I was having this very interesting experience I gained a hundred more pounds. I walked out of there at 320 pounds. I waddled out of there. It was so part of my healing, because I was getting so vulnerable physically from everything coming into me. Now I can protect myself emotionally so I can look like this and not have to work at issues, because I know what they are, and I can take care of myself.

At that point I needed every ounce of fat that I had, plus it kept me from—I would have killed myself had I not been that fat. My best friend said afterwards, "Thank God you were so fat. Because the doctor told me, had you not been that fat, you would have hit an artery and that would have been it, you would have been gone."

That was eight years ago and I took the better part of the following year, eight or nine months, and I stayed in bed, and I healed in my cocoon, with my golden retriever, Max. And I went to recovery meetings when I could, and I went to therapy when I could. I was in a DBT group: dialectical behavioral therapy. I still don't know what that is, but I showed up every day for God knows how long. And apparently it helped. Nobody seems to know how to define it but it helped. So I did that and I seem to remember that I started to get really simple and honest in pinpointing what it felt like to be me.

That's pretty much what I did. That's the core of what you have to do. Identify what it feels like where you are at the moment. When I was in treatment at nineteen we used to get out the feeling wheel. I'd look at that and think, "What's this?" There must have been thirty emotions depicted on drawings of faces. Happy, sad, angry, lonely, grumpy, horny—it bewildered me; I couldn't identify with what they were feeling. Because if you're an addict you are either furious or wasted. I mean, that was it. I didn't know any other feelings.

And really, you have to become like a child when you're getting sober. "Identify the feeling!" "I'm hungry!" "Eat something." . . . "I'm sleepy!"

"Well, if you don't have to work, take a fucking nap!" . . . "You know I'm angry?" "Tell me if you're angry. Tell me about it." . . . "I'm sad." "Cry!"

And you really can go on. For those of us who numbed ourselves with drugs for years of our lives, it "ain't natural." It doesn't come naturally. You have to learn how to express the basic things.

So I had to sort of get back to basics and figure out what it felt like just to feel. And it was unbelievably painful: the wreckage of my past. First of all, physically it was a nightmare, because I had done a lot of damage. My life was a mess. I was detoxing for the better part of two-and-a-half years of my sobriety.

Regeneration is an amazing thing. I have pictures of when I came in. The therapist of the first facility told me when I came in—I was twenty-five—she said, "You look like this fifty-year-old woman. Drugs have just kicked the shit out of you." And they do. It's not pretty. It really ravages you out. And it's not easy coming back.

The thing with the bypass surgery is that it's so funny. At my absolute heaviest I had been working out at the gym. I was always very athletic, and I was boxing and kickboxing and doing all this stuff at 300 pounds with a friend of mine, Wilton. To stay that fat was sick. He was the one, though, who got me to the gym and worked me out. He was the greatest thing, and since that time we became very good friends. (For my fortieth birthday I was home for a day between San Francisco and Italy and John the waiter decorated the whole back place of the diner, and Wilton and his girlfriends and a lot of my friends showed up.)

For a long time my golden retriever, Max, was my contact with the world. The great thing was that Max needed to go out and we went out. No matter how stoned or fat I was he needed his walk, and he was so beautiful that people would stop and talk to him. And no matter how fucked up or isolated I was, there was still that part of me that was very outgoing, so he would get me involved in the world. Max is pretty much the only reason that I got involved in the firehouse, because, you know, they always have cookies for dogs. So Max was eight months old when I brought him home, and the firemen kind of adopted Max, and they took care of me.

Maybe because I wasn't one of the flirty girls in the building, or one of the cute passersby. It wasn't that. I was so far away from that that I think, you see—now that I'm part of that family—we will joke when a pretty girl walks by. I know the way they talk about women because I'm with them when they do it. Because I was nothing like that, I had such low self-esteem or whatever. Obviously half those guys are dead now, and four retired since 9/11; it's a completely different crew.

On September 12, I was supposed to fly to Berlin to make a recording. September 11 was an election day, and my golden retriever and I got up in the morning and went and voted. We went to get a bagel. Someone at the bagel place said something about a plane or whatever and what I heard was—you know I am a native New Yorker—that some fucking helicopter, one of those rich people, flew their helicopter, and of course it was going to hit a building, and inevitably that was going to happen . . . That's what I heard. Then all hell broke loose, and needless to say I couldn't go to Berlin, I couldn't go anywhere. I spent the next couple of weeks at the fire station with the guys doing whatever had to be done . . . And it was a nightmare. You'd walk around this neighborhood that first day, and basically the first thing I did was, Max and I went to all the hardware stores to buy up all the industrial flashlights for the guys because they didn't have proper equipment to go down and do search and rescue. So I went and did that. Whatever you could think of because you'd walk on the street and somebody would be on a cell phone, and suddenly they'd just drop because they'd get some news. So you'd be walking down the street, pick up people and say, "Are you okay? Where can I take you?" You wouldn't believe what it was like. People were dropping like flies on the street, breaking down, and the diner was like ground central for our neighborhood. We would come in and we would check who was accounted for. So for the next however many weeks I was sort of living at the firehouse. My best friend was in New York at that point. She's a massage therapist and she'd had a back surgery but she would come in and work on the guys when they got down from the pit. They'd be down there digging all day. We got the guys food. We'd sit with them. Whatever. I'd known these guys for fifteen years.

The year after 9/11 they gave me this medal I wear which is the symbol of the firefighters. I'd sung a bunch of memorial services. In true fashion it's engraved on the back, "To Andrea from the guys." I'm not often rendered speechless but I was completely speechless when they gave this to me. It is my most treasured possession.

And something happened to me during this period. It was like life was so sort of—it's pathetic to say that, and I didn't want to spend another second preoccupied by how uncomfortable I was in my skin. It had nothing to do with the way I looked. And I didn't want to feel grossly overweight, and that was all there was to it.

I had to return to Buenos Aires and sing a concert. It had been mentioned to me a number of times about having surgery to reduce my weight. The first time it was mentioned to me, I said, "What? Are you talking about me? No way am I a hundred pounds overweight." I was mortified. Me? I didn't believe it. I already had a connection to the surgeon because my nutritionist worked with him, so I called him up. This was four years ago, so it was before the big craze. I made an appointment and when I got back from Buenos Aires, the next week I had the surgery.

My attitude was I didn't care if I ever sang again. It had nothing to do with that. First of all, I was in perfect health. I was just fat. So I was really a perfect candidate. I went in there totally healthy. I'm the poster child for the procedure. As you can see I can eat anything. I don't eat a lot. The weight came off. I was able to exercise.

The most important thing about having a gastric bypass, and this is the piece I don't think they'll ever be able to find out about, is that my obsession with food has been lifted. I have a huge bowl of Hersey's Kisses. I've got more sweets in my house: it's something I buy and it's there forever. My mother comes in and she says, "How can you have this stuff in your house?" She freaks because she herself is completely a food junkie. But that's how it is. My obsession with food has been lifted. I eat a piece of chocolate if I want a piece of chocolate, and then I'll be full. If I want a piece of cake I eat a few bites and then I'm done.

It's that simple. My obsession is over. It's got to be the surgery because, to draw a parallel, my obsession with drugs has not been lifted. I still have moments where my cravings just knock me off my ass, where the beast rears up in my belly and it's like, "God, I need my morphine now." It passes.

But I don't have that with food anymore, and I used to not be able to stop. Now I have an option. I didn't have that before the surgery. They have no explanation for that. They do surgery and people go on the table with diabetes and they come off the table not having lost an ounce, without diabetes. Why? How come? How does that happen?

I didn't have high cholesterol or high blood pressure, so I was healthy, but I'll never forget in the beginning the first time I went into a normal-sized clothing store I nearly cried. The first time I bought a piece of expensive clothing. I mean, I'm not a clothes horse, but I went through a period where I bought a lot of designer clothes just because I could. I went into Fendi and bought a coat or I bought a Chanel jacket. Unbelievable!

And as far as guys are concerned it's just bizarre. Because I'm the same girl I always was, and I always was very outgoing. Now I'm outgoing and lots of men want to sleep with me, and that's bizarre. Because I forget sometimes what I look like. So when I'm around people it doesn't occur to me they might be attracted to me physically. I was very blessed in the beginning in my recovery program: because I was fat no one hit on me. So I was able to just get sober. I mean, you see some of these girls come in and they're showing their bellies in the summer, and they're all cute and whatever, and they get completely sidetracked. So when I sponsor girls like that I become a Mama Bear. I'm like, "Don't you go near my sponsee! Get away! Bad boy! Back off!" No, really! I'm very protective because this is about life and death; recovery is not a game. And the girls, so many of them, not all of them, have sickness and craziness around them as we all do, and they come in and they've barely stopped drinking, and some guy's going to save your life, and make you well. And it's like, "Please, just go!"

So in some ways as pathetic as I felt, and as horrible as it was, I was very lucky because I didn't have to deal with any of that. I used to have long blond extensions and I cut them off when I got my hair auburn. Now I walk down the street and friends of mine who've known me for years, for example, will be checking me out. They'll say, "Oh my God, it's you, Andrea!" And I think it's so funny—you know me for ten years and don't even realize that it's me. And sometimes I find it a little disgusting. There are some people who can be really rude. But I'm a big girl. I'm forty years old. It's fine.

Now I feel like this person and not that person. And though eating now can be a pleasure, I think of it more as sustenance. I try to listen to what my body's hungry for. Sometimes I have cravings for a taste of something. Right now I have a herniated disk in my neck. I'm trying to avoid surgery so I've had a couple of epidurals, and when I have them a side effect for a week or so is weight loss. So I lost twenty more pounds that I really didn't want to, and I have next to no appetite. That's not good for my work as well as my life. It's ironic that I of all people have this side effect. But for me the surgery was exactly right. Today I face my emotions, I exercise because it makes me feel good, and I eat normally without obsession of any degree.

If I was unable to express my anger to my parents, at least I could express it to myself. I could grab, I could bite, I could gnaw. I could force as much food into myself as I wanted to, even when my body begged for rest. I could take the anger out on myself. And I could imagine my father or mother reading my body like a text.
See how angry I am at you? I was silently saying to them. It's written all over my body.

—Margaret Bullitt-Jonas,
Holy Hunger: A Memoir of Desire

Margaret Bullitt-Jonas
(pastor)

WITH HER PEACEFUL COUNTENANCE, mild professorial manner, and lilting laugh, it is hard to believe that Margaret Bullitt-Jonas, committed pastor and Harvard-trained scholar of literature, was ever governed by the demon of an eating disorder. Yet this arduous past is part of her spiritual quest and present activism.

Born in 1951 in Cambridge, Massachusetts, she grew up on the campus of Harvard University, where her father, a professor of eighteeth-century English literature, served as master of Quincy House. She eventually left for California, where she earned a B.A. with honors in Russian literature from Stanford University. After working as a VISTA volunteer in downtown Philadelphia, she returned to Harvard and completed a doctoral program in comparative literature. Taking time out from academic studies, Margaret worked for a year as residential coordinator for a group of schizophrenic men. At this time she also helped organize a family intervention into her own father's alcoholism.

Holy Hunger, her astonishing, elegantly written memoir, tells the story of how she broke loose from the grip of the secret eating disorder that had plagued her for two decades. As she discovered the source of her hunger, she clarified her fundamental life commitments and freed herself to pursue them.

In 1984, Margaret received her Ph.D. and entered seminary. Four years later she was ordained in the Episcopal Church. A parish priest in the Boston area for fifteen years, she now serves as priest associate at Grace Episcopal in Amherst, Massachusetts. From 1992 until 2005 she was also a lecturer at the Episcopal Divinity School, teaching courses on prayer, spiritual formation, and the spirituality of addiction. Margaret leads retreats and conferences around the country, and since the publication of *Holy Hunger* has been increasingly engaged in environmental activism. In recent years her retreats and speaking engagements have often focused on reclaiming the sacredness of the earth, and on placing care for it at the center of our moral and spiritual concerns.

Among the people profiled in this book, Margaret is perhaps the exception in that she is not, by most measures, a "celebrity." Her influence, however, can be profound. As I prepared to meet her, despite my own secular orientation, I acquired Margaret's second book, *Christ's Passion, Our Passions,* written after September 11. A collection of meditations on Jesus' last words, the book explores the dimensions of life's journey, the depths of loss and suffering, finding peace, and our search to become better people, true to ourselves. It is so rich in ideas, in language so clear and simple, that I pored over it night after night, taking spiritual nourishment.

—J.M.

I grew up in a home of privilege, education, and wealth. My father was a professor of English literature at Harvard, and was master of Quincy

House, one of Harvard's famed living quarters. My mother was a Radcliffe-educated, wealthy daughter of a newspaper family in the Midwest. Outwardly everything looked happy, secure, accomplished, and successful, but in fact, my family—like many other families, as I later discovered—was quite dysfunctional. My father was alcoholic, though I never realized that at the time and would never have named it that way: I always thought of an alcoholic as the bum sitting on the curb. And my mother was quite depressed in the years that I was growing up.

The way I remember the story of my developing an eating disorder is that it was a house where a great deal was unspeakable. The truth of our experience as individuals and as a family couldn't be named or shared. I later read in the literature that this is typical of alcoholics, or shame-based families: we grow up with rules such as, "Don't talk, don't trust, don't feel." I think Claudia Black came up with that formulation for the hidden family rules. I grew up believing that it was very important to look good, and very important to maintain appearances. In public each of us as individuals, and I think as a family, worked very hard to look good. And we passed. We passed as normal. But within the confines of the family itself, and within our own hearts, there was so much loneliness, and sadness, and anger. I later learned that children who grow up in alcoholic homes or shame-based families never witness real feelings, only the defenses against feelings. We may grow up with a lot of anxiety, or hearing a lot of rage, and we never learn how to make contact with another human being, how to simply share what's in our heart.

So I grew up feeling very isolated, and early on, food began to take on a much larger importance in my psychological life than it should have had. I found myself clinging to that extra bite, or slipping a little food in my pocket after a meal. There was some way in which I felt that food wouldn't let me down, that food would always be there for me, food would comfort me, food would keep me safe. I invested my relationship with food with enormous power.

I noticed food even when I was little, but it didn't take off as a real eating disorder until I reached adolescence. I know that this is true for many young women: we begin to have trouble in our relationship with food right around adolescence, as we embark on that struggle to differentiate and to separate ourselves from our family and confront all kinds of basic questions: Who am I as a separate self? And what's my life about? What am I going to do when I grow up? All the conflicts emerge about whether to grow up or to hold on. And of course I went through all that. The timing of my family's eventual breakup was also difficult for me. When I was fourteen, my parents separated, and my dad resigned as master of Quincy House and took a leave of absence to be in the Peace Corps for a couple of years. Harvard's administration asked him to leave because he was close to a nervous breakdown. His drinking was really taking a toll on him and on his capacity to function as a teacher.

This all came to a head in the mid-sixties. I finished in my middle school and I went off to boarding school in the fall of '66, and that was the great "fall" when we left the House at Harvard, and my father went off to start training for his job in the Peace Corps, and my mother decided not to join him in Bolivia but to stay in Cambridge. Our family was falling apart, and I was alone at boarding school, very lonely, sad, and confused, and I turned to sugar. Sugar became my great solace to get me through those very tough months and years. I discovered bingeing, and I discovered the whole subculture of girls in boarding schools who go on diets together and avidly compare notes about whether they are gaining weight or losing weight, and what they are going to eat and not going to eat.

What's tricky about addictions of any kind, and eating disorders in particular, is that at first they work. At first, when you take that handful of cookies or that drink or smoke, you do feel better. It does relieve the anxiety or the whatever-it-was, the uncomfortable feeling you'd been trying to avoid. So at first it seems like a really good move. But the nature of addiction is that it escalates.

I think there's a good distinction to be made between someone who goes through a spell of disordered eating for a time and someone with an eating disorder. Let's say you've broken up with your boyfriend or had some loss or shock in your life. Maybe you sit down and eat a quart of ice cream or something, but in the next day or two you find that your eating patterns are back on track. That is simply disordered eating.

But at a certain point disordered eating can develop into a full-blown eating disorder that takes on a life of its own. It feels like being possessed, like being suddenly transported to another planet. Sometimes it felt as if a dark cloud had come over me. Somehow I would find myself breathing this atmosphere in which suddenly I had to eat, and I'd feel a completely compulsive, compelling, urgent, anxious drive to put some food in my mouth. And I would hear an argument start up inside my head because the healthy part of me was still able to stand back and say, "What's going on? You're not hungry. Your body's full. You feel physically fine." I'd develop this inner combat of conflicting voices. Once I got into that battle, I always lost. I always ended up in the pantry or the refrigerator.

That, to me, is one of the first signs of addiction: loss of control over when you start the behavior and when you stop the behavior. When you lose control over starting, you think, "I didn't plan to be eating this bag of cookies but they just kind of jumped into my mouth." When you lose control over stopping, you say to yourself, "This is the last one. But maybe I'll take just one more. I promise I won't have any more after this one. Well, maybe I'll take just a couple more, and that will be the last one." And you find yourself unable to stop because you've lost control. I consider that one key sign of addiction.

What I did after bingeing was to exercise like mad. This is a form of bulimia: non-purging bulimia. I never used laxatives or made myself throw up, thank God. The more we do to harm our body, the harder it probably is to recover. But I did try to compensate for these binges of eating with long fasts. In college I would fast for five days at a time. I counted it up at the end of freshman year: I'd fasted thirty days out of however many days I had been in college. So I'd either fast or do some sort of white-knuckle diet, or go out on exercise binges and run seven miles a day rain or shine, in heat waves, in snow storms, it didn't matter. Feel sick? Too bad! I'd get out there and run, and it was very punishing and self-hating. I was trying to burn calories as fast as I could in order to make up for what I'd been putting in my mouth. It was basically crazy.

My family could see my weight going up and down, but I never got really fat. My weight went up and down between about twenty-five and thirty-five pounds. I'm sure I've gained and lost hundreds of pounds in my lifetime. I'd go up and I'd go down, and if anyone commented about my weight, I'd dodge the remark, or I'd lie. Except for a few dieting buddies in boarding school, I never told anyone what I was doing. It was a life of secrecy and isolation.

At school I worked very hard. I was a very successful student striving to please my father and to live up to his expectations. It took me a long time to realize that this was a game in which I was set up to fail, because there was no way I would ever win the ultimate approval from him that I was looking for. But for years I kept busy looking for good grades and for approval from my father and my teachers. I sailed through boarding school and went off to Stanford for college.

I started Stanford in 1969, at the height of the Vietnam War. I couldn't figure out how to place myself in the community because I was against the war but didn't want to throw rocks at the library. So I took a breather my sophomore year, what Erik Erickson would probably call a "moratorium": I went off to Newfoundland for a year, and it was wonderful. I taught in a kindergarten in a little village on the northern coast. Then I came back and finished at Stanford.

I was wrestling with what my life's work should be. I loved words and fiction and literature and the life of the imagination, but I was also very committed to social change and social justice. I was trying to put those two together. At Stanford I majored in Russian language and literature, and when I graduated, I decided to test out whether or not I should become a lawyer. I did a year in VISTA, the domestic Peace Corps, and worked in a public interest law center in Philadelphia. I understood pretty quickly that the law was not my calling. It required a kind of systematic, logical thinking and a taste for combat that I just didn't have. There are some lawyers on my father's side of the family, but I realized that law just wasn't the way that my love of words should be expressed. While working in the law center, I would sometimes lock myself in the ladies' room and memorize poetry. It was obvious that the law and I did not make a good match!

In the end I came back to Harvard as a graduate student in comparative literature. I chose Harvard partly because I dimly knew that I needed to confront my past and to get a handle on where I'd come from. I needed to begin to sort out my life. Even so, for a long time at Harvard I kept up the same old pattern of outwardly looking good, so that I was winning awards and looking like a stellar graduate student, but inwardly, oh, I was full of self-doubt and insecurity, and not sleeping, and bingeing in secret. And if I wasn't bingeing I was running, and if I wasn't bingeing or running, I was worrying about when was I going to start bingeing again.

I had a few close women friends but I didn't tell anyone what I was doing with food or how it was eating up my life. Early on I had one really dear boyfriend whom I now think of fondly as an exceptionally fine person, a good stable guy. But eventually we broke up, and I'm sure that my issues around intimacy and addiction contributed to that. After the end of that relationship I went through a long stretch of being drawn to men who were remarkably like the parts of my father that I didn't like. I suspect that this is very typical of women with complicated relationships with their dads.

I don't think I fully knew how unhappy I was. Addiction can keep a person quite numb and anesthetized. All I knew was that I was lonely and anxious and that my life felt out of control. For me the turning point came after struggling with my eating disorder for sixteen years.

Not long ago someone gave me a very helpful image for understanding the turning point in an addict's life. An addict is like someone pushing a wheelbarrow, and every time someone says to the addict, "I'm concerned about your drinking," or "I'm concerned about your eating," or "I'm concerned about what you're doing with sex or drugs or the Internet or gambling"—or whatever behavior the person is obsessively attached to—it is like putting a rock in the wheelbarrow. The wheelbarrow gets a bit harder to push. At some point, through the grace of God, the time may come when it becomes more painful to push that stupid wheelbarrow than to put it down and face the pain of recovery. I do think it's worth saying, very honestly, that recovery is painful. When you begin recovery, you go through the pain of withdrawal, which may be physical, psychological, or a combination of both. You also have to face the pain of finally feeling all those emotions that you've been avoiding and squashing down, lo these many years! But that's the kind of pain that leads to life. That's the kind of pain that leads us to wholeness and freedom, in contrast to the pain of going nowhere, forever pushing that idiot wheelbarrow.

One thing I like about the metaphor is that even if your rock isn't the final rock that gets the addict to drop the wheelbarrow, it's still worth putting your rock in. Your rock may add to other people's rocks, until finally the addict decides to choose life and to get into recovery. The metaphor is helpful, too, because it reminds us that we should put the rock in the wheelbarrow, not throw it at the addict. I say that because if you've ever been close to an addict, you know how frustrating it can be, how infuriating it can be to watch a person destroying himself and his relationships. It can be tempting to throw your rock at the addict, so I always tell people, "No, no, put it in the wheelbarrow!"

By the early eighties, plenty of people were putting their rocks in my wheelbarrow. My own turnaround started with confronting my father's alcoholism, which began with a good long year of preparation for a formal intervention into his drinking. This meant that I was beginning to learn about and study addiction and how it works. I was finally in conversation with an addiction counselor, talking about my father's drinking. I began to understand how his drinking had affected me, and I think that on some level I was beginning to take in the fact that my own relationship to food was completely analogous to his relationship to alcohol.

So that was a big rock. Other things conspired to make me face myself, including the apparent suicide of a coworker. I took a leave of absence from Harvard because I was perpetually stuck in writing my dissertation. I just couldn't get myself to finish it, and I was very conflicted about what the heck I was doing at Harvard in the first place, and what I wanted out of life. I took a year off and worked with a social service agency to help a group of men with schizophrenia make the move from a hospital setting into a halfway house. During that year one of my coworkers died, and as far as I know it was a suicide, even though her family denied that. Her death confronted me with the basic choice that I was facing. Was I going to continue along this deathly path, or was I going to choose life?

My eating disorder reached a level of crisis after my coworker's death and after the intervention into my father's drinking. I had poured a great deal of energy into paying attention to my father and his addiction, and as a result of the intervention he finally did agree to go into a thirty-day treatment program. The family had broken through its denial: my father was alcoholic; everyone in the family had been suffering; my childhood hadn't been the happy fantasy that I'd pretended to myself that it was. So a lot of pain from the past began to surface, and I couldn't face any of it. I couldn't face the mourning that I needed to do. My eating went crazy. I'd gobble down a pie before eating lunch with a friend and then go out afterwards and buy myself another pie and a loaf of bread and a box of English muffins, and eat them all, very fast. I'd eat stacks of pancakes in a sitting—what I used to call "suicide food." I gained eleven pounds in four days, and I still couldn't stop eating. I never ate in public. I did it all secretly, and I was becoming more and more withdrawn, more and more desperate and afraid. I felt completely out of control.

One of the last rocks in my wheelbarrow came from a friend. Addiction is a disease of isolation, but I did have one close friend who hung in there with me and who eventually confronted me with love. Her concern helped push me to turn my life around. My dear friend Gillian said, "Margaret, it's as if you're covered with Styrofoam—I can't make contact with you." She could see that I was putting up walls. And basically she said, "You need to face your pain. And if you don't face your pain we can't have any kind of relationship." It was just like the intervention into my father's drinking: she was pushing me to stop running from reality and to claim my life.

The final turnaround came shortly afterward when I woke up one morning from a dream. I dreamed that I was looking across a field and noticed that a curtain was covering the sky. And in the dream I was saying, in a dreamy sort of way, "Doesn't it feel cozy to be safely closed in like this?" I woke up in a rage, wanting to tear that curtain apart. I didn't want to be closed in any longer. I wanted to make contact with reality. I wanted to stop living inside a cocoon, inside an illusion, out of touch with either pain or joy.

I now have great respect for the power of anger as a source of energy to help us break out of depression or hopelessness or addiction. Anger can be an ally for life. When I woke up that morning, I felt a deep rage for life that announced, "I want to live, I want to find out who I am, I want to be real, I want to become my true self."

That night I went to church for the first time in years. I'd walked away from religious faith years before, but now I knew I needed God. I needed some Power greater than myself, some kind of ultimate something that could help me make meaning of my life and help me find a life worth living.

It turned out to be Good Friday. I have no idea whether or not I was particularly conscious of what that meant, but that night I made my way for the first time into the monastery of the Society of St. John the Evangelist, which is just outside of Harvard Square in Cambridge. I went through the Good Friday liturgy, which is a service all about facing the darkness, and acknowledging the pain, and admitting the guilt. As I stretched out my hands to receive Communion for the first time in years, I was touched to tears by the awareness that God was coming to me in the only way that I was able to take God in: in the form of food—a little bit of bread and a little sip of wine. For the first time in years I felt deeply fed. Something in my soul was satisfied. That was the night that I realized that addiction is fundamentally a spiritual quest and a religious journey.

It's a precious moment when an addict understands that the journey is ultimately a religious quest, but because of the nature of addiction, that insight by itself is never sufficient. You can have the most brilliant psychological insights in the world and understand all the factors in your childhood that contributed to your addiction. You can have the most powerful religious insights in the world, so that you understand addiction as basically a search for God. But insights by themselves have no power to heal an addiction.

Just a few days after that very powerful religious experience on Good Friday, I had my final binge. I made my stack of pancakes and ate my huge chocolate bars. I knew that this was the end; this was it. I couldn't do this anymore. And the next day I got myself into a Twelve Step program, which gave me the very concrete tools and support that I needed to live out those insights and to stay in recovery, a day at time.

My recovery began on April 13, 1982, which is now almost twenty-five years ago. In a way, that feels like a long time ago. But through the grace of God, I think I've learned a lot from the suffering I went through and through the hard work of recovery. One message I always want to express is that if you or someone you love is suffering from an addiction, there is still hope. There really are things you can do. There is support you can take hold of to get a life. At the same time I can't say any of that too glibly, because I know that some addicts don't make it—like my father, for instance, who went through a treatment program but was still never able to face his alcoholism. He died drinking.

Through the experience of addiction and recovery, I think I've learned some hard-won wisdom about how wonderful it is to have a self, how important it is to make honest connections with other people, and how important it is to keep listening to our deepest desires. I grew up believing that a good Christian, a good person and a good woman—in short, a saint—was someone who had no desires, someone who transcended desire. Good people didn't worry about what they themselves wanted, because they were busy taking care of everybody else and figuring out what other people wanted. Somehow it was okay for other people to have desires, but not oneself. I never really noticed the contradiction, but grew up believing in the importance of transcending the self, transcending the body, transcending desire. My journey has taught me to do just the reverse. I would say now that a saint is someone who knows what he or she most deeply desires and who has learned to align his or her life with that deep desire. We practice that a day at a time, as best we can.

I think of addicts as passionate people, people who are filled with desire. The Twelve Step program often speaks of the "God hole" within us, the space within that only God can fill. For years I tried to fill that hunger with other things. I asked myself, "Will good grades fill me?" "Will chasing after my father's or my mother's love fill me?" "Will eating a dozen doughnuts at a sitting fill me?" "Will having a boyfriend fill me?" And one thing after another never satisfied me. As they say in the Program, "people, places, and things" can never fill up the space that only God can occupy. There's a line from Saint Augustine's *Confessions* that means a lot to me, in which he says something like, "Lord, you have made us for yourself, and our hearts are restless until they rest in you." I say, hats off to Saint Augustine. His

Confessions was the first autobiography ever written, and his insight informs my own memoir, *Holy Hunger*. I think we all carry within us an infinite longing that only the Infinite can satisfy. We may name that ultimate longing in different ways—maybe as a longing for happiness, or for love, or for a life of meaning and purpose—but in the end I think it comes down to a longing for God, a longing to connect with the source of life.

If we don't know what we ultimately want, then we can be sure that the culture around us will be very quick to tell us what is worth wanting. I have a teenage son, and I think wearily of all the advertisements that he's subjected to. I remember the time we went to Boston's Fenway Park and together we counted forty different advertisements that we could see without moving from our seat. The culture around us is very quick to kidnap our religious longings and to tell us that we should invest our ultimate worship in things, in something that we can buy. We live in an addicted culture, and we get that message all the time: "This is what you want." I once followed a truck in Boston that had emblazoned in big letters on its rear the words, "What you are looking for." The truck was at some distance ahead of me, and I was curious what the smaller print would say. So I dodged and weaved a bit and got up to the truck. And on it was a picture of a woman reclining with a cigarette, with cigarette smoke encircling her head. "So that's it," I thought ironically to myself. "That's what I'm really looking for: a cigarette."

I think it's worth exploring our desires, because when we know what we love most, then we are free to let other things go. If we're connected to our deepest hunger, then we can see through the illusion that a cigarette or a snack is going to fill us, or that the huge bank account or impressive resume, the "perfect" body or "perfect" lover or enormous yacht—or whatever it is that we've been pining for or hustling to get—is going to satisfy us. I think it's worth digging into the question: What is most precious to me? What do I cherish most? To use the biblical image, what is my treasure hidden in the field? What is my pearl of great price? What is the North Star by which I want to navigate my life? To me those are very important questions, questions that can guide us home.

So in the years since getting into recovery I've been thinking a lot about desire and the education of desire, how we can learn to live, as Gerald

May says in his wonderful book *Addiction and Grace,* not with freedom from desire but with freedom of desire. When we know that God is ultimately important to us, then we are free to enjoy the things of this world without clinging to them for dear life.

After I got into recovery, I finished my doctorate at Harvard and went off to seminary. I wanted to bear witness to the love that had completely up-ended my life. In recovery I found a new vocation; I changed many of my friendships; I met the man that I eventually married. It was a whole new life. After seminary I was ordained in the Episcopal Church, and since then I've been trying to help other people make their own connection to the Holy so that they, too, can find a way to fill their "God hole." In addition to serving part-time in a parish, I've also spent these past two-plus decades leading spiritual retreats around the country and teaching courses on prayer at Episcopal Divinity School.

Since I got into recovery, I've also been thinking about the power of making peace with the body and of discovering how much God loves us in and through our bodies. I'm very concerned about global warming and the whole assault on the natural world that's now taking place. I have a sense that the first piece of my life was about making peace with my body and with learning to live in right-relationship to my body. This next piece of my life seems to be about falling in love with the whole body of the earth, and seeing it as filled with God, seeing it as sacred and blessed. God meets us not only in Holy Scripture and sacrament, but also in the trees and birds and air. I've become very interested in the whole mystery of how God comes to us through the natural world and what it means to stand up to protect this beautiful creation. In my next book I want to write something about that.

Credits and Permissions

About the Authors

Gary Stromberg cofounded Gibson & Stromberg, a large and influential public relations firm of the seventies. He represented such luminaries as the Rolling Stones, Pink Floyd, Muhammad Ali, Barbra Streisand, Boyz II Men, Neil Diamond, Ray Charles, The Doors, Earth, Wind & Fire, Elton John, Three Dog Night, and Crosby, Stills & Nash. Stromberg coproduced the motion pictures *Car Wash* and *The Fish That Saved Pittsburgh*. He currently runs The Blackbird Group, a small public relations firm in Westport, Connecticut, where he serves on the board of directors of Positive Directions, a center for prevention and recovery. He has a son in college and a daughter in high school. Gary and Jane Merrill are the coauthors of *The Harder They Fall: Celebrities Tell Their Real-Life Stories of Addiction and Recovery.*

Jane Merrill has written on popular history, art, style, and relationships for dozens of popular magazines, including *Cosmopolitan*, *New York*, *The New Republic, Penthouse, Town & Country, American Health, Redbook, Connoisseur, Gallery, The Christian Science Monitor*, and *Vogue*. She has written numerous books on diverse topics, including bilingual education, relationships, beauty, child rearing, jewelry, and China. In the nineties, she switched to ghostwriting and research for several of the most noted writers in America. She has three master's degrees from Harvard and Columbia, has worked and lived in Iran and France, and has raised four children.

Other titles that may interest you

The Harder They Fall
Celebrities Tell Their Real-Life Stories of Addiction and Recovery
Gary Stromberg and Jane Merrill
Foreword by Lewis Lapham; Introduction by Stephen Davis
This all-star account of hard-won recovery reveals what happens when fame and fortune meet addiction. From the authors of *Feeding the Fame*. Hardcover, 352 pp.
Order No. 7258

Locked Up for Eating Too Much
The Diary of a Food Addict in Rehab
Debbie Danowski, Ph.D.
This first-ever firsthand account of life in a food addiction treatment center is written with emotional honesty and a touch of humor. Softcover, 232 pp.
Order No. 1932

How to Make Almost Any Diet Work
Repair Your Disordered Appetite and Lose Weight
Anne Katherine
This breakthrough book on the biochemistry of overeating offers a step-by-step plan for restoring normal appetite. From the best-selling author of *Boundaries*. Softcover, 400 pp.
Order No. 2631

Food for Thought
Daily Meditations for Overeaters
Elisabeth L.
From an author recovering from compulsive overeating, this book offers guidance in the early days of living a Twelve Step program. Softcover, 400 pp.
Order No. 1074

◪ HAZELDEN®

Hazelden books are available at fine bookstores everywhere. To order directly from Hazelden, call 1-800-328-9000 or visit www.hazelden.org/bookstore.